Taste of Home EVERYDAY SLOW COOKER

TASTE OF HOME BOOKS • RDA ENTHUSIAST BRANDS, LLC • MILWAUKEE, WI

Visit us at **tasteofhome.com** for other Taste of Home
books and products.

International Standard Book Number: 978-1-62145-982-8

Chief Content Officer, Home & Garden: Jeanne Sidner
Content Director: Mark Hagen
Creative Director: Raeann Thompson
Senior Editor: Christine Rukavena
Editor: Hazel Wheaton

Senior Art Director: Courtney Lovetere
Senior Designer: Jazmin Delgado
Designer: Sierra Schuler
Deputy Editor, Copy Desk: Dulcie Shoener
Copy Editor: Kara Dennison

Photographer: Dan Roberts
Set Stylist: Stacey Genaw
Food Stylist: Josh Rink

Pictured on front cover:
Over-The-Rainbow Minestrone, p. 156; Steak Fajitas, p. 182; BBQ Bacon
Pulled Chicken Sandwiches, p. 130; Slow-Cooker Berry Cobbler, p. 224
Pictured on title page:
Pulled Turkey Tenderloin, p. 133
Pictured on back cover:
Moist & Tender Wings, p. 50; Root Beer Pulled Pork Nachos, p. 47;
Chocolate Pots de Creme, p. 252

Printed in China
1 3 5 7 9 10 8 6 4 2

**SLOW-COOKER DOUGHNUT
BREAKFAST BAKE P. 18**

CONTENTS

THE BUSY HOME COOK'S BEST FRIEND

For today's home cooks, time is always at a premium—and no tool works like the slow cooker to help navigate hectic schedules and still produce satisfying meals. The hands-free approach lets home cooks do other things—whether around the house or away from home. But all that convenience would be wasted if the food itself wasn't amazing!

Because of their low-and-slow cooking method, slow cookers are famously great for making tender pot roasts and savory stews. But that's not all they can do! If your slow cooker spends most of its time on the shelf, you're exploring only a fraction of this gadget's endless potential. This kitchen superstar turns out dips and spreads, drinks and breads, shredded meats for sandwiches and tacos, satisfying breakfasts, side dishes, and more—even a wide range of tempting snacks and sweet desserts.

With this new collection of recipes, you can use your slow cooker to make an entire meal in one for a busy weeknight, or to free up valuable oven space during holiday crunch time. The experts in the *Taste of Home* Test Kitchen test all recipes, so they'll work the first time—and every time after that. And each recipe comes with full nutritional information so you can always be sure you're feeding your family right.

What's more, we've included lots of extra bits of information, including the best slow-cooking tricks and techniques (see opposite page) and easy-to-follow advice for converting stovetop and oven recipes for the slow cooker (see inside back cover). Dozens of tips from our in-house experts help you make these recipes your own, and a helpful icon ❄ identifies freezer-friendly recipes, with instructions for freezing, storing and reheating.

So if you have your slow cooker tucked away in a cupboard, take it out and start exploring these fabulous recipes today. For everyday meals or special occasions, family dinners or office potlucks, casual entertaining or celebratory feasts, you'll find every day is a day for slow-cooking!

TOP SLOW-COOKER TIPS

1. CHOOSE THE RIGHT CUT OF MEAT.

Lower-cost cuts work better than higher-priced lean cuts. Trim extra fat from the outside, but look for good marbling on the inside—it will break down during cooking and make the meat tender.

2. MAKE SURE THE LID FITS.

Be sure the lid is secure, not askew. Steam held in during cooking creates a seal.

3. GO EASY ON THE ALCOHOL.

Alcohol won't evaporate from the slow cooker, so use it sparingly. If you brown the meat, use wine to deglaze the pan, then pour the liquid into the slow cooker. This will burn off the alcohol but leave the flavor.

4. FILL PROPERLY.

Fill the slow cooker between half and two-thirds full. Less than half full and the food may burn. More than two-thirds full, and it may not cook completely.

5. DON'T LET IT GET TOO COOL.

If you won't be home when the cooking time is up, be sure the cooker will switch itself to warm. Temperatures between 40° and 140° allow bacteria to thrive.

6. HALVE THE TIME BY DOUBLING THE SETTING.

On most models, low is 170° and high is 280°. For many recipes, cranking up the heat will cut down the cook time.

7. DON'T PEEK!

Each time you lift the lid, you'll need to add 15-30 minutes of cooking time. Open only when the recipe calls for it.

8. AVOID TEMPERATURE SHOCKS.

If your cooker has a ceramic insert, put a dish towel on a cold work surface before setting the hot insert down. Do not preheat your cooker. A cold insert should always be put into a cold base.

9. MAKE A SLING.

Some recipes call for a foil sling to help you lift food out. To make a sling, fold one or more pieces of heavy-duty foil into strips. Place the strips on the bottom and up the sides of the slow cooker; coat foil with cooking spray.

HOW TO KEEP YOUR SLOW COOKER CLEAN

ALLOW the stoneware insert to cool before rinsing it. Wash it in the dishwasher or in the sink with warm, soapy water.

DO NOT use abrasive cleansers.

USE a damp sponge to clean the metal base. Do not soak the base in water.

TO REMOVE white mineral stains from the insert, fill the cooker with hot water mixed with 1 cup white vinegar. Heat on high for 2 hours. Empty the insert, let it cool and wash as usual.

SLOW-COOKED
BIG BREAKFAST P. 21

SLOW & EASY BREAKFASTS

Whether your family prefers sweet treats or savory dishes for the morning meal, you can use the slow cooker to make precisely what they want!

OVERNIGHT FLAX OATMEAL

SPANAKOPITA FRITTATA SANDWICHES

Years ago my husband and I took a cruise through the Greek Islands for our tenth anniversary. Delicious and nutritious foods like this were served on our ship all day, every day. I enjoyed recreating the flavors in this brunch sandwich.
—*Laura Wilhelm, West Hollywood, CA*

PREP: 20 min.
COOK: 2 hours + standing
MAKES: 8 servings

- 12 large eggs
- ½ cup 2% milk
- 2 tsp. Greek seasoning
- 2 cups fresh baby spinach
- 1½ cups crumbled feta cheese
- 1 cup sliced fresh mushrooms
- ½ cup roasted sweet red pepper strips
- ½ cup shredded Italian cheese blend
- ¼ tsp. smoked paprika
- 8 ciabatta rolls, bagels or English muffins, split and toasted

1. In a large bowl, whisk the eggs, milk and Greek seasoning until blended. Stir in spinach, feta, mushrooms and pepper strips. Pour mixture into a greased 3.5-qt. slow cooker. Cook, covered, on high for 2-3 hours until eggs are set and a thermometer reads 160°.
2. Remove lid; sprinkle the frittata with shredded Italian cheese blend and paprika. Turn off slow cooker; remove insert. Let stand until the cheese is melted, about 10 minutes. Cut and serve on the bread of your choice.
1 SANDWICH: 481 cal., 14g fat (6g sat. fat), 296mg chol., 1115mg sod., 60g carb. (11g sugars, 3g fiber), 27g pro.

OVERNIGHT FLAX OATMEAL

Fans of the healthy benefits of flaxseed will enjoy this hearty oatmeal. It's full of yummy raisins and dried cranberries, too. Any combination of dried fruit will work, so get creative!
—*Susan Smith, Ocean View, NJ*

PREP: 10 min. • **COOK:** 7 hours
MAKES: 4 servings

- 3 cups water
- 1 cup old-fashioned oats
- 1 cup raisins
- ½ cup dried cranberries
- ½ cup ground flaxseed
- ½ cup 2% milk
- 1 tsp. vanilla extract
- 1 tsp. molasses
  Optional: Sliced almonds, 2% milk and additional molasses

In a 3-qt. slow cooker, combine the first 8 ingredients. Cover and cook on low for 7-8 hours or until liquid is absorbed and oatmeal is tender. If desired, top with sliced almonds, 2% milk and additional molasses.
1 CUP: 322 cal., 9g fat (1g sat. fat), 2mg chol., 28mg sod., 63g carb. (34g sugars, 8g fiber), 9g pro.

SPANAKOPITA FRITTATA
SANDWICHES

RASPBERRY COCONUT FRENCH TOAST SLOW-COOKER STYLE

I put the ingredients in the slow-cooker crock the night before, refrigerate it, then pop the crock into the slow cooker in the morning. You can use regular milk or half-and-half, your favorite jam, and substitute almond extract for the vanilla.
—Teri Rasey, Cadillac, MI

PREP: 20 min. + chilling
COOK: 2¾ hours.
MAKES: 12 servings

- 6 large eggs
- 1½ cups refrigerated sweetened coconut milk
- 1 tsp. vanilla extract
- 1 loaf (1 lb.) French bread, cubed
- 1 pkg. (8 oz.) cream cheese, cubed
- ⅔ cup seedless raspberry jam
- ½ cup sweetened shredded coconut
  Whipped cream, fresh raspberries and toasted sweetened shredded coconut

1. In a large bowl, whisk eggs, coconut milk and vanilla until blended. Place half of the bread in a greased 5- or 6-qt. slow cooker; layer with half each of the cream cheese, jam, coconut and egg mixture. Repeat layers. Refrigerate, covered, overnight.
2. Cook, covered, on low until a knife inserted in the center comes out clean, 2¾-3¼ hours. Serve warm with whipped cream, raspberries and toasted coconut.
1 CUP: 280 cal., 12g fat (7g sat. fat), 112mg chol., 338mg sod., 35g carb. (16g sugars, 1g fiber), 9g pro.

FRUITED OATMEAL WITH NUTS

The beauty of this breakfast is that it slow-cooks overnight and you can feed a crowd in the morning. If the oatmeal is too thick, add a little extra milk.
—Trisha Kruse, Eagle, ID

PREP: 15 min. • **COOK:** 6 hours
MAKES: 6 servings

- 3 cups water
- 2 cups old-fashioned oats
- 2 cups chopped apples
- 1 cup dried cranberries
- 1 cup fat-free milk
- 2 tsp. butter, melted
- 1 tsp. pumpkin pie spice
- 1 tsp. ground cinnamon
- 6 Tbsp. chopped almonds, toasted
- 6 Tbsp. chopped pecans, toasted
  Additional fat-free milk, optional

1. In a 3-qt. slow cooker coated with cooking spray, combine the first 8 ingredients. Cook, covered, on low until liquid is absorbed, 6-8 hours.
2. Spoon into bowls; sprinkle with almonds and pecans. If desired, drizzle with additional milk.
1 CUP: 306 cal., 13g fat (2g sat. fat), 4mg chol., 28mg sod., 45g carb. (20g sugars, 6g fiber), 8g pro. **DIABETIC EXCHANGES:** 3 starch, 2 fat.

EGG & BROCCOLI CASSEROLE

EGG & BROCCOLI CASSEROLE

For years, I have prepared this hearty casserole for brunches and potlucks. It's an unusual recipe for the slow cooker, but folks always welcome it and go back for seconds wherever I serve it.
—*Janet Sliter, Kennewick, WA*

PREP: 10 min. • **COOK:** 3½ hours
MAKES: 6 servings

- 3 cups 4% cottage cheese
- 3 cups frozen chopped broccoli, thawed and drained
- 2 cups shredded cheddar cheese
- 6 large eggs, lightly beaten
- ⅓ cup all-purpose flour
- ¼ cup butter, melted
- 3 Tbsp. finely chopped onion
- ½ tsp. salt
  Additional shredded cheddar cheese, optional

1. In a large bowl, combine the first 8 ingredients. Pour into a greased 3-qt. slow cooker. Cover and cook on high for 1 hour. Stir.
2. Reduce heat to low; cover and cook 2½-3 hours longer or until a thermometer reads 160°. Sprinkle with additional cheese if desired.
1 SERVING: 428 cal., 28g fat (17g sat. fat), 297mg chol., 953mg sod., 15g carb. (5g sugars, 2g fiber), 29g pro.

"Loved it. I recommend chopping up the frozen broccoli into smaller pieces. I definitely will make it again."
COLLEEN1734, TASTEOFHOME.COM

SPICED APPLE OATMEAL

SPICED APPLE OATMEAL

These easy appley oats let your family have a warm and cozy breakfast no matter how busy you are.
—*Teri Rasey, Cadillac, MI*

PREP: 15 min. • **COOK:** 4½ hours
MAKES: 10 servings

- ½ cup packed brown sugar
- 2 Tbsp. lemon juice
- 2 Tbsp. molasses
- 3 tsp. ground cinnamon
- 1 tsp. ground nutmeg
- ½ tsp. ground ginger
- ½ tsp. ground allspice
- ¼ tsp. salt
- 4 medium apples, peeled and cut into 1-in. slices
- 2 cups steel-cut oats
- 2 large eggs
- 2½ cups water
- 2 cups 2% milk
- 1 cup refrigerated vanilla dairy creamer
  Optional: Chopped pecans and additional milk

1. Mix first 8 ingredients. Place apples in a greased 4-qt. slow cooker. Top with brown sugar mixture, then with oats. Whisk together the eggs, water, milk and creamer; pour over oats. Cook, covered, on low until the oats are tender, 4½-5 hours. If desired, serve with pecans and additional milk.
NOTE: This recipe was tested with Coffee-mate Natural Bliss vanilla coffee creamer.
1 CUP: 290 cal., 7g fat (3g sat. fat), 49mg chol., 109mg sod., 53g carb. (30g sugars, 5g fiber), 7g pro.

SLOW-COOKER GOETTA

✳ SLOW-COOKER GOETTA

My husband's grandfather, a German, introduced goetta to me. I found a slow-cooker recipe and changed some of the ingredients to make this the best goetta around. It makes a lot, but it freezes well.
—*Sharon Geers, Wilmington, OH*

PREP: 45 min. + chilling
COOK: 4 hours
MAKES: 2 loaves (16 pieces each)

- 6 cups water
- 2½ cups steel-cut oats
- 6 bay leaves
- 3 Tbsp. beef bouillon granules
- ¾ tsp. salt
- 1 tsp. each garlic powder, rubbed sage and pepper
- ½ tsp. ground allspice
- ½ tsp. crushed red pepper flakes
- 2 lbs. bulk pork sausage
- 2 medium onions, chopped

1. In a 5-qt. slow cooker, combine water, oats and seasonings. Cook, covered, on high 2 hours. Remove bay leaves.
2. In a large skillet, cook sausage and onions over medium heat until the meat is no longer pink, breaking up sausage into crumbles, 8-10 minutes. Drain, reserving 2 Tbsp. drippings. Stir sausage mixture and reserved drippings into oats. Cook, covered, on low 2 hours.
3. Transfer mixture to 2 waxed paper-lined 9x5-in. loaf pans. Refrigerate, covered, overnight.
4. To serve, slice each loaf into 16 pieces. In a large skillet, cook goetta, in batches, over medium heat until lightly browned and heated through, 3-4 minutes on each side.
FREEZE OPTION: After shaping the goetta in loaf pans, cool and freeze, covered, until firm. Transfer to freezer containers or wrap securely in foil; return to freezer. Partially thaw in refrigerator overnight; slice and cook as directed.
1 PIECE: 121 cal., 7g fat (2g sat. fat), 15mg chol., 450mg sod., 10g carb. (1g sugars, 1g fiber), 5g pro.

APPLE CINNAMON FRENCH TOAST

My husband works nights delivering linens to hospitals and nursing homes. I often put this casserole together when I am making dinner and refrigerate it. I will put the insert into the slow-cooker about midnight, so when he gets home this meal is ready for breakfast. Although we are empty nesters, I make the full recipe—leftovers reheat well in the microwave.
—*Donna Gribbins, Shelbyville, KY*

PREP: 20 min. • **COOK:** 3 hours
MAKES: 14 servings

- 1 loaf (1 lb.) Italian bread, cubed
- 6 large eggs, room temperature
- 2 cups 2% milk
- 1 cup heavy whipping cream
- 2 tsp. vanilla extract
- ½ cup sugar
- 2 tsp. ground cinnamon
- ¼ tsp. salt
- 3 medium tart apples, peeled and chopped

CARAMEL SYRUP
- ½ cup caramel apple dip
- 1 cup maple syrup

1. In a greased 5- or 6-qt. slow cooker, combine bread and apples. In a large bowl, whisk eggs, milk, cream, sugar, cinnamon, vanilla and salt. Pour over bread mixture and stir to combine; gently press bread down into milk mixture. Cook, covered, on low until a knife inserted in the center comes out clean, 3-4 hours.
2. Meanwhile, combine caramel syrup ingredients in a small saucepan. Cook and stir over medium heat until smooth and heated through. Serve warm with French toast.

1 SERVING WITH ABOUT 2 TBSP. SYRUP: 343 cal., 12g fat (6g sat. fat), 103mg chol., 302mg sod., 51g carb. (34g sugars, 2g fiber), 8g pro.

SLOW-COOKER FRITTATA PROVENCAL

This meatless slow cooker meal makes an elegant brunch for lazy weekend mornings. It also makes an ideal breakfast-for-dinner, ready when I walk in the door from work.
—*Connie Eaton, Pittsburgh, PA*

PREP: 30 min. • **COOK:** 3 hours
MAKES: 6 servings

- ½ cup water
- 1 Tbsp. olive oil
- 1 medium Yukon Gold potato, peeled and sliced
- 1 small onion, thinly sliced
- ½ tsp. smoked paprika
- 12 large eggs
- 1 tsp. minced fresh thyme or ¼ tsp. dried thyme
- 1 tsp. hot pepper sauce
- ½ tsp. salt
- ¼ tsp. pepper
- 1 log (4 oz.) fresh goat cheese, coarsely crumbled
- ½ cup chopped soft sun-dried tomatoes (not packed in oil)

1. Layer two 24-in. pieces of aluminum foil; starting with a long side, fold up foil to create a 1-in.-wide strip. Shape strip into a coil to make a rack for bottom of a 6-qt. oval slow cooker. Add water to slow cooker; set foil rack in water.
2. In a large skillet, heat oil over medium-high heat. Add potato and onion; cook and stir until potato is lightly browned, 5-7 minutes. Stir in paprika. Transfer to a greased 1½-qt. baking dish (dish must fit in slow cooker).
3. In a large bowl, whisk eggs, thyme, pepper sauce, salt and pepper; stir in 2 oz. cheese. Pour over the potato mixture. Top with tomatoes and the remaining goat cheese. Place dish on foil rack.
4. Cook, covered, on low until eggs are set and a knife inserted in center comes out clean, 3-4 hours.

1 SERVING: 245 cal., 14g fat (5g sat. fat), 385mg chol., 338mg sod., 12g carb. (4g sugars, 2g fiber), 15g pro. **DIABETIC EXCHANGES:** 2 medium-fat meat, 1 starch, ½ fat.

TEST KITCHEN TIP

We tested this recipe with sun-dried tomatoes that are ready to use without soaking. When using whole sun-dried tomatoes that are not oil-packed, cover with boiling water and let stand until soft. Drain before chopping.

SLOW-COOKER
FRITTATA PROVENCAL

CHILI & CHEESE CRUSTLESS QUICHE

This filling Tex-Mex egg casserole makes a fantastic, filling breakfast, but is also perfect for any meal of the day. Add a salad and dinner is on!

—*Gail Watkins, West Haven, UT*

PREP: 15 min.
COOK: 3 hours + standing
MAKES: 6 servings

  3 corn tortillas (6 in.)
  2 cans (4 oz. each) whole green chiles
  1 can (15 oz.) chili con carne
1½ cups shredded cheddar cheese, divided
  4 large eggs
1½ cups 2% milk
  1 cup biscuit/baking mix
  ¼ tsp. salt
  ¼ tsp. pepper
  1 tsp. hot pepper sauce, optional
  1 can (4 oz.) chopped green chiles
  2 medium tomatoes, sliced
      Sour cream, optional

1. In a greased 4- or 5-qt. slow cooker, layer tortillas, whole green chiles, chili con carne and 1 cup cheese.

2. Whisk the eggs, milk, biscuit mix, salt, pepper and, if desired, pepper sauce until blended; pour into slow cooker. Top with chopped green chiles and tomatoes.

3. Cook, covered, on low until a thermometer reads 160°, 3-4 hours, sprinkling with remaining cheese during last 30 minutes of cooking. Turn off slow cooker; remove insert. Let stand for 15 minutes before serving. If desired, top with sour cream.

1 SERVING: 420 cal., 24g fat (11g sat. fat), 182mg chol., 1034mg sod., 32g carb. (7g sugars, 4g fiber), 20g pro.

CHILI & CHEESE CRUSTLESS QUICHE

OVERNIGHT PEACH OATMEAL

Hearty oatmeal combined with bright, sweet peaches make this slow-cooker recipe a perfect breakfast or brunch. This is an excellent make-ahead meal for busy mornings.
—*Rachel Lewis, Danville, VA*

PREP: 10 min. • **COOK:** 7 hours
MAKES: 6 servings

- 4 cups water
- 1 cup steel-cut oats
- 1 cup vanilla soy milk or vanilla almond milk
- 3 Tbsp. brown sugar
- ¼ tsp. salt
- ¼ tsp. vanilla or almond extract
- 2 medium peaches, sliced or 3 cups frozen unsweetened sliced peaches, thawed Optional: Sliced almonds, brown sugar, cinnamon and additional peaches

1. In a well-greased 3-qt. slow cooker, combine first 6 ingredients. Cook, covered, on low until the oats are tender, 7-8 hours.
2. Stir in peaches just before serving. The oatmeal will thicken upon standing. If desired, top with optional toppings.
¾ CUP: 163 cal., 2g fat (0 sat. fat), 0 chol., 116mg sod., 31g carb. (13g sugars, 4g fiber), 5g pro. **DIABETIC EXCHANGES:** 1½ starch, ½ fruit.
PRESSURE COOKER OPTION: Decrease water to 3 cups. Add to a 6-qt. electric pressure cooker coated with cooking spray. Stir in oats, soy milk, brown sugar, salt and vanilla. Lock lid; close pressure-release valve. Adjust to pressure-cook on high for 4 minutes. Let pressure release naturally. Stir in peaches just before serving.

BREAKFAST APPLE COBBLER

This is a lovely recipe to serve on Christmas or any other cold morning. The apples can be peeled if preferred.
—*Marietta Slater, Justin, TX*

PREP: 15 min. • **COOK:** 6 hours
MAKES: 6 servings

- 6 medium apples, cut into ½-in. wedges
- 1 Tbsp. butter
- 3 Tbsp. honey
- ½ tsp. ground cinnamon
- ¼ cup dried cranberries
- 2 cups granola without raisins Optional: Milk and maple syrup

1. Place apples in a greased 3-qt. slow cooker. In a microwave, melt butter; stir in honey and cinnamon. Drizzle over the apples. Sprinkle cranberries and granola over top.
2. Cook, covered, on low 6-8 hours, until apples are tender. If desired, serve with milk and syrup.
¾ CUP: 289 cal., 8g fat (1g sat. fat), 5mg chol., 31mg sod., 58g carb. (31g sugars, 11g fiber), 7g pro.

SLOW-COOKER DOUGHNUT BREAKFAST BAKE

This extravagant dish will be the star of your brunch table. Try serving it with sausage, fresh berries and yogurt.
—Rashanda Cobbins, Milwaukee, WI

PREP: 15 min.
COOK: 4 hours + standing
MAKES: 12 servings

- 24 cake doughnuts, cut into bite-sized pieces
- 2 apples, peeled and chopped
- 1 cup heavy whipping cream
- 4 large eggs
- 1 Tbsp. vanilla extract
- ½ cup packed brown sugar
- 1 tsp. ground cinnamon
  Optional: Whipped cream and fresh berries

1. Line a 5-qt. slow cooker with a double layer of heavy duty foil; spray with cooking spray. Layer half the doughnut pieces in slow cooker; top with half the apples. Repeat with remaining doughnut pieces and apples. In a large bowl, whisk together cream, eggs and vanilla; pour over top. In a small bowl, mix together brown sugar and cinnamon; sprinkle over doughnut mixture.

2. Cook, covered, on low until set, 4-5 hours. Remove insert. Let stand, uncovered, 20 minutes. If desired, serve with whipped cream and fresh berries.
1 SERVING: 609 cal., 36g fat (17g sat. fat), 95mg chol., 547mg sod., 64g carb. (32g sugars, 2g fiber), 8g pro

OVERNIGHT VEGETABLE & EGG BREAKFAST

My overnight eggs and veggies make a hearty breakfast for those who have to rush out the door. I use sliced potatoes, but frozen potatoes work, too.
—Kimberly Clark-Thiry, Anchor Point, AK

PREP: 15 min. • **COOK:** 7 hours
MAKES: 8 servings

- 4 lbs. potatoes, peeled and thinly sliced (about 8 cups)
- 1 medium green pepper, finely chopped
- 1 pkg. (10 oz.) frozen chopped spinach, thawed and squeezed dry
- 1 cup sliced fresh mushrooms
- 1 medium onion, finely chopped
- 8 large eggs
- 1 cup water
- 1 cup 2% milk
- 1¼ tsp. salt
- ¼ tsp. pepper
- 2 cups shredded cheddar cheese

In a greased 6-qt. slow cooker, layer the first 5 ingredients. Whisk the next 5 ingredients; pour over top. Sprinkle with cheese. Cook, covered, on low until potatoes are tender and eggs are set, 7-9 hours.
1½ CUPS: 354 cal., 15g fat (7g sat. fat), 217mg chol., 668mg sod., 37g carb. (5g sugars, 4g fiber), 19g pro.

APPLE PIE STEEL-CUT OATMEAL

I absolutely love this slow-cooker oatmeal. The oats have so much flavor and texture. My family loves to sprinkle toasted pecans on top.
—Angela Lively, Conroe, TX

PREP: 10 min. • **COOK:** 6 hours
MAKES: 8 servings

- 6 cups water
- 1½ cups steel-cut oats
- 1½ cups unsweetened applesauce
- ¼ cup maple syrup
- 1½ tsp. ground cinnamon
- ½ tsp. ground nutmeg
- ⅛ tsp. salt
- 1 large apple, chopped
  Optional: Sliced apples, toasted pecans and additional maple syrup

In a 4-qt. slow cooker, combine the first 7 ingredients. Cover and cook on low until liquid is absorbed, 6-8 hours. Stir in chopped apple. If desired, top servings with apple slices, pecans and syrup.
1¼ CUPS: 171 cal., 2g fat (0 sat. fat), 0 chol., 39mg sod., 36g carb. (13g sugars, 4g fiber), 4g pro.

TEST KITCHEN TIPS

- Keep an eye on this oatmeal as it nears the end of its cooking time to prevent overcooking at the edges, especially if your slow cooker runs hot.
- It's important in this recipe to use steel-cut oats, which need to cook longer than rolled oats. You might find them labeled as Irish oats.

APPLE PIE STEEL-CUT OATMEAL

SLOW-COOKER OATMEAL

Waking up to this wonderful aroma and piping hot meal is a wonderful way to start the day!
—*Brandy Schaefer, Glen Carbon, IL*

PREP: 10 min. • **COOK:** 3 hours
MAKES: 4 servings

- 2 cups 2% milk
- 1 cup old-fashioned oats
- 1 cup chopped peeled tart apple
- ½ cup raisins
- ¼ cup packed brown sugar
- ¼ cup chopped walnuts
- 1 Tbsp. butter, melted
- ½ tsp. ground cinnamon
- ¼ tsp. salt

In a 1½-qt. slow cooker coated with cooking spray, combine all ingredients. Cover and cook on low for 3-4 hours or until liquid is absorbed and oatmeal is tender. If desired, serve with additional milk, walnuts and cinnamon.
1 CUP: 340 cal., 13g fat (5g sat. fat), 20mg chol., 225mg sod., 51g carb. (32g sugars, 3g fiber), 10g pro.

SLOW-COOKED
BIG BREAKFAST

SLOW-COOKED BIG BREAKFAST

We make this during holidays or on mornings when we know we're going to have a busy day. You can substitute whatever vegetables your family prefers. It's also good made with steak.

—*Delisha Paris, Elizabeth City, NC*

PREP: 30 min.
COOK: 3 hours + standing
MAKES: 12 servings

- 1 lb. bulk pork sausage
- 2 lbs. potatoes (about 4 medium), peeled and cut into ½-in. cubes
- 1 large onion, finely chopped
- 1 medium sweet red pepper, chopped
- 2 cups fresh spinach
- 1 cup chopped fresh mushrooms
- 1 lb. deli ham, cubed
- 1 cup shredded cheddar cheese
- 12 large eggs
- ½ cup 2% milk
- 1 tsp. garlic powder
- 1 tsp. pepper
- ½ tsp. salt

1. In a large skillet, cook and crumble sausage over medium heat for 5-7 minutes or until no longer pink; drain.
2. Meanwhile, place potatoes and ¼ cup water in a large microwave-safe dish. Microwave, covered, on high until potatoes are tender, about 6 minutes; stir halfway. Drain and add to sausage.
3. Stir in onion, sweet red pepper, spinach, mushrooms, ham and cheese. Transfer to a greased 6-qt. slow cooker.
4. Whisk together the remaining ingredients until blended; pour over sausage mixture. Cook, covered, on low until eggs are set, 3-4 hours. Let stand, uncovered, 10 minutes.
1 CUP: 303 cal., 18g fat (6g sat. fat), 236mg chol., 873mg sod., 14g carb. (3g sugars, 1g fiber), 21g pro.

BACON BREAKFAST CASSEROLE

This easy breakfast dish allows me to make a comforting family favorite that doesn't take a lot of prep. It's also fantastic for big brunch gatherings.
—*Paula Lawson, Springfield, OH*

PREP: 30 min.
COOK: 4 hours + standing
MAKES: 12 servings

- 1 lb. bacon strips, chopped
- 1 pkg. (28 oz.) frozen potatoes O'Brien, thawed
- 3 cups shredded Mexican cheese blend
- 12 large eggs
- 1 cup 2% milk
- ½ tsp. salt
- ½ tsp. pepper
    Minced fresh parsley, optional

1. In a large skillet, cook bacon in batches over medium heat until crisp. Remove to paper towels to drain.
2. In a greased 4- or 5-qt. slow cooker, layer a third of each of the following: potatoes, reserved bacon and cheese. Repeat layers twice. In a large bowl, whisk eggs, milk, salt and pepper; pour over top. Cook, covered, on low until eggs are set, 4-5 hours.
3. Remove crock insert to a wire rack; let stand, uncovered, 30 minutes before serving. If desired, sprinkle with parsley.
1 SERVING: 306 cal., 19g fat (8g sat. fat), 226mg chol., 606mg sod., 13g carb. (2g sugars, 2g fiber), 18g pro.

TEST KITCHEN TIP

Letting this dish stand before serving helps prevent liquid from "weeping" out.

BACON BREAKFAST CASSEROLE

SLOW-COOKER SAUSAGE & WAFFLE BAKE

Here's an easy dish guaranteed to create excitement at the breakfast table! Nothing is missing from this sweet and savory combination. It's so wrong that it's right!
—Courtney Lentz, Boston, MA

PREP: 20 min.
COOK: 5 hours + standing
MAKES: 12 servings

- 2 lbs. bulk spicy breakfast pork sausage
- 1 Tbsp. rubbed sage
- ½ tsp. fennel seed
- 1 pkg. (12.3 oz.) frozen waffles, cut into bite-sized pieces
- 8 large eggs
- 1¼ cups half-and-half cream
- ¼ cup maple syrup
- ¼ tsp. salt
- ¼ tsp. pepper
- 2 cups shredded cheddar cheese
  Additional maple syrup

1. Fold two 18-in.-long pieces of foil into two 18x4-in. strips. Line the sides around the inside perimeter of a 5-qt. slow cooker with foil strips; spray with cooking spray.
2. In a large skillet, cook and crumble sausage over medium heat; drain. Add sage and fennel.
3. Place waffles in slow cooker; top with sausage. In a bowl, mix eggs, cream, syrup and seasonings. Pour over sausage and waffles. Top with cheese. Cook, covered, on low until set, 5-6 hours. Remove insert and let stand, uncovered, for 15 minutes. Serve with additional maple syrup.
1 SERVING: 442 cal., 31g fat (12g sat. fat), 200mg chol., 878mg sod., 20g carb. (7g sugars, 1g fiber), 19g pro.

APPLE-CRANBERRY BREAKFAST RISOTTO

Cranberries and apples are tart enough to balance the sweetness in this hearty dish that's fun for an after-presents breakfast on Christmas morning.
—Elizabeth King, Duluth, MN

PREP: 15 min. • **COOK:** 3 hours
MAKES: 10 servings

- ¼ cup butter, cubed
- 1½ cups uncooked arborio rice
- 2 medium apples, peeled and chopped
- ⅓ cup packed brown sugar
- ¼ tsp. kosher salt
- 1½ tsp. ground cinnamon
- ⅛ tsp. ground nutmeg
- ⅛ tsp. ground cloves
- 3 cups 2% milk
- 2 cups unsweetened apple juice
- 1 cup dried cranberries

1. Heat butter in a 4-qt. slow cooker on high heat until melted. Add rice; stir to coat. Add apples, brown sugar, salt and spices. Stir in milk and apple juice.
2. Cook, covered, on low until the rice is tender, 3-4 hours, stirring halfway through cooking. Stir in cranberries during the last 15 minutes of cooking.
¾ CUP: 298 cal., 7g fat (4g sat. fat), 18mg chol., 124mg sod., 57g carb. (30g sugars, 2g fiber), 5g pro.

SLOW-COOKED BLUEBERRY FRENCH TOAST

Your slow cooker can be your best friend on a busy morning. Just get this recipe going, run some errands and come back to the aroma of French toast ready to eat.
—*Elizabeth Lorenz, Peru, IN*

PREP: 30 min. + chilling
COOK: 3 hours
MAKES: 12 servings (2 cups syrup)

- 8   large eggs
- ½   cup plain yogurt
- ⅓   cup sour cream
- 1   tsp. vanilla extract
- ½   tsp. ground cinnamon
- 1   cup 2% milk
- ⅓   cup maple syrup
- 1   loaf (1 lb.) French bread, cubed
- 1½   cups fresh or frozen blueberries
- 12   oz. cream cheese, cubed

BLUEBERRY SAUCE
- 1   cup sugar
- 2   Tbsp. cornstarch
- 1   cup cold water
- ¾   cup fresh or frozen blueberries, divided
- 1   Tbsp. butter
- 1   Tbsp. lemon juice

1. In a large bowl, whisk eggs, yogurt, sour cream, vanilla and cinnamon. Gradually whisk in milk and maple syrup until blended.

2. Place half the bread in a greased 5- or 6-qt. slow cooker; layer with half the blueberries, cream cheese and egg mixture. Repeat layers. Refrigerate, covered, overnight.

3. Remove from refrigerator 30 minutes before cooking. Cook, covered, on low 3-4 hours, until a knife inserted in center comes out clean.

4. For sauce, in a small saucepan, mix sugar and cornstarch; stir in water until smooth. Stir in ¼ cup blueberries. Bring to a boil; cook, stirring, until berries pop, about 3 minutes. Remove from heat; stir in butter, lemon juice and remaining berries. Serve with French toast.

1 CUP WITH ABOUT 2 TBSP. SAUCE: 390 cal., 17g fat (9g sat. fat), 182mg chol., 371mg sod., 49g carb. (28g sugars, 2g fiber), 12g pro.

❄ POT ROAST HASH

I love to cook a Sunday-style pot roast for weeknights, then make pot roast hash for breakfast any day of the week.
—*Gina Jackson, Ogdensburg, NY*

PREP: 15 min. • **COOK:** 6½ hours
MAKES: 10 servings

- 1   cup warm water
- 1   Tbsp. beef base
- ½   lb. sliced fresh mushrooms
- 1   large onion, coarsely chopped
- 3   garlic cloves, minced
- 1   boneless beef chuck roast (3 lbs.)
- ½   tsp. pepper
- 1   Tbsp. Worcestershire sauce
- 1   pkg. (28 oz.) frozen potatoes O'Brien

EGGS
- 2   Tbsp. butter
- 10   large eggs
- ½   tsp. salt
- ½   tsp. pepper
   Minced chives

1. In a 5- or 6-qt. slow cooker, whisk water and beef base; add mushrooms, onion and garlic. Sprinkle the roast with pepper; transfer to slow cooker. Drizzle with Worcestershire sauce. Cook, covered, on low until meat is tender, 6-8 hours.

2. Remove roast; cool slightly. Shred meat with 2 forks. In a large skillet, cook potatoes according to package directions; stir in shredded beef. Using a slotted spoon, add vegetables from slow cooker to skillet; heat through. Discard cooking juices.

3. For eggs, in another skillet, heat 1 Tbsp. butter over medium-high heat. Break 5 eggs, 1 at a time, into pan. Sprinkle with half of the salt and pepper. Reduce heat to low. Cook until desired doneness, turning after whites are set if desired. Repeat with remaining butter, eggs, salt and pepper. Serve eggs over hash; sprinkle with chives.

FREEZE OPTION: Place shredded pot roast and vegetables in a freezer container; top with cooking juices. Cool and freeze. To use, partially thaw in refrigerator overnight. Heat through in a covered saucepan.
⅔ CUP HASH WITH 1 EGG: 429 cal., 24g fat (8g sat. fat), 281mg chol., 306mg sod., 15g carb. (2g sugars, 2g fiber), 35g pro.

TEST KITCHEN TIPS

You can find beef base near the broth and bouillon. You can serve this with scrambled eggs if you prefer. Top with fresh salsa, ketchup or Sriracha.

POT ROAST HASH

ONION-GARLIC
HASH BROWNS

ONION-GARLIC HASH BROWNS

Quick to assemble, these slow-cooked hash browns are one of my go-to breakfast sides. Stir in hot sauce if you like a bit of heat. I top my finished dish with a sprinkling of shredded cheddar cheese.
—*Cindi Boger, Ardmore, AL*

PREP: 20 min. • **COOK:** 3 hours
MAKES: 12 servings

- ¼ cup butter, cubed
- 1 Tbsp. olive oil
- 1 large red onion, chopped
- 1 small sweet red pepper, chopped
- 1 small green pepper, chopped
- 4 garlic cloves, minced
- 1 pkg. (30 oz.) frozen shredded hash brown potatoes
- ½ tsp. salt
- ½ tsp. pepper
- 3 drops hot pepper sauce, optional
- 2 tsp. minced fresh parsley

1. In a large skillet, heat butter and oil over medium heat. Add onion and peppers. Cook and stir until crisp-tender. Add garlic; cook 1 minute longer. Stir in hash browns, salt, pepper and, if desired, pepper sauce.
2. Transfer to a 5-qt. slow cooker coated with cooking spray. Cook, covered, 3-4 hours or until heated through. Sprinkle with parsley just before serving.
½ CUP: 110 cal., 5g fat (3g sat. fat), 10mg chol., 136mg sod., 15g carb. (1g sugars, 1g fiber), 2g pro. **DIABETIC EXCHANGES:** 1 starch, 1 fat.

CINNAMON BLUEBERRY FRENCH TOAST

CINNAMON BLUEBERRY FRENCH TOAST

I like to prep this breakfast in the evening, let it chill, then turn on the slow cooker when we wake up in the morning. It's done just right.
—*Angela Lively, Conroe, TX*

PREP: 15 min. + chilling
COOK: 3 hours • **MAKES:** 6 servings

- 3 large eggs
- 2 cups 2% milk
- ¼ cup sugar
- 1 tsp. ground cinnamon
- 1 tsp. vanilla extract
- ¼ tsp. salt
- 9 cups cubed French bread (about 9 oz.)
- 1 cup fresh or frozen blueberries, thawed
  Maple syrup

1. Whisk together the first 6 ingredients. Place half the bread in a greased 5-qt. slow cooker; top with ½ cup blueberries and half the milk mixture. Repeat layers. Refrigerate, covered, 4 hours or overnight.
2. Cook, covered, on low until a knife inserted in the center comes out clean, 3-4 hours. Serve warm with syrup.
1 CUP: 265 cal., 6g fat (2g sat. fat), 100mg chol., 430mg sod., 42g carb. (18g sugars, 2g fiber), 11g pro.

TEST KITCHEN TIP

To increase fiber, substitute whole wheat bread for the white French bread, or cube 100% whole wheat buns.

HONEY NUT GRANOLA

A friend gave me their recipe—
I lightened it up and changed the
add-ins to suit my family's tastes.
It's now one of our favorites! You
can use any type of nuts, seeds
or dried fruits you like.
—*Tari Ambler, Shorewood, IL*

PREP: 20 min.
COOK: 1½ hours + cooling
MAKES: 8 cups

  4½ cups old-fashioned oats
  ½   cup sunflower kernels
  ⅓   cup toasted wheat germ
  ¼   cup unsweetened
       shredded coconut
  ¼   cup sliced almonds
  ¼   cup chopped pecans
  ¼   cup chopped walnuts
  ¼   cup ground flaxseed
  ½   cup honey
  ⅓   cup water
  3   Tbsp. canola oil
  1   tsp. ground cinnamon
  1   tsp. vanilla extract
  ½   tsp. ground nutmeg
       Dash salt
  ¾   cup dried cranberries
  ¾   cup raisins
       Yogurt, optional

1. In a 3- or 4-qt. slow cooker,
combine the first 8 ingredients. In
a small bowl, whisk honey, water,
oil, cinnamon, vanilla, nutmeg and
salt until blended; stir into oat
mixture. Cook, covered, on high for
1½-2 hours or until crisp, stirring
well every 20 minutes.
2. Stir in cranberries and raisins.
Spread evenly onto waxed paper
or baking sheets; cool completely.
Store in airtight containers. If
desired, serve with yogurt.
½ CUP: 267 cal., 12g fat (2g sat. fat),
0 chol., 43mg sod., 39g carb. (19g
sugars, 5g fiber), 6g pro.

❄
CARNITAS HUEVOS RANCHEROS

When I was in college, I was a
church counselor in Colorado and
had my first taste of Mexican food.
Recently, I have learned to make
more authentic dishes, like these
pork huevos rancheros. It's a great
breakfast-for-dinner dish, too!
—*Lonnie Hartstack, Clarinda, IA*

PREP: 35 min. • **COOK:** 7 hours
MAKES: 12 servings

  1   boneless pork shoulder
       butt roast (3 lbs.), halved
  2   tsp. olive oil
  3   garlic cloves, thinly sliced
  ½   tsp. salt
  ½   tsp. pepper
  1   medium onion, chopped
  2   cans (4 oz. each)
       chopped green chiles
  1   cup salsa
  ½   cup minced fresh cilantro
  ½   cup chicken broth
  ½   cup tequila or additional
       chicken broth
  1   can (15 oz.) black beans,
       rinsed and drained
ASSEMBLY
  12 large eggs
  1   jar (16 oz.) salsa
  4   medium ripe avocados,
       peeled and sliced
  12 flour tortillas (6 in.),
       warmed and quartered

1. Rub roast with oil, garlic, salt and
pepper. Place in a 4- or 5-qt. slow
cooker. Top with onion, green chiles,
salsa, cilantro, broth and tequila.
Cook, covered, on low until meat
is tender, 7-8 hours.
2. Remove roast; shred with 2 forks.
Discard cooking juices, reserving
1 cup. Return meat and reserved
cooking juices to slow cooker. Stir
in beans; heat through.
3. Meanwhile, coat a large skillet
with cooking spray; place over
medium-high heat. Working in
batches, break eggs, 1 at a time,
into pan; reduce heat to low. Cook
until whites are set and yolks begin
to thicken, turning once if desired.
4. Divide pork mixture among
12 serving bowls. Top with salsa,
eggs, avocados and additional
cilantro. Serve with tortillas.
FREEZE OPTION: Freeze cooled meat
mixture and juices in freezer
containers. To use, partially thaw in
refrigerator overnight. Heat through
in a saucepan, stirring occasionally;
add water or broth if necessary.
1 SERVING: 509 cal., 27g fat (8g sat.
fat), 254mg chol., 858mg sod., 32g
carb. (3g sugars, 7g fiber), 31g pro.

CARNITAS HUEVOS RANCHEROS

SLOW-COOKER HAM & EGGS

This dish is appreciated any time of the year, but I especially love serving it on holiday mornings. Once started, it requires little attention—it's a fun meal for the family.
—*Andrea Schaak, Jordan, MN*

PREP: 15 min. • **COOK:** 3 hours
MAKES: 6 servings

- 6   large eggs
- 1   cup biscuit/baking mix
- ⅔   cup 2% milk
- ⅓   cup sour cream
- 2   Tbsp. minced fresh parsley
- 2   garlic cloves, minced
- ½   tsp. salt
- ½   tsp. pepper
- 1   cup cubed fully cooked ham
- 1   cup shredded Swiss cheese
- 1   small onion, finely chopped
- ⅓   cup shredded Parmesan cheese

1. In a large bowl, whisk the first 8 ingredients until blended; stir in remaining ingredients. Pour into a greased 3- or 4-qt. slow cooker.
2. Cook, covered, on low 3-4 hours or until the eggs are set. Cut into wedges.
1 SERVING: 315 cal., 18g fat (9g sat. fat), 256mg chol., 942mg sod., 17g carb. (4g sugars, 1g fiber), 21g pro.

EASY SLOW-COOKER CINNAMON ROLLS

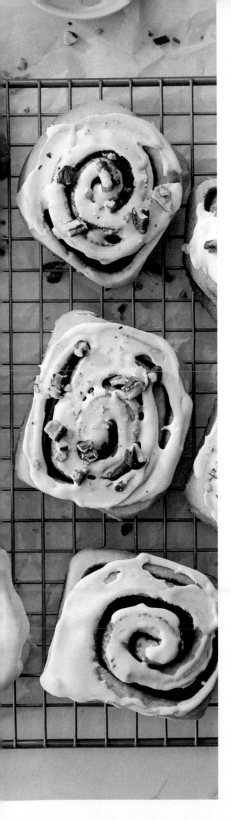

EASY SLOW-COOKER CINNAMON ROLLS

I love how these scrumptious treats make use of my slow cooker and are so easy! I can just walk away and come back to perfectly cooked cinnamon rolls ready for the taking.
—*Nina Ward, New Port Richey, FL*

PREP: 30 min. + standing
COOK: 2 hours • **MAKES:** 1 dozen

- 1   pkg. (¼ oz.) quick-rise yeast
- ¼   cup sugar, divided
- ¼   cup warm water (110° to 115°)
- ½   cup warm 2% milk (110° to 115°)
- 3   Tbsp. butter, softened
- 1   large egg, room temperature, lightly beaten
- 1   tsp. salt
- 2½ to 3 cups all-purpose flour

FILLING
- ¼   cup packed brown sugar
- 1   Tbsp. ground cinnamon
- 3   Tbsp. butter, softened
     Optional: Cream cheese frosting and chopped pecans

1. Place a piece of parchment in a 3½-qt. rectangular slow cooker, letting ends extend up side; spritz paper with cooking spray. In a small bowl, dissolve yeast and 1 tsp. sugar in warm water. In a large bowl, combine milk, remaining sugar, butter, egg, salt, yeast mixture and 2 cups flour; beat on medium speed until smooth. Stir in enough remaining flour to form a soft dough (dough will be sticky).

2. Turn dough onto a floured surface; knead until smooth and elastic, 6-8 minutes. Let stand for 10 minutes.

3. For filling, combine brown sugar and cinnamon. Punch down dough. Lightly flour the work surface again; roll dough into a 16x10-in. rectangle. Spread butter within ½ in. of edges; sprinkle with brown sugar mixture. Roll up jelly-roll style, starting with a long side; pinch seam to seal. Cut into 12 slices. Place rolls side by side, cut side down, into slow cooker.

4. Cover slow cooker with a double layer of white paper towels; place lid securely over towels. Cook, covered, on high, until rolls are set and edges begin to brown, about 2 hours. To avoid scorching, rotate slow cooker insert a half turn midway through cooking, lifting carefully with oven mitts.

5. Using parchment, lift rolls from slow cooker; cool slightly. If desired, top with cream cheese frosting and pecans.

1 CINNAMON ROLL: 195 cal., 7g fat (4g sat. fat), 32mg chol., 255mg sod., 30g carb. (9g sugars, 1g fiber), 4g pro.

TEST KITCHEN TIPS

- Condensation forms on the lid of the slow cooker during the cooking process; placing paper towels under the lid collects the condensation and prevents it from dripping down onto the cinnamon rolls.
- These rolls are best enjoyed the day they are made. If you have leftovers, cool completely, and place them in tightly sealed freezer containers. Freeze for up to 3 months. To reheat, place frozen cinnamon rolls on a baking sheet, and bake in a preheated oven at 375° for 12-15 minutes.

TACO JOE DIP P. 44

APPETIZERS, SNACKS & BEVERAGES

Let your slow cooker be the answer for party apps and between-meal cravings! Create zesty wings, delicious drinks, creamy dips and more—from elegant appetizers to game-day spreads.

ORANGE BLOSSOM
MINT REFRESHER

BUFFET MEATBALLS

I need only five ingredients to fix these easy appetizers. Grape juice and apple jelly are the secrets behind the sweet yet tangy sauce that complements convenient packaged meatballs.
—*Janet Anderson, Carson City, NV*

PREP: 10 min. • **COOK:** 4 hours
MAKES: about 10½ dozen

- 1   cup grape juice
- 1   cup apple jelly
- 1   cup ketchup
- 1   can (8 oz.) tomato sauce
- 1   pkg. (64 oz.) frozen fully cooked Italian meatballs
      Minced fresh parsley, optional

1. In a small saucepan, combine juice, jelly, ketchup and tomato sauce. Cook and stir over medium heat until jelly is melted.
2. Place meatballs in a 5-qt. slow cooker. Pour sauce over the top and gently stir to coat. Cover and cook on low for 4-5 hours or until heated through. If desired, sprinkle with parsley.
1 MEATBALL: 147 cal., 9g fat (4g sat. fat), 20mg chol., 411mg sod., 10g carb. (7g sugars, 1g fiber), 7g pro.

TEST KITCHEN TIPS

You can skip packaged and opt for homemade meatballs instead. If you like a sweeter sauce, use grape jelly instead of apple; to make things tarter, use cranberry juice instead of grape.

ORANGE BLOSSOM MINT REFRESHER

I came up with this recipe because I'm not a fan of regular iced tea. This tea has the perfect combination of freshness and sweetness; the orange blossom water gives it a distinctive flavor.
—*Juliana Gauss, Centennial, CO*

PREP: 10 min. + chilling
COOK: 6 hours
MAKES: 20 servings

- 20 cups water
- 1   bunch fresh mint (about 1 cup)
- 1   cup sugar
- 1   large navel orange
- 1   to 2 Tbsp. orange blossom water or 1½ to 2½ tsp. orange extract
      Optional: Orange slices and additional fresh mint

1. Place water and mint in a 6-qt. slow cooker. Cover and cook on high for 6 hours or until heated through. Strain mixture; discard mint.
2. Whisk in sugar until dissolved. Cut orange crosswise in half; squeeze juice from orange. Stir in juice and orange blossom water. Transfer to a pitcher. Refrigerate until cold, 4-6 hours. Serve over ice, with orange slices and additional mint if desired.
1 CUP: 43 cal., 0 fat (0 sat. fat), 0 chol., 0 sod., 11g carb. (11g sugars, 0 fiber), 0 pro.

BUFFET
MEATBALLS

SLOW-COOKED CHAI TEA

A friend of my mother's brought Chai to her house and told us in India it is served every day. I had never had it before. I liked it so much I came up with a recipe to re-create it.
—*Patty Crouse, Warren, PA*

PREP: 10 min. • **COOK:** 3 hours
MAKES: 8 servings

- 6 cups water
- 1 cup sugar
- 1 cup nonfat dry milk powder
- 6 black tea bags
- 1 tsp. ground ginger
- 1 tsp. ground cinnamon
- ½ tsp. pepper
- ½ tsp. ground cardamom
- ½ tsp. ground cloves
- ½ tsp. vanilla extract

Place all ingredients in a 3- or 4-qt. slow cooker. Cook, covered, on high until heated through, 3-4 hours. Discard tea bags. Serve tea warm.
¾ CUP: 131 cal., 0 fat (0 sat. fat), 2mg chol., 48mg sod., 30g carb. (30g sugars, 0 fiber), 3g pro.

FIVE-CHEESE SPINACH & ARTICHOKE DIP

FIVE-CHEESE SPINACH & ARTICHOKE DIP

This is the dish I am always asked to bring to events. I have made it for weddings, Christmas parties and more.
—*Noelle Myers, Grand Forks, ND*

PREP: 20 min. • **COOK:** 2½ hours
MAKES: 16 servings

- 1 jar (12 oz.) roasted sweet red peppers
- 1 jar (6½ oz.) marinated quartered artichoke hearts
- 1 pkg. (10 oz.) frozen chopped spinach, thawed and squeezed dry
- 8 oz. fresh mozzarella cheese, cubed
- 1½ cups shredded Asiago cheese
- 6 oz. cream cheese, softened and cubed
- 1 cup crumbled feta cheese
- ⅓ cup shredded provolone cheese
- ⅓ cup minced fresh basil
- ¼ cup finely chopped red onion
- 2 Tbsp. mayonnaise
- 2 garlic cloves, minced
  Assorted crackers

1. Drain peppers, reserving 1 Tbsp. liquid; chop peppers. Drain the artichokes, reserving 2 Tbsp. liquid; coarsely chop artichokes.
2. In a 3-qt. slow cooker coated with cooking spray, combine spinach, cheeses, basil, onion, mayonnaise, garlic, artichoke hearts and peppers. Stir in reserved pepper and artichoke liquids. Cook, covered, on high for 2 hours.
3. Stir dip; cook, covered, until cheese is melted, 30-60 minutes longer. Stir again before serving; serve with crackers.
¼ CUP: 197 cal., 16g fat (8g sat. fat), 38mg chol., 357mg sod., 4g carb. (2g sugars, 1g fiber), 9g pro.

BAKED FIVE-CHEESE SPINACH & ARTICHOKE DIP: Preheat oven to 400°. Bake, uncovered, until hot and bubbly, about 30 minutes.

BARBECUED PARTY STARTERS

These sweet and tangy bites are sure to tide everyone over until dinner. At the buffet, set out fun toothpicks for easy nibbling.
—*Anastasia Weiss, Punxsutawney, PA*

PREP: 30 min. • **COOK:** 2¼ hours
MAKES: 16 servings

- 1 lb. ground beef
- ¼ cup finely chopped onion
- 1 pkg. (16 oz.) miniature hot dogs, drained
- 1 jar (12 oz.) apricot preserves
- 1 cup barbecue sauce
- 1 can (20 oz.) pineapple chunks, drained

1. In a large bowl, combine beef and onion, mixing lightly but thoroughly. Shape into 1-in. balls. In a large skillet over medium heat, cook meatballs in 2 batches until cooked through, turning occasionally.
2. Using a slotted spoon, transfer meatballs to a 3-qt. slow cooker. Add hot dogs; stir in preserves and barbecue sauce. Cook, covered, on high or until heated through, 2-3 hours.
3. Stir in pineapple; cook, covered, until heated through, 15-20 minutes longer.
⅓ CUP: 237 cal., 11g fat (4g sat. fat), 36mg chol., 491mg sod., 26g carb. (20g sugars, 0 fiber), 9g pro.

ASIAN WRAPS

ASIAN WRAPS

This recipe is just like any other Asian wrap but with more flavor, a healthy twist and the convenience of a slow cooker. Instead of ordering takeout, try making these yourself.
—Melissa Hansen, Ellison Bay, WI

PREP: 30 min. • **COOK:** 3½ hours
MAKES: 1 dozen

- 2 lbs. boneless skinless chicken breast halves
- ¼ cup reduced-sodium soy sauce
- ¼ cup ketchup
- ¼ cup honey
- 2 Tbsp. minced fresh gingerroot
- 2 Tbsp. sesame oil
- 1 small onion, finely chopped
- 2 Tbsp. cornstarch
- 2 Tbsp. cold water
- 12 round rice paper wrappers (8 in.)
- 3 cups broccoli coleslaw mix
- ¾ cup crispy chow mein noodles

1. Place chicken in a 3-qt. slow cooker. In a small bowl, whisk soy sauce, ketchup, honey, ginger and oil; stir in onion. Pour over chicken. Cook, covered, on low 3-4 hours or until chicken is tender. Remove chicken; shred with 2 forks and refrigerate until assembly.
2. Meanwhile, in a small bowl, mix cornstarch and water until smooth; gradually stir into honey mixture. Cook, covered, on high until sauce is thickened, 20-30 minutes. Toss chicken with ¾ cup sauce; reserve remaining sauce for serving.
3. Fill a large shallow dish partway with water. Dip a rice paper wrapper into water just until pliable, about 45 seconds (do not soften completely); allow excess water to drip off.
4. Place wrapper on a flat surface. Layer ¼ cup coleslaw, ⅓ cup chicken mixture and 1 Tbsp. noodles across the bottom third of wrapper.

BLUEBERRY ICED TEA

Fold in both sides of wrapper; fold bottom over filling, then roll up tightly. Place on a serving plate, seam side down. Repeat with remaining ingredients. Serve with reserved sauce.
1 WRAP WITH 1 TSP. SAUCE: 195 cal., 5g fat (1g sat. fat), 42mg chol., 337mg sod., 21g carb. (8g sugars, 1g fiber), 17g pro. **DIABETIC EXCHANGES:** 2 lean meat, 1½ starch, ½ fat.

BLUEBERRY ICED TEA

I enjoy coming up with new ways to use my slow cooker in the kitchen. If it is going to take up space, it needs to earn its keep! Serve this refreshing tea over plenty of ice and garnish with blueberries if desired. For fun, freeze blueberries in your ice cubes.
—Colleen Delawder, Herndon, VA

PREP: 10 min.
COOK: 3 hours + cooling
MAKES: 11 servings (2¾ qt.)

- 12 cups water
- 2 cups fresh blueberries
- 1 cup sugar
- ¼ tsp. salt
- 4 family-sized tea bags
  Ice cubes
  Optional: Lemon slices. fresh mint leaves and additional fresh blueberries

1. In a 5-qt. slow cooker, combine water, blueberries, sugar and salt. Cook, covered, on low heat 3 hours.
2. Turn off slow cooker; add the tea bags. Cover and let stand for 5 minutes. Discard tea bags; cool 2 hours.
3. Strain and discard blueberries. Pour tea into a 3-qt. pitcher; serve over ice cubes. If desired, top each serving with lemon slices, fresh mint leaves and additional fresh blueberries.
1 CUP: 73 cal., 0 fat (0 sat. fat), 0 chol., 61mg sod., 19g carb. (18g sugars, 0 fiber), 0 pro.

HOT WING DIP

Since I usually have all the ingredients on hand for this recipe, it's a terrific go-to snack for friends and family.
—*Coleen Corner, Grove City, PA*

PREP: 10 min. • **COOK:** 1 hour
MAKES: 4½ cups

- 2 cups shredded cooked chicken
- 1 pkg. (8 oz.) cream cheese, cubed
- 2 cups shredded cheddar cheese
- 1 cup ranch salad dressing
- ½ cup Louisiana-style hot sauce
  Minced fresh parsley, optional
  Tortilla chips and celery sticks

In a 3- or 4-qt. slow cooker, mix the first 5 ingredients. Cook, covered, on low for 1-2 hours or until cheese is melted. If desired, sprinkle with parsley. Serve with tortilla chips and celery.
¼ CUP: 186 cal., 16g fat (7g sat. fat), 43mg chol., 235mg sod., 2g carb. (1g sugars, 0 fiber), 8g pro.
BAKED HOT WING DIP: Preheat oven to 350°. Spread dip mixture into an ungreased 9-in. square baking dish. Bake, uncovered, 20-25 minutes or until heated through.

SWEET & TANGY
CHICKEN WINGS

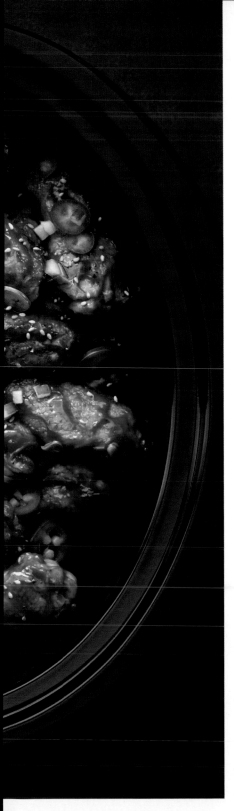

❄ SWEET & TANGY CHICKEN WINGS

I love the convenience of slow-cooker recipes for get-togethers. Start these wings a few hours ahead of time and you'll have fantastic appetizers ready when your guests arrive.
—*Ida Tuey, South Lyon, MI*

PREP: 20 min. • **COOK:** 2¼ hours
MAKES: 2 dozen

- 12 chicken wings (about 3 lbs.)
- ½ tsp. salt, divided
  Dash pepper
- 1½ cups ketchup
- ¼ cup packed brown sugar
- ¼ cup red wine vinegar
- 2 Tbsp. Worcestershire sauce
- 1 Tbsp. Dijon mustard
- 1 tsp. minced garlic
- 1 tsp. liquid smoke, optional
  Optional: Sliced jalapeno peppers, finely chopped red onion and sesame seeds

1. Preheat broiler. Using a sharp knife, cut through the 2 wing joints; discard wingtips. Sprinkle chicken with a dash of salt and pepper. Broil 4-6 in. from the heat until golden brown, 6-8 minutes on each side. Transfer to a greased 5-qt. slow cooker.
2. Combine the ketchup, brown sugar, vinegar, Worcestershire sauce, mustard, garlic, liquid smoke (if desired), and remaining salt; pour over wings. Toss to coat.
3. Cover and cook on low until chicken is tender, 2-3 hours. If desired, top with jalapenos, onion and sesame seeds to serve.

FREEZE OPTION: Freeze cooled fully cooked wings in freezer containers. To use, partially thaw in refrigerator overnight. Reheat in a foil-lined 15x10x1-in. baking pan in a preheated 325° oven until heated through, covering if necessary to prevent browning. Serve as directed.

NOTE: Wear disposable gloves when cutting hot peppers; the oils can burn skin. Avoid touching your face.

1 PIECE: 74 cal., 3g fat (1g sat. fat), 14mg chol., 282mg sod., 7g carb. (6g sugars, 0 fiber), 5g pro.

"Slow cooker wings, yes please! This was such an easy recipe to put together and made for an easy potluck contribution."
GINA.KAPFHAMER, TASTEOFHOME.COM

COCONUT GRANOLA

SLOW-COOKED CRAB DIP

Dips made in the slow cooker are ideal for entertaining since they free up the oven. Leftovers of this one are incredible the next day scooped over a baked potato.
—*Susan D'Amore, West Chester, PA*

PREP: 20 min. • **COOK:** 1½ hours
MAKES: 2¼ cups

- 1 pkg. (8 oz.) cream cheese, softened
- 2 green onions, chopped
- ¼ cup chopped sweet red pepper
- 2 Tbsp. minced fresh parsley
- 2 Tbsp. mayonnaise
- 1 Tbsp. Dijon mustard
- 1 tsp. Worcestershire sauce
- ¼ tsp. salt
- ¼ tsp. pepper
- 2 cans (6 oz. each) lump crabmeat, drained
- 2 Tbsp. capers, drained
  Dash hot pepper sauce
  Optional: Additional capers, minced fresh parsley and grated lemon zest
  Assorted crackers and lemon wedges

1. In a 1½-qt. slow cooker, combine the first 9 ingredients; stir in crab.
2. Cook, covered, on low 1-2 hours. Stir in capers and pepper sauce; cook 30 minutes longer to allow flavors to blend. If desired, top with additional capers, parsley and lemon zest. Serve with crackers and lemon wedges.
¼ CUP: 153 cal., 12g fat (6g sat. fat), 62mg chol., 387mg sod., 2g carb. (0 sugars, 0 fiber), 10g pro.

COCONUT GRANOLA

Here's a versatile treat with a taste of the tropics. Mix it up by subbing dried pineapple or tropical fruits for the cherries.
—Taste of Home *Test Kitchen*

PREP: 15 min.
COOK: 3½ hours + cooling
MAKES: 6 cups

- 4 cups old-fashioned oats
- 1 cup sliced almonds
- 1 cup unsweetened coconut flakes
- 1 tsp. ground cinnamon
- 1 tsp. ground ginger
- ¼ tsp. salt
- ½ cup coconut oil, melted
- ½ cup maple syrup
- 1 cup dried cherries

1. Combine oats, almonds, coconut, cinnamon, ginger and salt in a 3-qt. slow cooker. In small bowl, whisk together oil and maple syrup. Pour into slow cooker; stir to combine. Cook, covered, on low, stirring occasionally, 3½-4 hours. Stir in cherries.
2. Transfer mixture to a baking sheet; let stand until cool.
½ CUP: 343 cal., 19g fat (12g sat. fat), 0 chol., 55mg sod., 41g carb. (18g sugars, 5g fiber), 6g pro.

TEST KITCHEN TIP

Sprinkle this granola over yogurt or ice cream, or pack it in resealable bags for a portable snack throughout the work week.

SLOW-COOKED
CRAB DIP

CRANBERRY SAUERKRAUT MEATBALLS

I first tried these meatballs at a birthday party for a friend, and now I make them all the time. Super easy to prepare, they are perfect for a potluck or a Sunday afternoon football game.
—*Lisa Castelli, Pleasant Prairie, WI*

PREP: 15 min. • **COOK:** 4 hours
MAKES: about 5 dozen

- 1 can (14 oz.) whole-berry cranberry sauce
- 1 can (14 oz.) sauerkraut, rinsed and well drained
- 1 bottle (12 oz.) chili sauce
- ¾ cup packed brown sugar
- 1 pkg. (32 oz.) frozen fully cooked home-style meatballs, thawed
  Minced chives, optional

In a 4-qt. slow cooker, combine the cranberry sauce, sauerkraut, chili sauce and brown sugar. Stir in meatballs. Cook, covered, on low until heated through, 4-5 hours. If desired, top with chives to serve.
1 MEATBALL WITH ABOUT 1 TBSP. SAUCE: 76 cal., 4g fat (2g sat. fat), 6mg chol., 250mg sod., 8g carb. (6g sugars, 0 fiber), 2g pro.

TACO JOE DIP
(PICTURED ON P. 32)

My daughter was the first to try this recipe. She thought it was so good she passed it on to me. My husband and I think it's terrific. Because it's made in a slow cooker, it's perfect for parties or busy days.
—*Lang Secrest, Sierra Vista, AZ*

PREP: 5 min. • **COOK:** 5 hours
MAKES: about 7 cups

- 1 can (16 oz.) kidney beans, rinsed and drained
- 1 can (15¼ oz.) whole kernel corn, drained
- 1 can (15 oz.) black beans, rinsed and drained
- 1 can (14½ oz.) stewed tomatoes, undrained
- 1 can (8 oz.) tomato sauce
- 1 can (4 oz.) chopped green chiles, drained
- 1 envelope taco seasoning
- ½ cup chopped onion
  Thinly sliced green onions, optional
  Tortilla chips and fresh mini bell peppers

In a 5-qt. slow cooker, combine the first 8 ingredients. Cook, covered, on low for 5-6 hours. If desired, sprinkle with green onions. Serve with tortilla chips and mini peppers.
¼ CUP: 49 cal., 0 fat (0 sat. fat), 0 chol., 291mg sod., 9g carb. (2g sugars, 2g
TACO JOE SOUP: Add a 29-oz. can of tomato sauce to the slow cooker. Yield: 6-8.

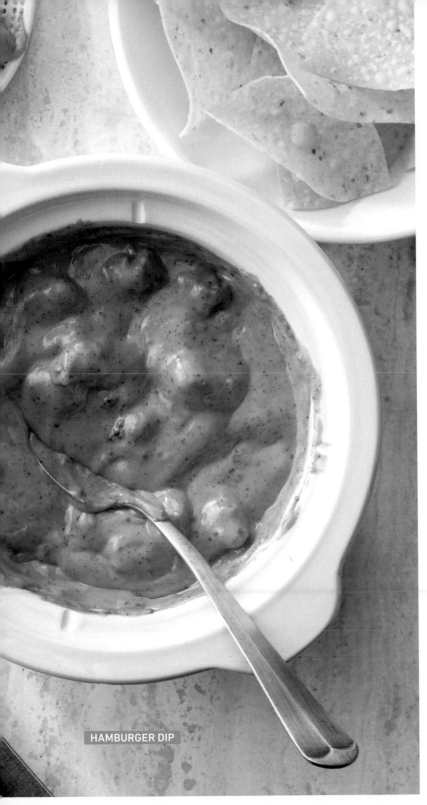

HAMBURGER DIP

HAMBURGER DIP

This is hands-down the easiest dip to make, and I never have leftovers. We have used venison in place of hamburger, as well as half hamburger and half spicy sausage.
—*Mary Kidder, Nappanee, IN*

PREP: 20 min. • **COOK:** 1½ hours
MAKES: 5 cups

- 1 lb. lean ground beef (90% lean)
- 12 oz. cubed Velveeta
- 1 can (10¾ oz.) condensed tomato soup, undiluted
- 1 can (10½ oz.) condensed cream of mushroom soup, undiluted
- 2 tsp. chili powder
- 1 tsp. ground cumin
  Tortilla chips

1. In a large skillet, cook beef over medium heat, breaking into crumbles, until no longer pink, 8-10 minutes; drain. Transfer to a greased 3- or 4-qt. slow cooker.
2. Stir in Velveeta, soups and seasonings. Cook, covered, on low until heated through, 1½-2 hours, stirring halfway through cooking. Serve warm with tortilla chips.
¼ CUP: 97 cal., 6g fat (3g sat. fat), 26mg chol., 330mg sod., 5g carb. (2g sugars, 1g fiber), 7g pro.

"I used smoked paprika and this was scarfed up by my friends in no time!"
REBELWITHOUTACLUE,
TASTEOFHOME.COM

ROOT BEER
PULLED PORK NACHOS

ROOT BEER PULLED PORK NACHOS

I count on my slow cooker to do the honors when I have a house full of summer guests. Teenagers especially love DIY nachos. Try cola, ginger ale or lemon-lime soda if you're not into root beer.
—*James Schend, Pleasant Prairie, WI*

PREP: 20 min. • **COOK:** 8 hours
MAKES: 12 servings

- 1 boneless pork shoulder butt roast (3 to 4 lbs.)
- 1 can (12 oz.) root beer or cola
- 12 cups tortilla chips
- 2 cups shredded cheddar cheese
- 2 medium tomatoes, chopped
  Optional: Pico de gallo, chopped green onions and sliced jalapeno peppers

1. In a 4- or 5-qt. slow cooker, combine pork roast and root beer. Cook, covered, on low 8-9 hours, until meat is tender.

2. Remove roast; cool slightly. When cool enough to handle, shred meat with 2 forks. Return to slow cooker; keep warm.

3. To serve, drain pork. Layer tortilla chips with pork, cheese, tomatoes and optional toppings as desired. Serve immediately.

NOTE: Wear disposable gloves when cutting hot peppers; the oils can burn skin. Avoid touching your face.

1 SERVING: 391 cal., 23g fat (8g sat. fat), 86mg chol., 287mg sod., 20g carb. (4g sugars, 1g fiber), 25g pro.

SPICED APRICOT CIDER

SPICED APRICOT CIDER

You'll need just six ingredients to simmer together this hot spiced beverage. Each delicious mugful is rich with apricot flavor.
—*Connie Cummings, Gloucester, NJ*

PREP: 5 min. • **COOK:** 2 hours
MAKES: 6 servings

- 2 cans (12 oz. each) apricot nectar
- 2 cups water
- ¼ cup lemon juice
- ¼ cup sugar
- 2 whole cloves
- 2 cinnamon sticks (3 in.)

In a 3-qt. slow cooker, combine all ingredients. Cook, covered, on low for 2 hours or until cider reaches desired temperature. Discard cloves and cinnamon sticks.

1 CUP: 70 cal., 0 fat (0 sat. fat), 0 chol., 2mg sod., 18g carb. (17g sugars, 0 fiber), 0 pro.

TEST KITCHEN TIP

If you can't find apricot nectar, try this recipe with peach nectar instead.

GREEK SHRIMP CANAPES

I grew up by the ocean and then moved to a landlocked state. I wanted to show people in my new area how to easily cook seafood, and this is the recipe I came up with. I think it's safe to say it has become a neighborhood favorite.
—*Amy Harris, Springville, UT*

PREP: 15 min. • **COOK:** 65 min.
MAKES: 2½ dozen

- 1½ cups olive oil
- ¾ cup lemon juice
- ⅔ cup dry white wine
- ¼ cup Greek seasoning
- 4 garlic cloves, minced
- 1 lb. uncooked shrimp (31-40 per lb.), peeled and deveined
- 2 large cucumbers
- 1 pkg. (8 oz.) cream cheese, softened
- Minced fresh parsley

1. In a large bowl, whisk the first 5 ingredients until blended. Pour 1½ cups marinade into a large bowl. Add shrimp and stir to coat. Cover; refrigerate 45 minutes.
2. Meanwhile, pour remaining marinade in a 4- or 5-qt. slow cooker. Cook, covered, on high for 45 minutes.
3. Drain shrimp, discarding marinade in bowl. Add shrimp to slow cooker. Cook, covered, on high until shrimp turn pink, about 20 minutes, stirring once; drain.
4. Cut each cucumber into ¼-in.-thick slices. Scoop out centers, leaving bottoms intact. Pipe cream cheese onto each cucumber slice; top with shrimp and parsley.

1 CANAPE: 68 cal., 6g fat (2g sat. fat), 26mg chol., 139mg sod., 1g carb. (1g sugars, 0 fiber), 3g pro.

GREEK SHRIMP CANAPES

OLE BEAN DIP

This rich, cheesy bean dip is a crowd-pleaser and so easy to prepare. Two kinds of cheese and sour cream balance the spicy flavor of chiles and taco sauce. Leftovers are great served cold in lunches.
—*Lorraine Wilson, Moses Lake, WA*

PREP: 20 min. • **COOK:** 4 hours
MAKES: 12 cups

- 4 cups shredded Monterey Jack cheese
- 4 cups shredded cheddar cheese
- 1 can (16 oz.) refried beans
- 1 bottle (16 oz.) taco sauce
- 2 cups sour cream
- 2 medium tomatoes, chopped
- 1 medium onion, chopped
- 1 can (6 oz.) pitted ripe olives, drained and chopped
- 1 can (4 oz.) chopped green chiles
- 1 Tbsp. lemon juice
  Tortilla chip scoops and thinly sliced green onions

Combine the first 10 ingredients in a greased 5- or 6-qt. slow cooker. Cook, covered, on low until cheese is melted, 4-5 hours, stirring every hour. Serve with tortilla chips and green onions.

¼ CUP: 114 cal., 9g fat (5g sat. fat), 20mg chol., 235mg sod., 3g carb. (1g sugars, 1g fiber), 5g pro.

TEST KITCHEN TIP

For a truly smooth dip it is best to shred your own cheese. Preshedded cheese tends not to melt as smoothly, leaving bits of cheese in your dip.

ITALIAN MEATBALLS & SAUSAGES

Here's a wonderful nibble for a tailgate or any family function. The snack is easy to prepare and also very tasty. I've doubled and even tripled the recipe for large groups. No matter how much I make, I always come home with an empty slow cooker.
—*Jan Kasinger, Graham, WA*

PREP: 10 min. • **COOK:** 4 hours
MAKES: 8 cups

- 2 lbs. frozen fully cooked Italian meatballs, thawed
- 1 bottle (16 oz.) zesty Italian salad dressing
- 1 pkg. (14 oz.) miniature smoked sausages
- 2 cups medium fresh mushrooms, stems removed
- 1 can (2¼ oz.) sliced ripe olives, drained

Combine all ingredients in a 4- or 5-qt. slow cooker. Cook, covered, on low until heated through, 4-6 hours, stirring every hour.

1 SERVING: 200 cal., 16g fat (6g sat. fat), 29mg chol., 663mg sod., 4g carb. (1g sugars, 1g fiber), 9g pro.

THAI CHICKEN
LETTUCE CUPS

MOIST & TENDER WINGS

Here are some irresistible,
fall-off-the-bone chicken wings
that everyone will love. Chili sauce
and chili powder give them just a bit
of heat, while molasses lends a hint
of sweetness. They make a fantastic
meal served with rice.
—*Sharon Morcilio, Joshua Tree, CA*

PREP: 15 min. • **COOK:** 3¼ hours
MAKES: about 4 dozen

- 5 lbs. chicken wings
  (about 25 wings)
- 1 bottle (12 oz.) chili sauce
- ¼ cup lemon juice
- ¼ cup molasses
- 2 Tbsp. Worcestershire sauce
- 6 garlic cloves, minced
- 1 Tbsp. chili powder
- 1 Tbsp. salsa
- 1 tsp. garlic salt
- 3 drops hot pepper sauce
  Optional: Ranch salad dressing
  and dill pickle slices

1. Cut chicken wings into 3 sections;
discard tips. Place wings in a 5-qt.
slow cooker.
2. In a small bowl, combine the next
9 ingredients; pour over chicken.
Stir to coat. Cook, covered, on low
3-4 hours or until chicken is tender.
3. To serve, remove wings to
a 15x10x1-in. pan; arrange in
a single layer. Preheat broiler.
4. Transfer cooking juices to
a skillet; skim fat. Bring juices
to a boil; cook until mixture is
reduced by half, 15-20 minutes,
stirring occasionally.
5. Meanwhile, broil wings 3-4 in.
from heat until lightly browned,
2-3 minutes. Brush with sauce
before serving. If desired, serve
with ranch dressing and pickles.
1 PIECE: 65 cal., 4g fat (1g sat. fat),
15mg chol., 165mg sod., 3g carb.
(3g sugars, 0 fiber), 5g pro.

❄ THAI CHICKEN LETTUCE CUPS

Lettuce wraps make light, lively
appetizers. The slow cooker does
most of the work—just load it up
and let things get cooking. When
the chicken is cooked, just shred
and serve.
—*Robin Haas, Hyde Park, MA*

PREP: 10 min. • **COOK:** 2½ hours
MAKES: 12 servings

- 1 lb. boneless skinless
  chicken breasts
- ½ cup reduced-sodium
  chicken broth
- 4 garlic cloves, minced
- 1 Tbsp. sugar
- 1 Tbsp. reduced-
  sodium soy sauce
- 2 tsp. oyster sauce
- ½ tsp. crushed red pepper flakes
- 2 cups torn basil leaves, divided
- 2 Tbsp. hoisin sauce
- 12 Bibb or Boston lettuce leaves
- 2 cups cooked long grain rice

- 4 green onions, chopped
  Shredded carrots and thinly
  sliced radishes

1. In a 1½-qt. slow cooker, combine
first 7 ingredients. Cook, covered,
on low until a thermometer inserted
in the chicken reads 165°, about
2½ hours.
2. Remove chicken; shred with
2 forks. Return to slow cooker.
Stir in 1½ cups basil and the
hoisin sauce; heat through.
3. Serve in lettuce leaves with rice,
green onions, carrots, radishes and
remaining ½ cup basil.
FREEZE OPTION: Freeze cooled
chicken mixture and juices in
freezer containers. To use, partially
thaw in refrigerator overnight. Heat
through in a saucepan, stirring
occasionally and adding broth
if necessary.
1 FILLED LETTUCE CUP: 93 cal., 1g fat
(0 sat. fat), 21mg chol., 162mg sod.,
11g carb. (2g sugars, 1g fiber), 9g pro.

MOIST & TENDER WINGS

SLOW-COOKED SMOKIES

I like to include these little smokies smothered in barbecue sauce on all my appetizer buffets—they're always popular with both children and adults.
—*Sundra Hauck, Bogalusa, LA*

PREP: 5 min. • **COOK:** 5 hours
MAKES: 8 servings

- 1 pkg. (14 oz.) miniature smoked sausages
- 1 bottle (28 oz.) barbecue sauce
- 1¼ cups water
- 3 Tbsp. Worcestershire sauce
- 3 Tbsp. steak sauce
- ½ tsp. pepper

In a 3-qt. slow cooker, combine all ingredients. Cover and cook on low for until heated through, 5-6 hours. Serve with a slotted spoon.
1 SERVING: 331 cal., 14g fat (5g sat. fat), 32mg chol., 1694mg sod., 44g carb. (35g sugars, 1g fiber), 7g pro.

SLOW-COOKED SALSA

I love the fresh taste of homemade salsa, but as a working mother, I don't have much time to make it. So I came up with this slow-cooked version that practically makes itself! It uses only five ingredients.
—*Toni Menard, Lompoc, CA*

PREP: 15 min.
COOK: 2½ hours + cooling
MAKES: about 2 cups

- 10 plum tomatoes
- 2 garlic cloves
- 1 small onion, cut into wedges
- 2 jalapeno peppers
- ¼ cup cilantro leaves
- ½ tsp. salt, optional

1. Core tomatoes. Cut a small slit in 2 tomatoes; insert a garlic clove into each slit. Place tomatoes and onion in a 3-qt. slow cooker.
2. Cut stems off jalapenos; remove seeds if a milder salsa is desired. Add jalapenos to the slow cooker.
3. Cover and cook on high for 2½-3 hours or until vegetables are softened (some may brown slightly); cool.
4. In a blender, combine the tomato mixture, cilantro and, if desired, salt; cover and process until blended. Refrigerate leftovers.
NOTE: Wear disposable gloves when cutting hot peppers; the oils can burn skin. Avoid touching your face.
¼ CUP: 20 cal., 0 fat (0 sat. fat), 0 chol., 5mg sod., 4g carb. (3g sugars, 1g fiber), 1g pro. **DIABETIC EXCHANGES:** 1 free food.

HOT BACON CHEESE DIP

HOT BACON CHEESE DIP

I've tried assorted appetizers before, but this one is a surefire people-pleaser. The thick dip has lots of bacon flavor and keeps my guests happily munching as long as it lasts. I serve it with tortilla chips or sliced French bread.
—*Suzanne Whitaker, Knoxville, TN*

PREP: 15 min. • **COOK:** 2 hours
MAKES: 4 cups

2 pkg. (8 oz. each) cream cheese, cubed
4 cups shredded cheddar cheese
1 cup half-and-half cream
2 tsp. Worcestershire sauce
1 tsp. dried minced onion
1 tsp. prepared mustard
16 bacon strips, cooked and crumbled
   Tortilla chips or toasted French bread slices

1. In a 1½-qt. slow cooker, combine first 6 ingredients. Cover and cook on low for 2-3 hours or until cheeses are melted, stirring occasionally.
2. Just before serving, stir in the bacon. If desired, top with additional crumbled bacon. Serve warm with tortilla chips or toasted bread.
¼ CUP: 261 cal., 23g fat (14g sat. fat), 77mg chol., 417mg sod., 3g carb. (1g sugars, 0 fiber), 11g pro.

TEST KITCHEN TIP

If you like, reserve some of the crumbled bacon to sprinkle on top of the dip before serving. Or, use some additional bacon for the topping—nothing's wrong with extra bacon!

NUTTY SLOW-COOKER
SNACK MIX

NUTTY SLOW-COOKER SNACK MIX

My three teenage boys inhale snacks so fast it's hard to keep up! This easy recipe makes a big batch that keeps them snacking happily for the day—and I appreciate that the nutrient-dense nuts add a little protein.
—*Jennifer Fisher, Austin, TX*

PREP: 10 min. • **COOK:** 1½ hours
MAKES: 7 cups

- 3 cups Cheerios
- 3 cups mixed nuts
- 2 cups Goldfish cheddar crackers
- ½ cup butter, melted
- 1 Tbsp. Worcestershire sauce
- 1 tsp. Greek seasoning

1. Combine Cheerios, nuts and crackers in a 4- or 5-qt. slow cooker. Whisk together butter, Worcestershire sauce and Greek seasoning. Pour over cereal mixture; toss to coat.
2. Cook, covered, on high for 1 hour, stirring frequently. Reduce heat to low; cook 30-45 minutes longer or until crisp, stirring frequently.
3. Spread onto a baking sheet to cool. Store in an airtight container.
½ CUP: 337 cal., 25g fat (7g sat. fat), 19mg chol., 399mg sod., 22g carb. (2g sugars, 4g fiber), 7g pro.

BUTTER CHICKEN MEATBALLS

✴ BUTTER CHICKEN MEATBALLS

My husband and I love meatballs, and we love butter chicken. Before an appetizer party, we had the idea to combine the two, and the result got rave reviews! For a main dish, just serve them with basmati rice.
—*Shannon Dobos, Calgary, AB*

PREP: 30 min. • **COOK:** 3 hours
MAKES: about 3 dozen

- 1½ lbs. ground chicken or turkey
- 1 large egg, lightly beaten
- ½ cup soft bread crumbs
- 1 tsp. garam masala
- ½ tsp. tandoori masala seasoning
- ½ tsp. salt
- ¼ tsp. cayenne pepper
- 3 Tbsp. minced fresh cilantro, divided
- 1 jar (14.1 oz.) butter chicken sauce

1. Combine the first 7 ingredients plus 2 Tbsp. cilantro; mix lightly but thoroughly. With wet hands, shape into 1-in. balls. Place meatballs in a 3-qt. slow cooker coated with cooking spray. Pour butter sauce over meatballs.
2. Cook, covered, on low until the meatballs are cooked through, 3-4 hours. Top with remaining 1 Tbsp. cilantro.
FREEZE OPTION: Omitting the last 1 Tbsp. cilantro, freeze the cooled meatball mixture in freezer containers. To use, partially thaw in refrigerator overnight. Microwave, covered, on high in a microwave-safe dish until heated through, stirring occasionally; add water if necessary. To serve, sprinkle with remaining cilantro.
NOTE: Look for butter chicken sauce in the international foods section.
1 MEATBALL: 40 cal., 2g fat (1g sat. fat), 18mg chol., 87mg sod., 1g carb. (1g sugars, 0 fiber), 3g pro.

TOMATO APPLE
CHUTNEY

CHEESY CHICKEN TACO DIP

We're huge college football fans (go Irish!), and my chicken taco dip hasn't missed a season opener in many years. A slow cooker keeps the dip warm for the whole game—if it lasts that long!

—Deanna Garretson, Yucaipa, CA

PREP: 15 min.
COOK: 4 hours 10 min.
MAKES: 8 cups

- 1 jar (16 oz.) salsa
- 1 can (30 oz.) refried beans
- 1½ lbs. boneless skinless chicken breasts
- 1 Tbsp. taco seasoning
- 2 cups shredded cheddar cheese
- 3 green onions, chopped
- 1 medium tomato, chopped
- ¼ cup chopped fresh cilantro Tortilla chips

1. In a greased 3- or 4-qt. slow cooker, mix salsa and beans. Top with chicken; sprinkle with taco seasoning. Cook, covered, on low until chicken is tender, 4-5 hours.
2. Remove chicken; shred finely using 2 forks. Return to slow cooker; stir in cheese. Cook, covered, on low until cheddar cheese is melted, 10-15 minutes, stirring occasionally.
3. To serve, top with green onions, tomato and cilantro. Serve with tortilla chips.

¼ CUP DIP: 82 cal., 3g fat (2g sat. fat), 19mg chol., 238mg sod., 5g carb. (1g sugars, 1g fiber), 7g pro.

TOMATO APPLE CHUTNEY

During the fall and winter, I love to make different kinds of chutney to give as hostess gifts. Cook this chutney in a slow cooker, and you don't have to fuss with it until you are ready to serve it.

—Nancy Heishman, Las Vegas, NV

PREP: 15 min. • **COOK:** 5 hours
MAKES: 7½ cups

- 3 cans (14½ oz. each) fire-roasted diced tomatoes with garlic, undrained
- 2 medium red onions, chopped
- 1 large apple, peeled and chopped
- 1 cup golden raisins
- ¾ cup cider vinegar
- ½ cup packed brown sugar
- 1 Tbsp. chopped seeded jalapeno pepper
- 1 Tbsp. minced fresh cilantro
- 2 tsp. curry powder
- ½ tsp. salt
- ¼ tsp. ground allspice Baked pita chips

Combine the first 11 ingredients in a greased 3-qt. slow cooker. Cook, uncovered, on high 5-6 hours or until thickened. Serve warm with pita chips.

NOTE: Wear disposable gloves when cutting hot peppers; the oils can burn skin. Avoid touching your face.

¼ CUP: 48 cal., 0 fat (0 sat. fat), 0 chol., 152mg sod., 11g carb. (8g sugars, 1g fiber), 1g pro.

TEST KITCHEN TIP

It's unusual to cook something uncovered in the slow cooker, but it is essential for this chutney. Keeping the cover off allows the liquid to evaporate during cooking.

CHEESY CHICKEN
TACO DIP

ITALIAN OYSTER CRACKERS

My friends and family love these crackers that are easily made in the slow cooker. Often I leave them in the slow cooker and everyone eats them warm.
—*Angela Lively, Conroe, TX*

PREP: 10 min. • **COOK:** 1 hour
MAKES: 6 cups

- 2 pkg. (9 oz. each) oyster crackers
- ¼ cup canola oil
- 3 garlic cloves, minced
- 1 envelope Italian salad dressing mix
- 1 tsp. dill weed
- ¼ cup butter, melted
- ½ cup grated Parmesan cheese

1. Combine crackers, oil, garlic, Italian salad dressing mix and dill weed in a 6-qt. slow cooker. Cook, covered, on low for 1 hour.
2. Drizzle melted butter over crackers; sprinkle with cheese. Stir to coat.
3. Transfer mixture to a baking sheet; let stand until cool. Store in an airtight container.
¾ CUP: 407 cal., 20g fat (6g sat. fat), 20mg chol., 1057mg sod., 49g carb. (2g sugars, 2g fiber), 8g pro.

ITALIAN OYSTER CRACKERS

ONE-BITE TAMALES

Clever little meatballs deliver the flavor and rich sauce of a traditional tamale in a bite-sized portion. They're a delightfully different addition to a party spread.
—*Dolores Jaycox, Gretna, LA*

PREP: 40 min.
COOK: 3 hours 20 min.
MAKES: about 5½ dozen

1¼ cups cornmeal
½ cup all-purpose flour
5¾ cups V8 juice, divided
4 tsp. chili powder, divided
4 tsp. ground cumin, divided
2 tsp. salt, divided
1 tsp. garlic powder
½ to 1 tsp. cayenne pepper
1 lb. bulk spicy pork sausage
Tortilla chip scoops

1. Preheat oven to 350°. Mix cornmeal, flour, ¾ cup V8 juice, 2 tsp. chili powder, 2 tsp. cumin, 1 tsp. salt, the garlic powder and cayenne. Add sausage; mix lightly but thoroughly. Divide mixture and shape into 1-in. balls.
2. Place meatballs on a greased rack in a 15x10-in. pan. Bake until cooked through, 20-25 minutes.
3. In a 4-qt. slow cooker, mix the remaining 5 cups V8 juice, 2 tsp. chili powder, 2 tsp. cumin and 1 tsp. salt. Gently stir in meatballs. Cook, covered, on low until heated through, 3-4 hours. Place each meatball in a tortilla chip scoop to serve.

1 TAMALE: 37 cal., 2g fat (0g sat. fat), 4mg chol., 172mg sod., 4g carb. (1g sugars, 0g fiber), 1g pro.

MEXICAN FONDUE

This irresistible fondue has become such a favorite with family and friends, I make it often for all kinds of occasions. It's fun to serve with fondue forks if you have them.
—*Nella Parker, Hersey, MI*

PREP: 15 min. • **COOK:** 1½ hours
MAKES: 4½ cups

1 can (14¾ oz.) cream-style corn
1 can (14½ oz.) diced tomatoes, drained
3 Tbsp. chopped green chiles
1 tsp. chili powder
1 pkg. (16 oz.) Velveeta, cubed
French bread cubes

1. In a small bowl, combine the corn, tomatoes, green chiles and chili powder. Stir in cheese. Pour mixture into a 1½-qt. slow cooker coated with cooking spray.
2. Cover and cook on high until cheese is melted, 1½ hours, stirring every 30 minutes. Serve warm with bread cubes.

¼ CUP: 105 cal., 6g fat (4g sat. fat), 20mg chol., 421mg sod., 7g carb. (3g sugars, 1g fiber), 5g pro.

BLACK BEAN CHICKEN NACHOS

SPICY HONEY SRIRACHA GAME-DAY DIP

You can easily whip up this creamy, spicy and salty dip. I love dips in the slow cooker for parties—just turn the slow cooker to low once the dip is cooked and let your guests help themselves. No need to worry about the dip getting cold and having to reheat it.
—Julie Peterson, Crofton, MD

PREP: 20 min. • **COOK:** 3 hours
MAKES: 3 cups

- 1 lb. ground chicken
- 1 pkg. (8 oz.) cream cheese, cubed
- 1 cup shredded white cheddar cheese
- ¼ cup chicken broth
- 2 to 4 Tbsp. Sriracha chili sauce
- 2 Tbsp. honey
  Tortilla chips
  Chopped green onions, optional

1. In a large skillet, cook chicken over medium heat until no longer pink, 6-8 minutes, breaking into crumbles; drain. Transfer to a greased 3-qt. slow cooker. Stir in cream cheese, cheddar cheese, broth, chili sauce and honey.
2. Cook, covered, on low until cheese is melted, 3-4 hours, stirring every 30 minutes. Serve with tortilla chips. If desired, sprinkle with green onions.
¼ CUP: 168 cal., 13g fat (6g sat. fat), 54mg chol., 243mg sod., 5g carb. (4g sugars, 0 fiber), 9g pro.

BLACK BEAN CHICKEN NACHOS

The best chicken nachos are found at Zeppelins in Cedar Rapids, Iowa. Their famous dish inspired me to make my own nachos—but with the added convenience of a slow cooker. I always use cilantro because it is economical and makes the dish pop.
—Natalie Hess, Pennsville, NJ

PREP: 10 min. • **COOK:** 4 hours
MAKES: 8 servings

- 1½ lbs. boneless skinless chicken breast
- 2 jars (16 oz. each) black bean and corn salsa
- 1 each medium green pepper and sweet red pepper, chopped
  Tortilla chips
- 2 cups shredded Mexican cheese blend

Optional: Minced fresh cilantro, pickled jalapeno slices and sour cream

1. Place chicken, salsa and peppers in a 3- or 4-qt. slow cooker. Cook, covered, on low until meat is tender, 4-5 hours.
2. Remove chicken; shred with 2 forks. Return to slow cooker to heat through. Using a slotted spoon, serve chicken over chips; sprinkle with cheese and optional toppings.
½ CUP CHICKEN MIXTURE: 280 cal., 11g fat (5g sat. fat), 72mg chol., 708mg sod., 20g carb. (5g sugars, 8g fiber), 27g pro

SPICY HONEY SRIRACHA
GAME-DAY DIP

SLOW-COOKER
CAPONATA

SLOW-COOKER CAPONATA

This Italian eggplant dip preps quickly and actually gets better as it stands. Serve it at room temperature or warm right from the slow cooker.
—*Nancy Beckman, Helena, MT*

PREP: 20 min. • **COOK:** 5 hours
MAKES: 6 cups

- 2 medium eggplants, cut into ½-in. pieces
- 1 medium onion, chopped
- 1 can (14½ oz.) diced tomatoes, undrained
- 12 garlic cloves, sliced
- ½ cup dry red wine
- 3 Tbsp. olive oil
- 2 Tbsp. red wine vinegar
- 4 tsp. capers, undrained
- 5 bay leaves
- 1½ tsp. salt
- ¼ tsp. coarsely ground pepper
  French bread baguette slices, toasted
  Optional: Fresh basil leaves, toasted pine nuts and additional olive oil

1. Place the first 11 ingredients in a 6-qt. slow cooker (do not stir). Cook, covered, on high for 3 hours.
2. Stir gently; replace lid. Cook on high 2 hours longer or until vegetables are tender.
3. Cool slightly; discard bay leaves. Serve with toasted baguette slices, adding toppings as desired.
¼ CUP: 34 cal., 2g fat (0 sat. fat), 0 chol., 189mg sod., 4g carb. (2g sugars, 2g fiber), 1g pro.

TEST KITCHEN TIP

Try adding a little leftover caponata to scrambled eggs for a savory breakfast.

CHEESY MEATBALLS

CHEESY MEATBALLS

Can meatballs be lucky? My guys think so, and they want them on game days! My recipe has a big fan following.
—*Jill Hill, Dixon, IL*

PREP: 1 hour • **COOK:** 4 hours
MAKES: about 9 dozen

- 1 large egg
- ½ cup 2% milk
- 2 Tbsp. dried minced onion
- 4 Tbsp. chili powder, divided
- 1 tsp. salt
- 1 tsp. pepper
- 1½ cups crushed Ritz crackers (about 1 sleeve)
- 2 lbs. ground beef
- 1 lb. bulk pork sausage
- 2 cups shredded Velveeta
- 3 cans (10¾ oz. each) condensed tomato soup, undiluted
- 2½ cups water
- ½ cup packed brown sugar

1. Preheat oven to 400°. In a large bowl, whisk egg, milk, minced onion, 2 Tbsp. chili powder, salt and pepper; stir in crushed crackers. Add beef, sausage and cheese; mix lightly but thoroughly.
2. Shape mixture into 1-in. balls. Place meatballs on greased racks in 15x10x1-in. baking pans. Bake until browned, 15-18 minutes.
3. Meanwhile, in a 5- or 6-qt. slow cooker, combine soup, water, brown sugar and remaining chili powder. Gently stir in meatballs. Cook, covered, on low until meatballs are cooked through, 4-5 hours.
FREEZE OPTION: Freeze cooled meatball mixture in freezer containers. To use, partially thaw in refrigerator overnight. Heat through in a covered saucepan, stirring and add water if necessary. Serve as directed.
1 MEATBALL: 52 cal., 3g fat (1g sat. fat), 11mg chol., 134mg sod., 4g carb. (2g sugars, 0 fiber), 3g pro.

VEGETABLES WITH
CHEESE SAUCE P. 100

SIDE DISHES

A side dish should do more than just fill up space on the plate—a delicious side dish might just steal the show! Here are some amazing options full of flavor and slow-cooked convenience.

SAUSAGE-HERB DRESSING

SIMPLE SAUCY POTATOES

These rich and creamy potatoes are simple to prepare for potlucks. The saucy side dish always gets rave reviews wherever I take it.
—*Gloria Schroeder, Ottawa Lake, MI*

PREP: 10 min. • **COOK:** 4 hours
MAKES: 12 servings

- 4 cans (14½ oz. each) sliced potatoes, drained
- 2 cans (10¾ oz. each) condensed cream of celery soup, undiluted
- 2 cups sour cream
- 10 bacon strips, cooked and crumbled, divided
- 6 green onions, thinly sliced
  Optional: Chopped chives and coarse cracked pepper

Place potatoes in a 3-qt. slow cooker. Combine next 4 ingredients, reserving ⅓ cup bacon crumbles; pour mixture over potatoes and mix well. Cover and cook on high for 4-5 hours. Top with reserved bacon and, if desired, chopped chives and coarse cracked pepper.
¾ CUP: 144 cal., 10g fat (6g sat. fat), 32mg chol., 369mg sod., 7g carb. (2g sugars, 1g fiber), 4g pro.

SAUSAGE-HERB DRESSING

To make time for last-minute Thanksgiving essentials, I prep the sausage part of this recipe a day ahead of time, then finish the dressing in my slow cooker on the big day. It has stood the test two years running!
—*Judy Batson, Tampa, FL*

PREP: 20 min. • **COOK:** 2 hours
MAKES: 10 servings

- 1 lb. bulk sage pork sausage
- 1 medium sweet onion, chopped (about 2 cups)
- 2 celery ribs, chopped
- ¼ cup brewed coffee
- ½ tsp. poultry seasoning
- ½ tsp. dried oregano
- ½ tsp. rubbed sage
- ½ tsp. dried thyme
- ½ tsp. pepper
- 1½ cups chicken or turkey broth
- 1 pkg. (12 oz.) seasoned stuffing cubes (8 cups)
  Chopped fresh parsley

1. In a 6-qt. stockpot, cook and crumble sausage with onion and celery over medium heat until no longer pink, 5-7 minutes; drain. Stir in coffee and seasonings; cook 3 minutes, stirring occasionally.
2. Add broth; bring to a boil. Remove from heat; stir in stuffing cubes. Transfer to a greased 4- or 5-qt. slow cooker.
3. Cook, covered, on low until heated through and edges are lightly browned, 2-2½ hours, stirring once. Sprinkle with parsley.
¾ CUP: 254 cal., 11g fat (3g sat. fat), 25mg chol., 919mg sod., 29g carb. (4g sugars, 2g fiber), 9g pro.

TEST KITCHEN TIP

Don't be tempted to add more broth than is called for—the dressing will moisten as it cooks. Stir once during cooking so the mixture heats evenly.

SIMPLE SAUCY
POTATOES

GLAZED SPICED CARROTS

Glazed carrots are a classic side dish for special occasions. This side is easy to put together, and people really enjoy it.
—Taste of Home *Test Kitchen*

PREP: 10 min. • **COOK:** 6 hours
MAKES: 6 servings

- 2 lbs. small carrots
- ½ cup peach preserves
- ½ cup butter, melted
- ¼ cup packed brown sugar
- 1 tsp. vanilla extract
- ½ tsp. ground cinnamon
- ¼ tsp. salt
- ⅛ tsp. ground nutmeg
- 2 Tbsp. cornstarch
- 2 Tbsp. water
  Toasted chopped pecans, optional

1. Place carrots in a 3-qt. slow cooker. Combine preserves, butter, brown sugar, vanilla, cinnamon, salt and nutmeg. In a small bowl, combine cornstarch and water until smooth; stir into preserve mixture. Pour over carrots.
2. Cook, covered, on low until tender, 6-8 hours. Stir; sprinkle with pecans if desired.
¾ CUP: 290 cal., 15g fat (10g sat. fat), 40mg chol., 327mg sod., 39g carb. (32g sugars, 3g fiber), 1g pro.

BUTTERNUT COCONUT CURRY

I love my slow cooker—it makes it so easy to make dinner! This flavorful curry was first created for a potluck, and since then the recipe has been requested often.
—Jess Apfe, Berkeley, CA

PREP: 35 min. • **COOK:** 4 hours
MAKES: 9 servings

- 1 cup chopped carrots
- 1 small onion, chopped
- 1 Tbsp. olive oil
- 1½ tsp. brown sugar
- 1½ tsp. curry powder
- 1 garlic clove, minced
- ½ tsp. ground cinnamon
- ¼ tsp. ground ginger
- ⅛ tsp. salt
- 1 medium butternut squash (about 2½ lbs.), cut into 1-in. cubes
- 2½ cups vegetable broth
- ¾ cup coconut milk
- ½ cup uncooked basmati or jasmine rice

1. In a large skillet, saute carrots and onion in oil until onion is tender. Add the brown sugar, curry, garlic, cinnamon, ginger and salt. Cook and stir 2 minutes longer.
2. In a 3- or 4-qt. slow cooker, combine the butternut squash, broth, coconut milk, rice and carrot mixture. Cover and cook on low until rice is tender, 4-5 hours.
¾ CUP: 200 cal., 6g fat (4g sat. fat), 0 chol., 312mg sod., 34g carb. (5g sugars, 5g fiber), 3g pro.

SPICED ACORN SQUASH

SPICED ACORN SQUASH

When I was working full time, I found I couldn't always cook the meals my family loved when I got home in the evening. So I re-created many of those dishes in the slow cooker. This treatment for squash is one of our favorites.
—*Carol Greco, Centereach, NY*

PREP: 15 min. • **COOK:** 3½ hours
MAKES: 4 squash halves

- ¾ cup packed brown sugar
- 1 tsp. ground cinnamon
- 1 tsp. ground nutmeg
- 2 small acorn squash, halved and seeded
- ¾ cup raisins
- 4 Tbsp. butter
- ½ cup water

1. In a small bowl, mix brown sugar, cinnamon and nutmeg; spoon into squash halves. Sprinkle with the raisins. Top each with 1 Tbsp. butter. Wrap each half individually in heavy-duty foil, sealing tightly.
2. Pour water into a 5-qt. slow cooker. Place the squash in slow cooker, cut side up (packets may be stacked). Cook, covered, on high until squash is tender, 3½-4 hours. Open foil carefully to allow steam to escape.
1 FILLED SQUASH HALF: 433 cal., 12g fat (7g sat. fat), 31mg chol., 142mg sod., 86g carb. (63g sugars, 5g fiber), 3g pro.

CITRUS CARROTS

CITRUS CARROTS

These carrots are yummy and so simple. The recipe is from my mom, who tweaked it a bit to suit her tastes. You can make this dish a day in advance and refrigerate it until needed. Then just reheat it before serving!
—*Julie Puderbaugh, Berwick, PA*

PREP: 10 min. • **COOK:** 4¼ hours
MAKES: 12 servings

- 12 cups frozen sliced carrots (about 48 oz.), thawed
- 1¾ cups orange juice
- ½ cup sugar
- 3 Tbsp. butter, cubed
- ½ tsp. salt
- 3 Tbsp. cornstarch
- ¼ cup cold water
  Minced fresh parsley, optional

1. In a 3- or 4-qt. slow cooker, combine the first 5 ingredients. Cook, covered, on low until carrots are tender, 4-5 hours.
2. In a small bowl, mix cornstarch and water until smooth; gradually stir into slow cooker. Cook, covered, on high until sauce is thickened, 15-30 minutes. Garnish with fresh parsley if desired.
¾ CUP: 136 cal., 4g fat (2g sat. fat), 8mg chol., 208mg sod., 25g carb. (18g sugars, 5g fiber), 1g pro.

SCALLOPED POTATOES & HAM

SCALLOPED POTATOES & HAM

I adapted a favorite oven recipe so it could be made in the slow cooker. It's ready to serve when I get home, making it a real winner in my book!
—*Joni Hilton, Rocklin, CA*

PREP: 25 min. • **COOK:** 8 hours
MAKES: 16 servings

- 1 can (10¾ oz.) condensed cheddar cheese soup, undiluted
- 1 can (10¾ oz.) condensed cream of mushroom soup, undiluted
- 1 cup 2% milk
- 10 medium potatoes, peeled and thinly sliced
- 3 cups cubed fully cooked ham
- 2 medium onions, chopped
- 1 tsp. paprika
- 1 tsp. pepper

1. In a small bowl, combine the soups and milk. In a greased 5-qt. slow cooker, layer half of the potatoes, ham, onions and soup mixture. Repeat layers. Sprinkle with paprika and pepper.
2. Cover and cook on low until potatoes are tender, 8-10 hours.
¾ CUP: 167 cal., 4g fat (1g sat. fat), 17mg chol., 630mg sod., 25g carb. (4g sugars, 2g fiber), 8g pro.

LOADED
MASHED POTATOES

LOADED MASHED POTATOES

Every holiday season, my mom could be counted on to deliver her cream cheese mashed potatoes. I keep the tradition going but boost the cheese factor.
—*Ann Nolte, Riverview, FL*

PREP: 25 min. + chilling
COOK: 3 hours • **MAKES:** 10 servings

- 3   lbs. cubed peeled potatoes (about 9 medium)
- 1   pkg. (8 oz.) cream cheese, softened
- 1   cup sour cream
- ½   cup butter, cubed
- ¼   cup 2% milk
- ½   lb. bacon strips, cooked and crumbled
- 1½ cups shredded cheddar cheese
- 1½ cups shredded pepper jack cheese
- 4   green onions, thinly sliced
- ½   tsp. onion powder
- ½   tsp. garlic powder
     Salt and pepper to taste

1. Place potatoes in a Dutch oven, adding water to cover. Bring to a boil; reduce heat and simmer, uncovered, 10-15 minutes or until tender. Drain; return to pan. Mash with cream cheese, sour cream, butter and milk. Stir in bacon, cheeses, onions and seasonings. Cover; refrigerate overnight.
2. Transfer to a greased 3- or 4-qt. slow cooker. Cook, covered, on low 3-3½ hours.
¾ CUP: 505 cal., 36g fat (20g sat. fat), 109mg chol., 530mg sod., 31g carb. (3g sugars, 3g fiber), 16g pro.

SLOW-COOKED BROCCOLI

SLOW-COOKED BROCCOLI

This crumb-topped side dish is quick to assemble and full of flavor. Since it simmers in a slow cooker, it frees up my oven for other things. This is a tremendous help when I'm preparing a big meal at home.
—*Connie Slocum, Antioch, TN*

PREP: 10 min.
COOK: 2 hours 40 min.
MAKES: 10 servings

- 6   cups frozen chopped broccoli, partially thawed
- 1   can (10¾ oz.) condensed cream of celery soup, undiluted
- 1½   cups shredded sharp cheddar cheese, divided
- ¼   cup chopped onion
- ½   tsp. Worcestershire sauce
- ¼   tsp. pepper
- 1   cup crushed butter-flavored crackers (about 25)
- 2   Tbsp. butter

1. In a large bowl, combine the broccoli, soup, 1 cup cheese, onion, Worcestershire sauce and pepper. Pour into a greased 3-qt. slow cooker. Sprinkle crackers on top; dot with butter.
2. Cook, covered, on high for 2½-3 hours. Sprinkle with the remaining ½ cup cheese. Cook 10 minutes longer or until cheese is melted.
½ CUP: 159 cal., 11g fat (6g sat. fat), 25mg chol., 431mg sod., 11g carb. (2g sugars, 1g fiber), 6g pro.

SAUCY SCALLOPED POTATOES

MOIST CORN SPOON BREAD

Enjoy this easy take on a southern specialty by using the convenient slow cooker. It's an excellent side dish for Thanksgiving, Easter or any special feast.
—Taste of Home *Test Kitchen*

PREP: 20 min. • **COOK:** 4 hours
MAKES: 8 servings

- 1 pkg. (8 oz.) cream cheese, softened
- 2 Tbsp. sugar
- 2 large eggs, beaten
- 1 cup 2% milk
- 2 Tbsp. butter, melted
- ½ tsp. salt
- ¼ tsp. cayenne pepper
- ⅛ tsp. pepper
- 2 cups frozen corn
- 1 can (14¾ oz.) cream-style corn
- 1 cup yellow cornmeal
- 1 cup shredded Monterey Jack cheese
- 3 green onions, thinly sliced

1. In a large bowl, beat cream cheese and sugar until smooth. Gradually beat in eggs. Beat in the milk, butter, salt, cayenne and pepper until blended. Stir in the next 5 ingredients.
2. Pour into a greased 3-qt. slow cooker. Cook, covered, on low until a toothpick inserted in the center comes out clean, 4-5 hours. Top with additional pepper and green onions if desired.
1 SERVING: 350 cal., 18g fat (11g sat. fat), 54mg chol., 525mg sod., 38g carb. (8g sugars, 3g fiber), 12g pro.

SAUCY SCALLOPED POTATOES

For old-fashioned flavor, try these scalloped potatoes. They cook up tender, creamy and comforting. Chopped ham adds a hearty touch.
—Elaine Kane, Keizer, OR

PREP: 15 min. • **COOK:** 4 hours
MAKES: 8 servings

- 4 cups thinly sliced peeled potatoes (about 2 lbs.)
- 1 can (10¾ oz.) condensed cream of celery soup or cream of mushroom soup, undiluted
- 1 can (12 oz.) evaporated milk
- 1 large onion, sliced
- 2 Tbsp. butter
- ½ tsp. salt
- ¼ tsp. pepper
- 1½ cups chopped fully cooked ham

In a 3-qt. slow cooker, combine the first 7 ingredients. Cook, covered, on high 1 hour. Stir in ham. Reduce heat to low; cook until the potatoes are tender, 3-5 hours longer.
½ CUP: 555 cal., 10g fat (5g sat. fat), 36mg chol., 831mg sod., 101g carb. (9g sugars, 9g fiber), 17g pro.

"Finally! A great recipe for scalloped potatoes without using flour or cheese. It turned out perfectly!"

HARTMAN213, TASTEOFHOME.COM

MOIST CORN
SPOON BREAD

**GARLIC-ROSEMARY
CAULIFLOWER PUREE**

CORN & ONION STUFFING

I like something different for a side dish and this stuffing is it. It's perfect with pork, beef or chicken. Leave it in the slow cooker until it's time to eat—or make it early, refrigerate it until almost serving time and then simply reheat it.
—*Patricia Swart, Galloway, NJ*

PREP: 10 min. • **COOK:** 3 hours
MAKES: 8 servings

- 1 can (14¾ oz.) cream-style corn
- 1 pkg. (6 oz.) stuffing mix
- 1 small onion, chopped
- 1 celery rib, chopped
- ¼ cup water
- 2 large eggs
- 1 tsp. poultry seasoning
- ⅛ tsp. pepper
- ¼ cup butter, melted

Combine first 8 ingredients. Transfer to a greased 3-qt. slow cooker. Drizzle with butter. Cook, covered, on low until set, 3-4 hours.
½ CUP: 192 cal., 8g fat (4g sat. fat), 63mg chol., 530mg sod., 26g carb. (4g sugars, 1g fiber), 5g pro.

"This was really good corn stuffing. I didn't have enough time to put it in the slow cooker, so I baked it in the oven at 400° for 30 minutes. It still turned out great."
RWIPPEL, TASTEOFHOME.COM

GARLIC-ROSEMARY
CAULIFLOWER PUREE

I love this delicious fake take on mashed potatoes, and it doesn't heat up my kitchen! Treat leftovers as you would leftover mashed potatoes and make mock potato pancakes.
—*Sharon Gibson, Hendersonville, NC*

PREP: 15 min. • **COOK:** 3 hours
MAKES: 6 servings

- 2 Tbsp. butter, melted
- 1 medium onion, chopped
- 1 large head cauliflower, cut into florets
- 1 pkg. (6½ oz.) spreadable garlic and herb cheese
- ½ cup grated Parmesan cheese
- ½ tsp. Montreal steak seasoning
- ¼ tsp. pepper
- 1 tsp. minced fresh rosemary or ½ tsp. dried rosemary, crushed
- ¼ cup heavy cream, warmed
  Optional: Additional minced fresh rosemary and pepper

1. Place melted butter and onion in a 4- or 5-qt. slow cooker. Add cauliflower; cook, covered, on high 3-4 hours or until the cauliflower is tender.
2. Process in batches in a food processor to desired consistency. Add the next 6 ingredients and process until blended. If desired, serve with additional rosemary and pepper.
⅔ CUP: 245 cal., 20g fat (12g sat. fat), 54mg chol., 386mg sod., 11g carb. (5g sugars, 3g fiber), 6g pro.

CORN & ONION STUFFING

SLOW-COOKED
SUMMER SQUASH

SLOW-COOKED SUMMER SQUASH

We love squash, but I got tired of fixing just plain squash and cheese. I decided to jazz it up a bit.
—*Joan Hallford,*
North Richland Hills, TX

PREP: 15 min. • **COOK:** 2½ hours
MAKES: 8 servings

- 1 lb. medium yellow summer squash
- 1 lb. medium zucchini
- 2 medium tomatoes, chopped
- ¼ cup thinly sliced green onions
- ½ tsp. salt
- ¼ tsp. pepper
- 1 cup vegetable broth
- 1½ cups Caesar salad croutons, coarsely crushed
- ½ cup shredded cheddar cheese
- 4 bacon strips, cooked and crumbled

1. Cut squash and zucchini into ¼-in.-thick slices. In a 3- or 4-qt. slow cooker, combine squash, zucchini, tomatoes and green onions. Add the salt, pepper and broth. Cook, covered, on low until tender, 2½-3½ hours. Remove with a slotted spoon.
2. To serve, top with croutons, cheese and bacon.

¾ CUP: 111 cal., 6g fat (2g sat. fat), 12mg chol., 442mg sod., 10g carb. (4g sugars, 2g fiber), 6g pro.
DIABETIC EXCHANGES: 1 vegetable, 1 fat.

"To give this a little more spice but make it gluten free, I added spicy corn chips instead of croutons."
KRSW, TASTEOFHOME.COM

STUFFED SWEET ONIONS WITH BACON

STUFFED SWEET ONIONS WITH BACON

This unique side dish is perfect alongside grilled steak or pork chops. Even if you're not an onion fan, the low heat and long cooking time of this dish mellows and sweetens the naturally sharp onion flavors.
—*Erin Chilcoat, Central Islip, NY*

PREP: 45 min. • **COOK:** 4 hours
MAKES: 4 servings

- 4 medium sweet onions
- 2 small zucchini, shredded
- 1 large garlic clove, minced
- 1 Tbsp. olive oil
- 1 tsp. dried basil
- 1 tsp. dried thyme
- ¼ tsp. salt
- ¼ tsp. pepper
- ½ cup dry bread crumbs
- 4 thick-sliced bacon strips, cooked and crumbled
- ¼ cup grated Parmesan cheese
- ¼ cup reduced-sodium chicken broth

1. Peel onions and cut a ¼-in. slice from the top and bottom. Carefully cut and remove the center of each onion, leaving a ½-in. shell; chop removed onion.
2. In a large skillet, saute zucchini, garlic and chopped onions in oil until tender and juices are reduced. Stir in the basil, thyme, salt and pepper. Remove from the heat. Stir in the bread crumbs, bacon and Parmesan cheese. Fill onion shells with zucchini mixture.
3. Place in a greased 3- or 4-qt. slow cooker. Add broth to the slow cooker. Cook, covered, on low until onions are tender, 4-5 hours.

1 STUFFED ONION: 284 cal., 11g fat (3g sat. fat), 14mg chol., 641mg sod., 38g carb. (19g sugars, 5g fiber), 11g pro.

STEWED ZUCCHINI
& TOMATOES

STEWED ZUCCHINI & TOMATOES

A fresh take on traditional vegetable sides, this make-ahead dish stars zucchini, tomatoes and green peppers. Bubbly cheddar cheese adds a down-home feel.
—*Barbara Smith, Salem, OR*

PREP: 20 min. • **COOK:** 3½ hours
MAKES: 6 servings

- 3 medium zucchini, cut into ¼-in. slices
- 1 tsp. salt, divided
- ½ tsp. pepper, divided
- 1 medium onion, thinly sliced
- 1 medium green pepper, thinly sliced
- 3 medium tomatoes, sliced
- ⅔ cup condensed tomato soup, undiluted
- 1 tsp. dried basil
- 1 cup shredded cheddar cheese
  Minced fresh basil, optional

1. Place zucchini in a greased 3-qt. slow cooker. Sprinkle with ½ tsp. salt and ¼ tsp. pepper. Layer with onion, green pepper and tomatoes.
2. In a small bowl, combine soup, basil and the remaining ½ tsp. salt and ¼ tsp. pepper; spread mixture over the tomatoes.
3. Cook, covered, on low until vegetables are tender, 3-4 hours. Sprinkle with cheese. Cover and cook 30 minutes longer or until cheese is melted. If desired, top with fresh basil.
¾ CUP: 126 cal., 6g fat (4g sat. fat), 20mg chol., 678mg sod., 14g carb. (8g sugars, 3g fiber), 7g pro.
DIABETIC EXCHANGES: 1 vegetable, 1 fat, ½ starch.

MUSHROOM RICE PILAF

MUSHROOM RICE PILAF

A few modifications to our dear Great-Aunt Bernice's recipe have made this an always-requested dish for potlucks, barbecues and get-togethers.
—*Amy Williams, Rialto, CA*

PREP: 20 min. • **COOK:** 3 hours
MAKES: 6 servings

- 1 cup medium-grain rice
- ¼ cup butter
- 6 green onions, chopped
- 2 garlic cloves, minced
- ½ lb. sliced baby portobello mushrooms
- 2 cups warm water
- 4 tsp. beef base
  Thinly sliced green onions, optional

1. In a large skillet, saute rice in butter until lightly browned. Add green onions and garlic; cook and stir until tender. Stir in mushrooms. Transfer to a 1½-qt. slow cooker.
2. In a small bowl, whisk water and beef base; pour over rice mixture. Cook, covered, on low 3-3½ hours or until rice is tender and liquid is absorbed. Fluff with a fork. Sprinkle with sliced green onions if desired.
⅔ CUP: 210 cal., 8g fat (5g sat. fat), 20mg chol., 512mg sod., 30g carb. (2g sugars, 1g fiber), 4g pro.
DIABETIC EXCHANGES: 2 starch, 2 fat.

SLOW-COOKER
SRIRACHA CORN

SLOW-COOKER SRIRACHA CORN

A restaurant in our town advertised Sriracha corn on the cob, but I knew I could make my own. The golden ears cooked up a little sweet, a little smoky and a little hot—perfect, if you ask my three teenage boys!
—*Julie Peterson, Crofton, MD*

PREP: 15 min. • **COOK:** 3 hours
MAKES: 8 servings

- ½ cup butter, softened
- 2 Tbsp. honey
- 1 Tbsp. Sriracha chili sauce
- 1 tsp. smoked paprika
- ½ tsp. kosher salt
- 8 small ears sweet corn, husked
- ¼ cup water
   Additional smoked paprika, optional

1. Mix first 5 ingredients. Place each ear of corn on a 12x12-in. piece of heavy-duty foil and spread with 1 Tbsp. butter mixture. Wrap foil around corn, sealing tightly. Place in a 6-qt. slow cooker.
2. Add water; cook, covered, on low until corn is tender, 3-4 hours. If desired, sprinkle with additional paprika before serving.
1 EAR OF CORN: 209 cal., 13g fat (8g sat. fat), 31mg chol., 287mg sod., 24g carb. (11g sugars, 2g fiber), 4g pro.

❄ YUMMY PINTO BEANS

I love pinto beans, but I always feel the flavor can easily turn too bland. I added a little this and a little that and came out with this amazing but easy slow-cooker recipe.
—*Erica Vanderpool, Clarksville, TN*

PREP: 15 min. • **COOK:** 8 hours
MAKES: 8 servings

- 1 lb. dried pinto beans
- ¼ cup sliced onions
- 8 cups water
- 1 garlic clove, minced
- 1 Tbsp. chicken bouillon granules
- 1 Tbsp. kosher salt
- 1 tsp. pepper
- 1 tsp. ground cumin
- ½ tsp. dried thyme
- ¼ tsp. dried marjoram
- ¼ tsp. ground coriander
   Fresh thyme sprigs, optional

1. Sort beans and rinse in cold water. Add beans to a greased 3-qt. slow cooker. Add the next 10 ingredients; stir.
2. Cook, covered, on high 2 hours. Reduce heat to low; cook until the beans are tender, 6-7 hours. Serve with a slotted spoon. If desired, top with fresh thyme sprigs.
FREEZE OPTION: Freeze cooled beans in freezer containers. To use, partially thaw in refrigerator overnight. Heat through in a covered saucepan, stirring occasionally; add broth or water if necessary.
¾ CUP: 203 cal., 1g fat (0 sat. fat), 0 chol., 1043mg sod., 37g carb. (2g sugars, 9g fiber), 12g pro.

YUMMY
PINTO BEANS

SLOW-COOKER RATATOUILLE

Not only does this classic recipe make a phenomenal side dish, you can also serve it with sliced French bread for a warm and easy appetizer. Try it in the summer with garden-fresh vegetables.
—*Jolene Walters, North Miami, FL*

PREP: 20 min. + standing
COOK: 3 hours • **MAKES:** 10 servings

- 1 large eggplant, peeled and cut into 1-in. cubes
- 2 tsp. salt, divided
- 3 medium tomatoes, chopped
- 3 medium zucchini, halved lengthwise and sliced
- 2 medium onions, chopped
- 1 large green pepper, chopped
- 1 large sweet yellow pepper, chopped
- 1 can (6 oz.) pitted ripe olives, drained and chopped
- 1 can (6 oz.) tomato paste
- ½ cup minced fresh basil
- 2 garlic cloves, minced
- ½ tsp. pepper
- 2 Tbsp. olive oil

1. Place eggplant in a colander over a plate; sprinkle with 1 tsp. salt and toss. Let stand for 30 minutes. Rinse and drain well. Transfer to a 5-qt. slow cooker coated with cooking spray.

2. Stir in the tomatoes, zucchini, onions, green and yellow peppers, olives, tomato paste, basil, garlic, pepper and remaining 1 tsp. salt. Drizzle with oil. Cook, covered, on high until vegetables are tender, 3-4 hours.

¾ CUP: 116 cal., 5g fat (1g sat. fat), 0 chol., 468mg sod., 18g carb. (10g sugars, 6g fiber), 3g pro. **DIABETIC EXCHANGES:** 1 starch, 1 fat.

STOVETOP RATATOUILLE: Increase olive oil to 3 Tbsp. and substitute 1 can (14½ oz.) undrained diced tomatoes for the 3 tomatoes. Prepare eggplant as directed. In a Dutch oven, saute the eggplant, zucchini, onions and peppers in oil in batches until crisp-tender. Add the diced tomatoes, olives, tomato paste, basil, garlic, pepper and remaining salt. Bring to a boil. Reduce heat; cover and simmer 15-20 minutes or until vegetables are tender, stirring occasionally.

"I made this recipe with butternut squash because my farmers market didn't have any eggplant. Everyone, including my children, loved it. In fact, my husband was excited we had leftovers."
GINAMARIE550, TASTEOFHOME.COM

SLOW-COOKER RATATOUILLE

MUSHROOM WILD RICE

This is one of my favorite recipes from my mother. With only seven ingredients, it's quick to assemble in the morning before I leave for work. By the time I get home, mouthwatering aromas have filled the house.
—*Bob Malchow, Monon, IN*

PREP: 5 min. • **COOK:** 3 hours
MAKES: 12 servings

- 2¼ cups water
- 1 can (10½ oz.) condensed beef consomme, undiluted
- 1 can (10½ oz.) condensed French onion soup, undiluted
- 3 cans (4 oz. each) mushroom stems and pieces, drained
- ½ cup butter, melted
- 1 cup uncooked brown rice
- 1 cup uncooked wild rice

In a 3-qt. slow cooker, combine all ingredients. Cook, covered, on low until rice is tender, 3-4 hours.
¾ CUP: 192 cal., 9g fat (5g sat. fat), 21mg chol., 437mg sod., 24g carb. (2g sugars, 2g fiber), 5g pro.

JAZZED-UP GREEN BEAN CASSEROLE

After trying many variations of this old standby, I decided to give it a little extra kick. The crunchy texture, cheesy goodness and bacon make it a hit at any holiday get-together.
—*Stephan-Scott Rugh, Portland, OR*

PREP: 20 min. • **COOK:** 5½ hours
MAKES: 10 servings

- 2 pkg. (16 oz. each) frozen cut green beans, thawed
- 2 cans (10¾ oz. each) condensed cream of mushroom soup, undiluted
- 1 can (8 oz.) sliced water chestnuts, drained
- 1 cup 2% milk
- 6 bacon strips, cooked and crumbled
- 1 tsp. pepper
- ⅛ tsp. paprika
- 4 oz. cubed Velveeta
- 1 can (2.8 oz.) french-fried onions

In a 4-qt. slow cooker, combine the green beans, soup, water chestnuts, milk, bacon, pepper and paprika. Cook, covered, on low until beans are tender, 5-6 hours; stir in cheese. Cover and cook for 30 minutes or until cheese is melted. Sprinkle with onions.
¾ CUP: 200 cal., 11g fat (4g sat. fat), 18mg chol., 862mg sod., 19g carb. (5g sugars, 3g fiber), 7g pro.

"Excellent upgrade to typical green bean casserole. It's easy to make—I also have made it on the stovetop but it is a great go-to slow-cooker recipe. Hearty, full of flavor and yummy!"

DARLYN29, TASTEOFHOME.COM

SMOKY BAKED BEANS

SMOKY BAKED BEANS

They'll be lining up for this saucy bean recipe, full of that hard-to-capture campfire flavor. A combination of colorful calico beans, it makes a lovely side dish with many summer entrees.
—*Lynne German, Buford, GA*

PREP: 25 min. • **COOK:** 7 hours
MAKES: 16 servings

- 1 lb. bulk spicy pork sausage
- 1 medium onion, chopped
- 2 cans (15 oz. each) pork and beans
- 1 can (16 oz.) kidney beans, rinsed and drained
- 1 can (16 oz.) butter beans, rinsed and drained
- 1 can (15½ oz.) navy beans, rinsed and drained
- 1 can (15 oz.) black beans, rinsed and drained
- 1 can (10 oz.) diced tomatoes and green chiles, drained
- ½ cup hickory smoke-flavored barbecue sauce
- ½ cup ketchup
- ½ cup packed brown sugar
- 1 tsp. ground mustard
- 1 tsp. steak seasoning
- 1 tsp. liquid smoke, optional

1. In a large skillet, cook sausage and onion over medium heat until meat is no longer pink, breaking it into crumbles; drain.
2. In a 5-qt. slow cooker, combine the beans, tomatoes and sausage mixture. In a small bowl, combine the barbecue sauce, ketchup, brown sugar, mustard, steak seasoning and, if desired, liquid smoke. Stir into bean mixture.
3. Cover and cook on low until heated through, 7-8 hours.
¾ CUP: 244 cal., 6g fat (2g sat. fat), 10mg chol., 896mg sod., 39g carb. (15g sugars, 8g fiber), 11g pro.

CRANBERRY-APPLE RED CABBAGE

When I was looking for something new, I started playing with flavors and came up with this tasty dish. My German grandmother would be impressed, I think! The colorful side dish is just right with pork.
—*Ann Sheehy, Lawrence, MA*

PREP: 15 min. • **COOK:** 3 hours
MAKES: 8 servings

- 1 medium head red cabbage, coarsely chopped (8 cups)
- 1 can (14 oz.) whole-berry cranberry sauce
- 2 medium Granny Smith apples, peeled and coarsely chopped
- 1 large white onion, chopped
- ½ cup cider vinegar
- ¼ cup sweet vermouth or white wine, optional
- 1 tsp. kosher salt
- ¾ tsp. caraway seeds
- ½ tsp. coarsely ground pepper

Combine all ingredients; transfer to a 5-qt. slow cooker. Cook, covered, on low 3-4 hours or until cabbage is tender. Serve with a slotted spoon.
¾ CUP: 131 cal., 0 fat (0 sat. fat), 0 chol., 295mg sod., 32g carb. (20g sugars, 4g fiber), 2g pro.

CRANBERRY-APPLE
RED CABBAGE

EASY SLOW-COOKER MAC & CHEESE

My sons always cheer, "You're the best mom in the world!" whenever I make this creamy mac and cheese perfection. You can't beat a response like that!
—*Heidi Fleek, Hamburg, PA*

PREP: 25 min. • **COOK:** 1 hour
MAKES: 8 servings

- 2 cups uncooked elbow macaroni
- 1 can (10¾ oz.) condensed cheddar cheese soup, undiluted
- 1 cup 2% milk
- ½ cup sour cream
- ¼ cup butter, cubed
- ½ tsp. onion powder
- ¼ tsp. white pepper
- ⅛ tsp. salt
- 1 cup shredded cheddar cheese
- 1 cup shredded fontina cheese
- 1 cup shredded provolone cheese

1. Cook macaroni according to package directions for al dente. Meanwhile, in a large saucepan, combine soup, milk, sour cream, butter and seasonings; cook and stir over medium-low heat until blended. Stir in cheeses until melted.
2. Drain macaroni; transfer to a greased 3-qt. slow cooker. Stir in cheese mixture. Cook, covered, on low 1-2 hours or until heated through.
¾ CUP: 346 cal., 23g fat (14g sat. fat), 71mg chol., 712mg sod., 20g carb. (4g sugars, 1g fiber), 15g pro.

SLOW-COOKED CREAMY RICE

This wonderful side dish goes well with any meat stew. I use whatever fresh herbs I have on hand along with the chopped parsley to add even more flavor.
—*Laura Crane, Leetonia, OH*

PREP: 25 min. • **COOK:** 2½ hours
MAKES: 8 servings

- 3 cups cooked rice
- 2 large eggs, lightly beaten
- 1 can (12 oz.) evaporated milk
- 1 cup shredded Swiss cheese
- 1 cup shredded cheddar cheese
- 1 medium onion, chopped
- ½ cup minced fresh parsley
- 6 Tbsp. water
- 2 Tbsp. canola oil
- 1 garlic clove, minced
- 1½ tsp. salt
- ¼ tsp. pepper

In a 3-qt. slow cooker, combine all ingredients. Cook, covered, on low for 2½-3 hours or until a thermometer reads 160°.
¾ CUP: 290 cal., 15g fat (8g sat. fat), 94mg chol., 624mg sod., 24g carb. (6g sugars, 1g fiber), 13g pro.

**CORN & BROCCOLI
IN CHEESE SAUCE**

BROWN RICE &
VEGETABLES

This nutritious rice dish, full of big chunks of butternut squash and sweet potatoes, is a standout combination of sweet and savory flavors.
—Taste of Home *Test Kitchen*

PREP: 20 min. • **COOK:** 5 hours
MAKES: 12 servings

- 1 cup uncooked brown rice
- 1 medium butternut squash (about 3 lbs.), cubed
- 2 medium apples, coarsely chopped
- 1 medium sweet potato, peeled and cubed
- 1 medium onion, chopped
- 1 tsp. salt
- ½ tsp. pepper
- 1 can (14½ oz.) reduced-sodium chicken broth
- ½ cup raisins
- 1 Tbsp. minced fresh tarragon or 1 tsp. dried tarragon

1. Place rice in a greased 4- or 5-qt. slow cooker. In a large bowl, combine the squash, apples, sweet potato, onion, salt and pepper; add to slow cooker. Pour broth over vegetables.
2. Cook, covered, on low until vegetables are tender, 5-6 hours. Stir in raisins and tarragon.
¾ CUP: 148 cal., 1g fat (0 sat. fat), 0 chol., 303mg sod., 35g carb. (11g sugars, 5g fiber), 3g pro. **DIABETIC EXCHANGES:** 2 starch.

CORN & BROCCOLI
IN CHEESE SAUCE

Save room in the oven by making this savory side in your slow cooker. It is a standby in my house. My daughter likes to add leftover ham to create a hearty main course.
—*Joyce Johnson, Uniontown, OH*

PREP: 10 min. • **COOK:** 3 hours
MAKES: 8 servings

- 1 pkg. (16 oz.) frozen corn, thawed
- 1 pkg. (16 oz.) frozen broccoli florets, thawed
- 4 oz. reduced-fat Velveeta, cubed
- ½ cup shredded cheddar cheese
- 1 can (10¼ oz.) reduced fat, reduced-sodium condensed cream of chicken soup, undiluted
- ¼ cup fat-free milk

1. In a 4-qt. slow cooker, combine the corn, broccoli and cheeses. In a small bowl, combine soup and milk; pour over vegetable mixture.
2. Cook, covered, on low until heated through, 3-4 hours. Stir before serving.
¾ CUP: 148 cal., 5g fat (3g sat. fat), 16mg chol., 409mg sod., 21g carb. (4g sugars, 3g fiber), 8g pro. **DIABETIC EXCHANGES:** 1 starch, 1 medium-fat meat.

BROWN RICE
& VEGETABLES

MUSHROOMS MARSALA WITH BARLEY

This filling vegetarian recipe is a tasty mashup of chicken Marsala and mushroom barley soup. It's great as a main dish, but it can also be served, with or without the barley, as a side.
—*Arlene Erlbach, Morton Grove, IL*

PREP: 20 min. • **COOK:** 4¼ hours
MAKES: 6 servings

- 1½ lbs. baby portobello mushrooms, cut into ¾-in. chunks
- 1 cup thinly sliced shallots
- 3 Tbsp. olive oil
- ½ tsp. minced fresh thyme
- ¾ cup Marsala wine, divided
- 3 Tbsp. reduced-fat sour cream
- 2 Tbsp. all-purpose flour
- 1½ tsp. grated lemon zest
- ¼ tsp. salt
- ¼ cup crumbled goat cheese
- ¼ cup minced fresh parsley
- 2½ cups cooked barley

1. In a 4- or 5-qt. slow cooker, combine mushrooms, shallots, olive oil and thyme. Add ¼ cup Marsala wine. Cook, covered, on low 4 hours or until vegetables are tender.

2. Stir in sour cream, flour, lemon zest, salt and remaining ½ cup Marsala. Cook, covered, on low 15 minutes longer. Sprinkle with goat cheese and parsley. Serve with hot cooked barley.

¾ CUP MUSHROOMS WITH ABOUT ⅓ CUP BARLEY: 235 cal., 9g fat (2g sat. fat), 7mg chol., 139mg sod., 31g carb. (6g sugars, 5g fiber), 7g pro.
DIABETIC EXCHANGES: 2 starch, 2 fat, 1 vegetable.

TEST KITCHEN TIPS

- Marsala is an Italian wine fortified with alcohol. Its distinctive flavor is found in many Italian desserts, entrees and side dishes. You can substitute red or white wine, beer or broth for the Marsala, but be prepared—this will change the flavor dramatically.
- When fresh wild mushrooms are in season, swap in a medley of them for the baby portobellos.

SPANISH HOMINY

SPANISH HOMINY

I received this recipe from a good friend who is a fabulous cook. The colorful side dish gets its zesty flavor from spicy canned tomatoes with green chiles.
—*Donna Brockett, Kingfisher, OK*

PREP: 15 min. • **COOK:** 6 hours
MAKES: 12 servings

- 4 cans (15½ oz. each) hominy, rinsed and drained
- 1 can (14½ oz.) diced tomatoes, undrained
- 1 can (10 oz.) diced tomatoes and green chiles, undrained
- 1 can (8 oz.) tomato sauce
- ¾ lb. bacon strips, diced
- 1 large onion, chopped
- 1 medium green pepper, chopped

1. In a 5-qt. slow cooker, combine the hominy, tomatoes and tomato sauce.
2. In a large skillet, cook bacon until crisp; remove with a slotted spoon to paper towels. Drain drippings from pan, reserving 1 Tbsp.
3. In the same skillet, saute onion and green pepper in reserved drippings until tender.
4. Stir onion mixture and bacon into hominy mixture. Cover and cook on low until heated through, 6-8 hours.
¾ CUP: 150 cal., 5g fat (2g sat. fat), 11mg chol., 1039mg sod., 20g carb. (2g sugars, 5g fiber), 6g pro.

SLOW-COOKER
SAUERKRAUT

SLOW-COOKER SAUERKRAUT

This recipe was made by a special someone in my life. I was never a fan of sauerkraut until I tried this and fell in love. It's terrific on hot dogs or Reuben sandwiches.
—*Karen Tringali, Minooka, IL*

PREP: 20 min. • **COOK:** 1 hour
MAKES: 10 servings

- ½ lb. bacon strips, chopped
- 1 medium onion, chopped
- ¾ cup white vinegar
- ¾ cup sugar
- 2 cans (14 oz. each) sauerkraut, rinsed and well drained
- ½ tsp. caraway seeds

1. In a large skillet, cook chopped bacon and onions over medium heat until bacon is crisp and onions are just tender, 5-7 minutes. Add vinegar and sugar to skillet; cook and stir 5 minutes. Add sauerkraut and caraway seeds to skillet; stir to combine.
2. Transfer mixture to a 4-qt. slow cooker. Cover and cook on low to allow flavors to blend, 1-2 hours.
½ CUP: 173 cal., 9g fat (3g sat. fat), 15mg chol., 675mg sod., 20g carb. (17g sugars, 2g fiber), 4g pro.

TEST KITCHEN TIP

If the sauerkraut gets too dry, add a little water.

AU GRATIN GARLIC POTATOES

AU GRATIN GARLIC POTATOES

Cream cheese and a can of cheese soup turn ordinary sliced potatoes into a rich and flavorful side dish.
—*Tonya Vowels, Vine Grove, KY*

PREP: 10 min. • **COOK:** 6 hours
MAKES: 8 servings

- ½ cup 2% milk
- 1 can (10¾ oz.) condensed cheddar cheese soup, undiluted
- 1 pkg. (8 oz.) cream cheese, cubed
- 1 garlic clove, minced
- ¼ tsp. ground nutmeg
- ⅛ tsp. pepper
- 2 lbs. potatoes, peeled and sliced
- 1 small onion, chopped
  Paprika, optional

1. In a large saucepan, heat milk over medium heat until bubbles form around side of saucepan. Remove from the heat. Add soup, cream cheese, garlic, nutmeg and pepper; stir until smooth.
2. Place the potatoes and onion in a 3-qt. slow cooker. Pour the milk mixture over the potato mixture; mix well. Cook, covered, on low until potatoes are tender, 6-7 hours. If desired, sprinkle with paprika.
1 CUP: 206 cal., 13g fat (8g sat. fat), 38mg chol., 386mg sod., 21g carb. (4g sugars, 2g fiber), 5g pro.

SPICE TRADE
BEANS & BULGUR

SPICE TRADE BEANS & BULGUR

A rich blend of spices adds flavor to tender, nutritious bulgur and garbanzo beans in this tangy dish that has just the right amount of heat. A hint of sweetness from golden raisins is the perfect accent.
—*Faith Cromwell, San Francisco, CA*

PREP: 30 min. • **COOK:** 3½ hours
MAKES: 10 servings

- 3 Tbsp. canola oil, divided
- 2 medium onions, chopped
- 1 medium sweet red pepper, chopped
- 5 garlic cloves, minced
- 1 Tbsp. ground cumin
- 1 Tbsp. paprika
- 2 tsp. ground ginger
- 1 tsp. pepper
- ½ tsp. ground cinnamon
- ½ tsp. cayenne pepper
- 1½ cups bulgur
- 1 can (28 oz.) crushed tomatoes
- 1 can (14½ oz.) diced tomatoes, undrained
- 1 carton (32 oz.) vegetable broth
- 2 Tbsp. brown sugar
- 2 Tbsp. soy sauce
- 1 can (15 oz.) garbanzo beans or chickpeas, rinsed and drained
- ½ cup golden raisins
  Minced fresh cilantro, optional

1. In a large skillet, heat 2 Tbsp. oil over medium-high heat. Add onions and pepper; cook and stir until tender, 3-4 minutes. Add garlic and seasonings; cook 1 minute longer. Transfer to a 5-qt. slow cooker.
2. In same skillet, heat remaining 1 Tbsp. oil over medium-high heat. Add bulgur; cook and stir until lightly browned, 2-3 minutes.
3. Add the bulgur, tomatoes, broth, brown sugar and soy sauce to slow cooker. Cook, covered, on low until bulgur is tender, 3-4 hours. Stir in beans and raisins; cook 30 minutes longer. If desired, sprinkle with minced cilantro.
1¼ CUPS: 245 cal., 6g fat (0 sat. fat), 0 chol., 752mg sod., 45g carb. (15g sugars, 8g fiber), 8g pro.

SWEET & TANGY BEETS

Fresh beets are delicious when combined with aromatic spice and a hint of orange. These have the ideal balance of sweet and sour flavors.
—*Taste of Home Test Kitchen*

PREP: 15 min. • **COOK:** 7 hours
MAKES: 6 servings

- 2 lbs. small fresh beets, peeled and halved
- ½ cup sugar
- ¼ cup packed brown sugar
- 2 Tbsp. cornstarch
- ½ tsp. salt
- ¼ cup orange juice
- ¼ cup cider vinegar
- 2 Tbsp. butter
- 1½ tsp. whole cloves

1. Place beets in a 3-qt. slow cooker. Mix sugar, brown sugar, cornstarch and salt. Stir in orange juice and vinegar. Pour over beets; dot with butter.
2. Place cloves on a double thickness of cheesecloth. Gather corners of cloth to enclose cloves; tie securely with string. Place bag in slow cooker. Cook, covered, on low until beets are tender, 7-8 hours. Discard spice bag.
¾ CUP: 214 cal., 4g fat (2g sat. fat), 10mg chol., 344mg sod., 44g carb. (38g sugars, 3g fiber), 3g pro.

SLOW-COOKER MASHED POTATOES

Sour cream and cream cheese give richness to these smooth make-ahead potatoes. They are wonderful for holiday dinners that require getting multiple dishes to the table, as there is no last-minute mashing required.
—*Trudy Vincent, Valles Mines, MO*

PREP: 20 min. • **COOK:** 2 hours
MAKES: 10 servings

- 3 oz. cream cheese, softened
- ½ cup sour cream
- ¼ cup plus 1 Tbsp. softened butter, divided
- 1 envelope ranch salad dressing mix
- 1 Tbsp. minced fresh parsley
- 6 cups warm mashed potatoes (without added milk or butter)

In a large bowl, combine the cream cheese, sour cream, ¼ cup butter, salad dressing mix and parsley; stir in mashed potatoes. Transfer to a 3-qt. slow cooker. Cook, covered, on low for 2-3 hours. Top with remaining 1 Tbsp. butter.
¾ CUP: 210 cal., 11g fat (7g sat. fat), 27mg chol., 670mg sod., 23g carb. (1g sugars, 4g fiber), 3g pro.

CELEBRATION BRUSSELS SPROUTS

CELEBRATION BRUSSELS SPROUTS

This recipe hits all the flavor points and makes a fantastic Thanksgiving or Christmas side. You've got to love a dish that requires minimal effort and doesn't take up oven space! You can omit the bacon if you need a vegetarian option.
—*Lauren McAnelly, Des Moines, IA*

PREP: 20 min. • **COOK:** 2 hours
MAKES: 10 servings

- 2 lbs. fresh Brussels sprouts, thinly sliced
- 2 large apples (Fuji or Braeburn), chopped
- ⅓ cup dried cranberries
- 8 bacon strips, cooked and crumbled, divided
- ⅓ cup cider vinegar
- ¼ cup maple syrup
- 2 Tbsp. olive oil
- 1 tsp. salt
- ½ tsp. fresh ground pepper
- ¾ cup chopped hazelnuts or pecans, toasted

1. Combine Brussels sprouts, apples, cranberries and ¼ cup bacon. In a small bowl, whisk vinegar, syrup, oil, salt and pepper; pour over the Brussels sprouts mixture, tossing to coat. Transfer to a 5-qt. slow cooker.
2. Cook, covered, on low, stirring once, until sprouts reach desired tenderness, 2-4 hours. To serve, sprinkle with hazelnuts and remaining bacon.
¾ CUP: 204 cal., 11g fat (2g sat. fat), 7mg chol., 375mg sod., 24g carb. (15g sugars, 5g fiber), 6g pro.

SMASHED SWEET POTATOES & APPLES

SMASHED SWEET POTATOES & APPLES

I was looking for ways to cut down on the number of dishes that require oven time on Thanksgiving, so I devised a sweet potato dish that can be made ahead in a slow cooker. It's not too sweet, and it makes a perfect side for turkey or ham.
—*Judy Batson, Tampa, FL*

PREP: 20 min. • **COOK:** 5 hours
MAKES: 10 servings

- 3 lbs. sweet potatoes, peeled and cubed (about 8 cups)
- 1½ lbs. tart apples, peeled and cubed (about 4 cups)
- 1½ cups unsweetened apple juice
- 1 bottle (12 oz.) light beer or additional unsweetened apple juice
- 1 cup packed brown sugar
- 1 cup sour cream
- 2 Tbsp. butter
  Minced chives, optional

1. Place potatoes and apples in a 6-qt. slow cooker. Add apple juice and beer. Cook, covered, on low until potatoes are tender, 5-6 hours.
2. Drain; return to slow cooker. Add brown sugar, sour cream and butter. Mash potato mixture to reach desired consistency. Top with minced chives if desired.
¾ CUP: 338 cal., 7g fat (4g sat. fat), 12mg chol., 48mg sod., 67g carb. (45g sugars, 5g fiber), 3g pro.
PRESSURE COOKER: Place potatoes and apples in a 6-qt. electric pressure cooker; add apple juice and beer. Lock lid; close pressure-release valve. Adjust to pressure-cook on high for 12 minutes. Let pressure release naturally. Drain; return to pressure cooker. Add the brown sugar, sour cream and butter. Mash the potato mixture to reach desired consistency. If desired, top with minced chives.

VEGETABLES WITH CHEESE SAUCE

Who can pass up veggies smothered in cheese? No one I know! This is an inviting recipe to serve kids who normally shy away from vegetables.
—*Teresa Flowers, Sacramento, CA*

PREP: 5 min. • **COOK:** 3 hours
MAKES: 6 servings

- 1 pkg. (16 oz.) frozen Italian vegetables, thawed
- 3 cups frozen broccoli florets, thawed
- 1 pkg. (8 oz.) Velveeta, cubed
- 1½ cups frozen cut kale, thawed and squeezed dry
- ⅓ cup chicken broth
- 1 Tbsp. butter
- ¼ tsp. salt
- ¼ tsp. pepper

Place all ingredients in a 3- or 4-qt. slow cooker. Cook, covered, on low until cheese is melted, 3-4 hours. Stir before serving.

¾ CUP: 209 cal., 16g fat (7g sat. fat), 42mg chol., 704mg sod., 14g carb. (6g sugars, 4g fiber), 10g pro.

PRESSURE COOKER: Increase broth to 1 cup; place in a 6-qt. electric pressure cooker. Add Italian vegetables, broccoli, kale, butter, salt and pepper. Lock lid; close pressure-release valve. Adjust to pressure-cook on high for 3 minutes. Quick-release pressure. Drain vegetables and return to pressure cooker. Select saute setting; adjust for low heat. Add cheese; cook and stir until melted, 1-2 minutes.

VEGETABLES WITH CHEESE SAUCE

FALL GARDEN MEDLEY

I like to make this recipe in the fall and winter for special occasions because it's very colorful, tasty and healthy. It's a hearty side that complements many different meat dishes.
—*Krystine Kercher, Lincoln, NE*

PREP: 20 min. • **COOK:** 5 hours
MAKES: 8 servings

- 4 large carrots, cut into 1½-in. pieces
- 3 fresh beets, peeled and cut into 1½-in. pieces
- 2 medium sweet potatoes, peeled and cut into 1½-in. pieces
- 2 medium onions, peeled and quartered
- ½ cup water
- 2 tsp. salt
- ½ tsp. pepper
- ¼ tsp. dried thyme
- 1 Tbsp. olive oil
  Fresh parsley or dried parsley flakes, optional

1. Place the carrots, beets, sweet potatoes, onions and water in a greased 3-qt. slow cooker. Sprinkle with salt, pepper and thyme. Drizzle with olive oil. Cook, covered, on low until tender, 5-6 hours.
2. Stir vegetables and, if desired, sprinkle with parsley.
¾ CUP: 83 cal., 2g fat (0 sat. fat), 0 chol., 633mg sod., 16g carb. (8g sugars, 3g fiber), 2g pro.
DIABETIC EXCHANGES: 1 vegetable, ½ starch.

BACON LIMA BEANS

An unusual twist on traditional baked beans, this sweet and spicy version is easy to make and is a surefire crowd pleaser any time of the year!
—*E.M. Banjack, Norristown, PA*

PREP: 15 min. + soaking
COOK: 6 hours • **MAKES:** 8 servings

- 1 lb. dried lima beans
- ½ lb. bacon strips, cooked and crumbled
- 1 can (10¾ oz.) condensed tomato soup, undiluted
- 1⅓ cups water
- 1 cup packed brown sugar
- 1 garlic clove, minced
- 1 tsp. salt
- 1 tsp. paprika
- ½ tsp. ground mustard

Rinse and sort the beans; soak according to package directions. Drain and rinse beans, discarding liquid. In a 3-qt. slow cooker, combine beans and remaining ingredients. Cook, covered, on low until beans are tender, 6-8 hours.
¾ CUP: 375 cal., 5g fat (1g sat. fat), 10mg chol., 635mg sod., 69g carb. (35g sugars, 12g fiber), 16g pro.

SLAW-TOPPED
BEEF SLIDERS P. 111

SANDWICHES

Subs, sliders, wraps and more—the
slow cooker is the key to tender, tempting
fillings for sandwiches of all kinds.

FRENCH DIP SANDWICHES

FRENCH DIP SANDWICHES

These sandwiches make a standout addition to any buffet line. Make sure to have plenty of small cups of broth for everyone to grab. Dipping perfection!
—Holly Neuharth, Mesa, AZ

PREP: 15 min. • **COOK:** 8 hours
MAKES: 12 servings

- 1 beef rump or bottom round roast (about 3 lbs.)
- 1½ tsp. onion powder
- 1½ tsp. garlic powder
- ½ tsp. Creole seasoning
- 1 carton (26 oz.) beef stock
- 12 whole wheat hoagie buns, split
- 6 oz. Havarti cheese, cut into 12 slices

1. Cut roast in half. Mix onion powder, garlic powder and Creole seasoning; rub onto beef. Place in a 5-qt. slow cooker; add stock. Cook, covered, on low until meat is tender, 8-10 hours.

2. Remove beef; cool slightly. Skim fat from cooking juices. When cool enough to handle, shred beef with 2 forks and return to slow cooker.
3. Place buns on ungreased baking sheets, cut side up. Using tongs, place beef on bun bottoms. Place cheese on bun tops. Broil 3-4 in. from heat until cheese is melted, 1-2 minutes. Close sandwiches; serve with cooking juices.
1 SANDWICH WITH ⅓ CUP JUICES: 456 cal., 14g fat (5g sat. fat), 81mg chol., 722mg sod., 50g carb. (9g sugars, 7g fiber), 35g pro.

TEST KITCHEN TIP

This recipe uses a beef rump or bottom round roast, but you could also use a chuck roast if you prefer.

CHICKEN CAESAR WRAPS

I first created this recipe for our daughter who loves Caesar salads, then later for our extended family on vacation. It's such an easy meal—perfect for when you'd rather be outside than inside cooking all day.
—Christine Hadden, Whitman, MA

PREP: 10 min. • **COOK:** 3 hours
MAKES: 6 servings

- 1½ lbs. boneless skinless chicken breast halves
- 2 cups chicken broth
- ¾ cup creamy Caesar salad dressing
- ½ cup shredded Parmesan cheese
- ¼ cup minced fresh parsley
- ½ tsp. pepper
- 6 flour tortillas (8 in.)
- 2 cups shredded lettuce
  Optional: Salad croutons, crumbled cooked bacon and additional shredded Parmesan cheese

1. Place chicken and broth in a 1½- or 3-qt. slow cooker. Cook, covered, on low 3-4 hours or until a thermometer inserted in chicken reads 165°. Remove chicken and discard cooking juices. Shred chicken with 2 forks; return to slow cooker.
2. Stir in dressing, Parmesan, parsley and pepper; heat through. Serve in tortillas with lettuce and, if desired, salad croutons, crumbled bacon and additional shredded Parmesan cheese.
1 WRAP: 472 cal., 25g fat (5g sat. fat), 79mg chol., 795mg sod., 29g carb. (1g sugars, 2g fiber), 31g pro.

CHICKEN CAESAR WRAPS

CHILI SANDWICHES

No one will be able to resist these special sandwiches stuffed with spicy chili. The chili also makes a wonderfully filling meal by itself.
—*Kerry Haglund, WY, MN*

PREP: 30 min. + standing
COOK: 5 hours
MAKES: 30 servings

- 1 lb. dried navy beans
- 2 lbs. beef stew meat
- 2 cups water
- 1 lb. sliced bacon, diced
- 1 cup chopped onion
- 1 cup shredded carrots
- 1 cup chopped celery
- ⅓ cup chopped green pepper
- ⅓ cup chopped sweet red pepper
- 4 garlic cloves, minced
- 3 cans (14½ oz. each) diced tomatoes, undrained
- 1 cup barbecue sauce
- 1 cup chili sauce
- ½ cup honey
- ¼ cup hot pepper sauce
- 1 Tbsp. chili powder
- 1 Tbsp. baking cocoa
- 1 Tbsp. Dijon mustard
- 1 Tbsp. Worcestershire sauce
- 1 bay leaf
- 4 tsp. beef bouillon granules
- 30 hamburger buns, split

1. Place beans in a large saucepan; add water to cover by 2 in. Bring to a boil; boil for 2 minutes. Remove from the heat; cover and let stand for 1 to 4 hours or until beans are softened. Drain and rinse beans, discarding liquid.
2. In a large kettle or Dutch oven, simmer beans and beef in water for 2 hours or until very tender; drain. Place beef and beans in a 5-qt. slow cooker.
3. In a large skillet, cook bacon over medium heat until crisp. Using a slotted spoon, remove bacon to slow cooker. Discard all but 3 Tbsp. drippings. Saute the onion, carrots, celery and peppers in reserved drippings until tender. Add garlic; cook 1 minute longer. Transfer to the slow cooker. Add all the remaining ingredients except buns.
4. Cook, covered, on high for 3-4 hours, stirring often. Discard bay leaf. Spoon ½ cup onto each bun.
1 SANDWICH: 289 cal., 7g fat (2g sat. fat), 23mg chol., 686mg sod., 41g carb. (12g sugars, 6g fiber), 15g pro.

TEST KITCHEN TIP

Navy beans (also known as haricot beans or pea beans) can be swapped out for Great Northern beans, cannellini (white kidney) beans, or pinto beans.

BISTRO BEEF BARBECUE SANDWICHES

BISTRO BEEF BARBECUE SANDWICHES

These zippy barbecue sandwiches make for fun late-summer dinners and are also wonderful for potluck gatherings. The coleslaw topping adds the perfect tangy crunch.
—*Gilda Lester, Millsboro, DE*

PREP: 25 min. • **COOK:** 8 hours
MAKES: 16 servings

- 1½ cups ketchup
- ½ cup packed brown sugar
- ½ cup picante sauce
- ½ cup dry red wine
- ¼ cup balsamic vinegar
- 2 Tbsp. Worcestershire sauce
- ½ tsp. salt
- ½ tsp. pepper
- ¼ tsp. ground allspice
- 1 beef sirloin tip roast (4 lbs.)
- 4 garlic cloves, sliced
- 16 kaiser rolls, split and toasted
- 2 cups deli coleslaw

1. Mix the first 9 ingredients. Cut roast in half; cut slits in roast and insert garlic. Place in a 5-qt. slow cooker. Pour sauce over top. Cook, covered, on low until tender, 8-10 hours.
2. Remove beef. Skim fat from cooking liquid. Shred meat with 2 forks; return to slow cooker and heat through. Serve on rolls with coleslaw.

FREEZE OPTION: Freeze cooled meat mixture and sauce in freezer containers. To use, partially thaw in refrigerator overnight. Heat through in a saucepan, stirring occasionally.

1 SANDWICH: 411 cal., 11g fat (3g sat. fat), 76mg chol., 832mg sod., 49g carb. (18g sugars, 2g fiber), 29g pro.

EASY ITALIAN BEEF SANDWICHES

EASY ITALIAN BEEF SANDWICHES

These party-sized sandwiches make the meal—just add your favorite salad. If you like, top the sandwiches with sliced provolone.
—*Troy Parkos, Verona, WI*

PREP: 20 min. • **COOK:** 5 hours
MAKES: 12 servings

- 1 boneless beef chuck roast (3 lbs.)
- 1 tsp. Italian seasoning
- ¼ tsp. cayenne pepper
- ¼ tsp. pepper
- ¼ cup water
- 1 jar (16 oz.) sliced pepperoncini, undrained
- 1 medium sweet red pepper, julienned
- 1 medium green pepper, julienned
- 1 garlic clove, minced
- 1 envelope reduced-sodium onion soup mix
- 2 Tbsp. Worcestershire sauce
- 2 loaves (1 lb. each) Italian bread, split

1. Cut roast in half; place in a 5-qt. slow cooker. Sprinkle with Italian seasoning, cayenne and pepper. Add the water. Cook, covered, on high until meat is tender, 4 hours.
2. Remove roast; shred meat with 2 forks and return to the slow cooker. In a large bowl, combine the pepperoncini, peppers, garlic, soup mix and Worcestershire sauce; pour over meat. Cook, covered, on high for 1 hour or until peppers are tender.
3. Spoon beef mixture over the bottom halves of bread loaves; replace tops. Cut each loaf into 6 sandwiches.
1 SANDWICH: 428 cal., 14g fat (5g sat. fat), 74mg chol., 661mg sod., 43g carb. (2g sugars, 3g fiber), 29g pro.

LAMB PITAS WITH YOGURT SAUCE

❄ LAMB PITAS WITH YOGURT SAUCE

The spiced lamb in these stuffed pita pockets goes perfectly with cool cucumber and yogurt. It's like having your own Greek gyro stand in the kitchen!
—*Angela Leinenbach, Mechanicsville, VA*

PREP: 35 min. • **COOK:** 6 hours
MAKES: 8 servings

- 2 Tbsp. olive oil
- 2 lbs. lamb stew meat (¾-in. pieces)
- 1 large onion, chopped
- 1 garlic clove, minced
- ⅓ cup tomato paste
- ½ cup dry red wine
- 1¼ tsp. salt, divided
- 1 tsp. dried oregano
- ½ tsp. dried basil
- 1 medium cucumber
- 1 cup plain yogurt
- 16 pita pocket halves, warmed
- 4 plum tomatoes, sliced

1. In a large skillet, heat oil over medium-high heat; brown lamb in batches. Transfer lamb to a 3- or 4-qt. slow cooker, reserving drippings in skillet.
2. In drippings, cook and stir onion over medium heat until tender, 4-6 minutes. Add garlic and tomato paste; cook and stir 2 minutes. Stir in wine, 1 tsp. salt, oregano and basil. Add to lamb. Cook, covered, on low until the lamb is tender, 6-8 hours.
3. To serve, dice enough cucumber to measure 1 cup; thinly slice the remaining cucumber. Combine diced cucumber with yogurt and remaining ¼ tsp. salt. Fill pita halves with lamb mixture, tomatoes, sliced cucumbers and yogurt mixture.
FREEZE OPTION: Freeze the cooled lamb mixture in freezer containers. To use, partially thaw in refrigerator overnight. Heat through in a saucepan, stirring occasionally; add broth or water if necessary.
2 FILLED PITA HALVES: 383 cal., 11g fat (3g sat. fat), 78mg chol., 766mg sod., 39g carb. (5g sugars, 3g fiber), 31g pro. **DIABETIC EXCHANGES:** 3 lean meat, 2½ starch, 1 fat.

TURKEY SLOPPY JOES

The combination of chili sauce and ground turkey in these sloppy joes creates a delicious flavor. The avocado adds a special spring-summer touch to the sandwiches.
—*Nichole Jones, ID Falls, ID*

PREP: 35 min. • **COOK:** 4 hours
MAKES: 8 servings

1½ lbs. lean ground turkey
2 medium onions, finely chopped
4 garlic cloves, minced
1 jar (12 oz.) chili sauce
1 jalapeno pepper, seeded and chopped
1 Tbsp. Worcestershire sauce
2 tsp. dried oregano
1 tsp. ground cumin
1 tsp. paprika
½ tsp. salt
½ tsp. pepper
2 cups shredded Monterey Jack cheese
8 onion rolls, split
2 medium ripe avocados, peeled and mashed

1. In a large skillet coated with cooking spray, cook turkey, onions and garlic over medium heat, breaking the meat into crumbles, until meat is no longer pink; drain.
2. Transfer to a 1½-qt. slow cooker. Stir in the chili sauce, jalapeno, Worcestershire sauce, oregano, cumin, paprika, salt and pepper. Cook, covered, on low for 4-5 hours or until heated through. Just before serving, stir in cheese. Serve on rolls topped with avocado.
NOTE: Wear disposable gloves when cutting hot peppers; the oils can burn skin. Avoid touching your face.
1 SANDWICH: 515 cal., 25g fat (9g sat. fat), 92mg chol., 1231mg sod., 44g carb. (13g sugars, 5g fiber), 29g pro.

TURKEY SLOPPY JOES

SLAW-TOPPED BEEF SLIDERS
(PICTURED ON P. 102)

When I was working full time, I would rely on these fast-to-fix beef sliders for simple meals. To ease on prep time, I used bagged coleslaw mix and bottled slaw dressing.
—*Jane Whittaker, Pensacola, FL*

PREP: 20 min. • **COOK:** 6 hours
MAKES: 1 dozen

- 3 cups coleslaw mix
- ½ medium red onion, chopped (about ⅔ cup)
- ⅛ tsp. celery seed
- ¼ tsp. pepper
- ⅓ cup coleslaw salad dressing

SANDWICHES
- 1 boneless beef chuck roast (2 lbs.)
- 1 tsp. salt
- ½ tsp. pepper
- 1 can (6 oz.) tomato paste
- ¼ cup water
- 1 tsp. Worcestershire sauce
- 1 small onion, diced
- 1 cup barbecue sauce
- 12 slider buns or dinner rolls, split

1. Combine coleslaw, onion, celery seed and pepper. Add the salad dressing; toss to coat. Refrigerate until serving.
2. Sprinkle roast with salt and pepper; transfer to a 5-qt. slow cooker. Mix tomato paste, water and Worcestershire sauce; pour over roast. Top with onion. Cook, covered, on low until meat is tender, 6-8 hours.
3. Shred meat with 2 forks; return to slow cooker. Stir in barbecue sauce; heat through. Place beef on buns; top with coleslaw. Replace bun tops.
1 SLIDER: 322 cal., 12g fat (4g sat. fat), 67mg chol., 726mg sod., 34g carb. (13g sugars, 3g fiber), 20g pro.

TEX-MEX BEEF BARBECUES

This recipe came from my mom. Slow-cooking is ideal for brisket—the longer it cooks, the more tender it gets. The sauce tastes just as good with ground beef.
—*Lynda Zuniga, Crystal City, TX*

PREP: 20 min. • **COOK:** 8 hours
MAKES: 14 servings

- 1 fresh beef brisket (3½ lbs.)
- 1 jar (18 oz.) hickory smoke-flavored barbecue sauce
- ½ cup finely chopped onion
- 1 envelope chili seasoning
- 1 Tbsp. Worcestershire sauce
- 1 tsp. minced garlic
- 1 tsp. lemon juice
- 14 hamburger buns, split

1. Cut brisket in half; place in a 5-qt. slow cooker.
2. Combine barbecue sauce, onion, chili seasoning, Worcestershire sauce, garlic and lemon juice. Pour over beef. Cook, covered, on low for 8-9 hours or until meat is tender.
3. Remove beef; cool slightly. Shred and return to the slow cooker; heat through. Serve on buns.
1 SANDWICH: 294 cal., 7g fat (2g sat. fat), 47mg chol., 732mg sod., 28g carb. (8g sugars, 2g fiber), 28g pro.
DIABETIC EXCHANGES: 3 lean meat, 2 starch.

MOROCCAN CHICKEN TAGINE POCKETS

MOROCCAN CHICKEN TAGINE POCKETS

I enjoy shredded chicken dishes, Moroccan seasonings and pita sandwiches. The addition of the carrot salad laced with dates and pomegranate seeds lends an extra punch and crunch. Mini flour tortillas can be substituted for pitas.
—Arlene Erlbach, Morton Grove, IL

PREP: 20 min. • **COOK:** 5 hours
MAKES: 14 sandwiches

- 1½ lbs. boneless skinless chicken thighs
- 1 cup chunky salsa
- ½ cup pomegranate juice, divided
- ½ cup pitted dates, chopped and divided
- 2 Tbsp. honey
- 1 Tbsp. Moroccan seasoning (ras el hanout)
- 1½ tsp. garlic powder
- 1¼ cups shredded carrots
- 3 Tbsp. mayonnaise
- 2 Tbsp. pomegranate seeds
- 7 miniature pita pockets, halved Minced fresh cilantro, optional

1. Place chicken in a greased 3- or 4-qt. slow cooker. Combine the salsa, 6 Tbsp. pomegranate juice, ⅓ cup dates, the honey, Moroccan seasoning and garlic powder; pour over chicken. Cook, covered, on low, until chicken is tender, 5-6 hours.
2. Meanwhile, combine the carrots, mayonnaise, pomegranate seeds and remaining dates. Refrigerate, covered, until serving.
3. Remove chicken from slow cooker; cool slightly. Skim fat from cooking juices. Shred chicken with 2 forks. Return chicken and juices to slow cooker. Stir in remaining 2 Tbsp. pomegranate juice; heat through. Serve in pitas with carrot slaw and, if desired, cilantro.
1 FILLED PITA HALF: 164 cal., 6g fat (1g sat. fat), 33mg chol., 194mg sod., 17g carb. (7g sugars, 1g fiber), 11g pro.

LUAU PORK LETTUCE WRAPS

I first made this recipe when our family took a trip to a beach house in Florida. On my night to cook, I did a luau theme and used this recipe as the appetizer. These are still a favorite today!
—Joyce Conway, Westerville, OH

PREP: 30 min. • **COOK:** 6 hours
MAKES: 2 dozen

- 3 tsp. sea salt
- 1 tsp. pepper
- 1 boneless pork shoulder butt roast (3 to 4 lbs.)
- ½ cup ketchup
- ½ cup hoisin sauce
- ⅓ cup chili garlic sauce
- 1 lb. baby portobello mushrooms, chopped
- 1 large onion, chopped
- 1 can (20 oz.) unsweetened crushed pineapple
- 2 cans (8 oz. each) sliced water chestnuts, drained and chopped Bibb lettuce leaves Chopped green onions, optional

1. Rub salt and pepper over roast; transfer to a 5- or 6-qt. slow cooker. Combine ketchup, hoisin and chili sauce; pour over roast. Top with mushrooms, onion and pineapple. Cook, covered, on low until pork is tender, 6-8 hours.
2. Remove roast; cool slightly. Strain the cooking juices. Reserve vegetables and ½ to 1½ cups juices; discard remaining juices. Skim fat from reserved juices. Shred pork with 2 forks; return pork and reserved vegetables slow cooker. Pour desired amount of reserved cooking juices over pork mixture; stir to combine. Stir in water chestnuts; heat through. Serve in lettuce leaves; top with green onions, if desired.
FREEZE OPTION: Freeze cooled meat mixture in freezer containers. To use, partially thaw in refrigerator overnight. Microwave, covered, on high until heated through, stirring occasionally; add broth if necessary. Serve with lettuce.
2 FILLED LETTUCE WRAPS: 242 cal., 6g fat (2g sat. fat), 57mg chol., 1017mg sod., 23g carb. (16g sugars, 2g fiber), 24g pro.

LUAU PORK
LETTUCE WRAPS

CHIPOTLE BEEF
SANDWICHES

CHIPOTLE BEEF SANDWICHES

A jar of chipotle salsa makes it easy to spice up beef sirloin for these mouthwatering sandwiches. Keep this no-stress recipe in mind the next time you have to feed a hungry crowd.
—*Jessica Ring, Madison, WI*

PREP: 25 min. • **COOK:** 7 hours
MAKES: 10 sandwiches

- 1 large sweet onion, halved and thinly sliced
- 1 beef sirloin tip roast (3 lbs.)
- 1 jar (16 oz.) chipotle salsa
- ½ cup beer or nonalcoholic beer
- 1 envelope Lipton beefy onion soup mix
- 10 kaiser rolls, split

1. Place onion in a 5-qt. slow cooker. Cut roast in half; place over onion. Combine salsa, beer and soup mix; pour over top. Cook, covered, on low for 7-8 hours or until meat is tender.
2. Remove roast. Shred meat with 2 forks and return to the slow cooker; heat through. Using a slotted spoon, spoon shredded meat onto rolls.
1 SANDWICH: 362 cal., 9g fat (3g sat. fat), 72mg chol., 524mg sod., 37g carb. (6g sugars, 2g fiber), 31g pro.
DIABETIC EXCHANGES: 3 lean meat, 2½ starch.

TEST KITCHEN TIP

When choosing a beer to cook with, pick one with good flavor that you'd actually want to drink. A light ale or lager would be a safe choice here—but not an IPA, which would taste bitter.

ITALIAN SAUSAGE HOAGIES

ITALIAN SAUSAGE HOAGIES

In southeastern Wisconsin, our cuisine is influenced by both Germans and Italians who immigrated to this area. When preparing this recipe, we'll often substitute bratwurst for the Italian sausage, so we blend the two influences with delicious results.
—*Craig Wachs, Racine, WI*

PREP: 15 min. • **COOK:** 4 hours
MAKES: 10 servings

- 10 Italian sausage links
- 2 Tbsp. olive oil
- 1 jar (24 oz.) meatless spaghetti sauce
- ½ medium green pepper, julienned
- ½ medium sweet red pepper, julienned
- ½ cup water
- ¼ cup grated Romano cheese
- 2 Tbsp. dried oregano
- 2 Tbsp. dried basil
- 2 loaves French bread (20 in.)

1. In a large skillet over medium-high heat, brown sausage in oil; drain. Transfer to a 5-qt. slow cooker. Add the spaghetti sauce, peppers, water, cheese, oregano and basil. Cook, covered, on low for 4 hours or until sausage is no longer pink.
2. Slice each French bread loaf lengthwise but not all the way through; cut each loaf widthwise into 5 pieces. Fill each with sausage, peppers and sauce.
1 SANDWICH: 509 cal., 21g fat (7g sat. fat), 48mg chol., 1451mg sod., 56g carb. (7g sugars, 5g fiber), 22g pro.

POT ROAST SLIDERS

SHREDDED BUFFALO CHICKEN SANDWICHES

My family loves Buffalo chicken wings, but the frying makes them unhealthy. This recipe takes out some of the fat yet lets us enjoy the same amazing taste.
—Terri McKenzie, Wilmington, OH

PREP: 10 min. • **COOK:** 3 hours
MAKES: 6 servings

- 4 boneless skinless chicken breast halves (6 oz. each)
- 3 celery ribs, chopped
- 2 cups Buffalo wing sauce
- ½ cup chicken stock
- 2 Tbsp. butter
- 4 tsp. ranch salad dressing mix
- 6 hoagie buns, toasted
  Optional: Blue cheese or ranch salad dressing, and celery ribs

In a 3- or 4-qt. slow cooker, combine first 6 ingredients. Cook, covered, on low until the chicken is tender, 3-4 hours. Remove from slow cooker. Cool slightly; shred meat with 2 forks and return to slow cooker. Using tongs, serve on hoagie buns. If desired, top with dressing and serve with celery ribs.
1 SANDWICH: 398 cal., 12g fat (4g sat. fat), 73mg chol., 2212mg sod., 42g carb. (6g sugars, 2g fiber), 32g pro.

TEST KITCHEN TIP

If you prefer dark meat, substitute chicken thighs for the breasts. Top sandwiches with coleslaw for added crunch.

POT ROAST SLIDERS

This recipe reminds me of my mom's famous pot roast. Best of all, these sandwiches are simple to make with only a few ingredients. I love that I can enjoy the flavors of Mom's roast with the delicious portability of a slider.
—Lauren Drafke, Cape Coral, FL

PREP: 20 min. • **COOK:** 5 hours
MAKES: 2 dozen

- 1 boneless beef chuck roast (3 lbs.)
- 1½ cups water
- 1 envelope (1 oz.) onion soup mix
- 1 envelope (1 oz.) au jus gravy mix
- 2 pkg. (12 oz. each) Hawaiian sweet rolls, halved
- 12 slices Swiss cheese (¾ oz. each), cut in half
  Optional: Horseradish sauce, sliced tomato and baby arugula

1. Place roast in a 4-qt. slow cooker. In a small bowl, whisk together water and the soup and gravy mixes. Pour seasoning mixture over roast. Cook, covered, on low until tender, 5-6 hours. Remove from cooker. Cool slightly; shred meat with 2 forks.
2. Preheat broiler. Place halved rolls on a baking sheet. On each bottom half, place a cheese piece. Broil buns 4-6 in. from heat until cheese is melted and rolls start to brown, 1-2 minutes. Remove from broiler. Using tongs, place meat mixture on roll bottoms. If desired, layer with horseradish sauce, tomato and baby arugula. Replace roll tops.
2 SLIDERS: 487 cal., 22g fat (11g sat. fat), 124mg chol., 721mg sod., 36g carb. (12g sugars, 2g fiber), 36g pro.

SHREDDED BUFFALO CHICKEN SANDWICHES

MACHACA BEEF DIP SANDWICHES

MACHACA BEEF DIP SANDWICHES

The winning combination of beef, cumin, chili powder and the spicy heat of chipotle peppers makes these sandwiches game-day food at its finest!
—*Karol Chandler-Ezell, Nacogdoches, TX*

PREP: 20 min. • **COOK:** 8 hours
MAKES: 6 servings

- 1 boneless beef chuck roast (2 to 3 lbs.)
- 1 large sweet onion, thinly sliced
- 1 can (14½ oz.) reduced-sodium beef broth
- ½ cup water
- 3 chipotle peppers in adobo sauce, chopped
- 1 Tbsp. adobo sauce
- 1 envelope au jus gravy mix
- 1 Tbsp. Creole seasoning
- 1 Tbsp. chili powder
- 2 tsp. ground cumin
- 6 French rolls, split
   Optional: Guacamole and salsa

1. Place roast in a 3- to 4-qt. slow cooker; top with onion. Combine broth, water, chipotle peppers, adobo sauce, gravy mix, Creole seasoning, chili powder and cumin; pour over meat. Cook, covered, on low until meat is tender, 8-10 hours.
2. Remove roast; cool slightly. Skim fat from cooking juices. Shred beef with 2 forks and return to slow cooker; heat through. Using a slotted spoon, place meat on rolls. Serve with guacamole or salsa if desired and the cooking juices.
FREEZE OPTION: Freeze individual portions of cooled meat mixture and juices in freezer containers. To use, partially thaw in refrigerator overnight. Heat through in a saucepan, stirring occasionally. Serve as directed.

SLOW-COOKED REUBEN BRATS

1 SANDWICH: 476 cal., 18g fat (6g sat. fat), 100mg chol., 1288mg sod., 39g carb. (5g sugars, 3g fiber), 37g pro.

SLOW-COOKED REUBEN BRATS

Sauerkraut gives these beer-simmered brats a big flavor boost, but it's the special chili sauce and melted cheese that put them over the top. Top your favorite burger with some of the sauce; you won't be sorry.
—*Alana Simmons, Johnstown, PA*

PREP: 30 min. • **COOK:** 7¼ hours
MAKES: 10 servings

- 10 uncooked bratwurst links
- 3 bottles (12 oz. each) light beer or nonalcoholic beer
- 1 large sweet onion, sliced
- 1 can (14 oz.) sauerkraut, rinsed and well-drained
- ¾ cup mayonnaise
- ¼ cup chili sauce
- 2 Tbsp. ketchup
- 1 Tbsp. finely chopped onion
- 2 tsp. sweet pickle relish
- 1 garlic clove, minced
- ⅛ tsp. pepper
- 10 hoagie buns, split
- 10 slices Swiss cheese

1. In a large skillet, brown bratwurst in batches; drain. In a 5-qt. slow cooker, combine beer, sliced onion and sauerkraut; add bratwurst. Cook, covered, on low 7-9 hours or until sausages are cooked through.
2. Preheat oven to 350°. In a small bowl, mix mayonnaise, chili sauce, ketchup, chopped onion, relish, garlic and pepper until blended. Spread sauce over cut sides of buns; top with cheese, bratwurst and sauerkraut mixture. Place on an ungreased baking sheet. Bake 8-10 minutes or until cheese is melted.
1 SANDWICH: 733 cal., 50g fat (16g sat. fat), 94mg chol., 1643mg sod., 45g carb. (10g sugars, 2g fiber), 26g pro.

SPICY PORTUGUESE CACOILA

SPICY PORTUGUESE CACOILA

You're probably used to pulled pork coated with barbecue sauce and made into sandwiches. Portuguese pulled pork is a spicy dish often served at our large family functions. Each cook generally adds his or her own touches that reflect their taste and Portuguese heritage. A mixture of beef roast and pork can be used.

—*Michele Merlino, Exeter, RI*

PREP: 20 min. + marinating
COOK: 6 hours • **MAKES:** 12 servings

- 4 lbs. boneless pork shoulder butt roast, cut into 2-in. pieces
- 1½ cups dry red wine or reduced-sodium chicken broth
- 4 garlic cloves, minced
- 4 bay leaves
- 1 Tbsp. salt
- 1 Tbsp. paprika
- 2 to 3 tsp. crushed red pepper flakes
- 1 tsp. ground cinnamon
- 1 large onion, chopped
- ½ cup water
- 12 bolillos or hoagie buns, split, optional

1. Place pork roast in a large bowl; add the wine, garlic and seasonings. Turn to coat; cover and refrigerate overnight.
2. Transfer pork mixture to a 5- or 6-qt. slow cooker; add onion and water. Cook, covered, on low until meat is tender, 6-8 hours.
3. Skim fat. Remove bay leaves. Shred the meat with 2 forks. If desired, serve with a slotted spoon on bolillos.

1 SANDWICH: 489 cal., 20g fat (7g sat. fat), 90mg chol., 1075mg sod., 38g carb. (6g sugars, 2g fiber), 34g pro.

❄ CHICKEN ENCHILADA MELTS

After tasting a similar recipe at a sandwich shop, I knew I had to try my own version at home. I like mine even more! I enjoy mixing equal parts salsa and ranch dressing to make a tasty sauce for these sandwiches.

—*Blair Lonergan, Rochelle, VA*

PREP: 25 min. • **COOK:** 4 hours
MAKES: 6 servings

- 1½ lbs. boneless skinless chicken breasts
- 1 jar (16 oz.) salsa
- 1 envelope reduced-sodium taco seasoning
- 4 medium tomatoes, seeded and chopped
- ½ cup minced fresh cilantro
- 12 diagonally sliced French bread slices (1 in. thick)
- 1 cup shredded cheddar cheese Optional: Sliced ripe olives and additional chopped tomatoes

1. In a greased 3-qt. slow cooker, combine chicken, salsa and taco seasoning. Cook, covered, on low until chicken is tender, 4-5 hours.
2. Preheat broiler. Shred chicken with 2 forks; stir in the tomatoes and cilantro.
3. Place bread on ungreased baking sheets; broil 2-3 in. from heat until tops are lightly browned. Using tongs, place rounded ⅓ cup chicken mixture on each toast. Sprinkle with cheese. Broil until cheese is melted, 2-3 minutes. If desired, top with olives and additional tomatoes.
FREEZE OPTION: Cool chicken mixture without tomatoes and cilantro; freeze in freezer containers. To use, partially thaw in refrigerator overnight. Heat through in a saucepan, stirring occasionally; stir in tomatoes and cilantro and serve as directed.
2 OPEN-FACED SANDWICHES: 377 cal., 10g fat (5g sat. fat), 81mg chol., 1082mg sod., 36g carb. (7g sugars, 2g fiber), 32g pro.

CHICKEN
ENCHILADA MELTS

✽ BEER-BRAISED PULLED HAM

To jazz up ham, I slow-cooked it with a beer sauce. Buns loaded with ham and topped with pickles and mustard are irresistible.
—Ann Sheehy, Lawrence, MA

PREP: 10 min. • **COOK:** 7 hours
MAKES: 16 servings

- 2 bottles (12 oz. each) beer or nonalcoholic beer
- ¾ cup German or Dijon mustard, divided
- ½ tsp. coarsely ground pepper
- 1 fully cooked bone-in ham (about 4 lbs.)
- 4 fresh rosemary sprigs
- 16 pretzel hamburger buns, split
  Dill pickle slices, optional

1. In a 5-qt. slow cooker, whisk together beer and ½ cup mustard. Stir in pepper. Add ham and rosemary. Cook, covered, on low until tender, 7-9 hours.

2. Remove ham; cool slightly. Discard rosemary sprigs. Skim fat. When ham is cool enough to handle, shred meat with 2 forks. Discard bone. Return to slow cooker; heat through.

3. Using tongs, place shredded ham on pretzel buns; top with remaining ¼ cup mustard and, if desired, dill pickle slices.

FREEZE OPTION: Freeze cooled ham mixture in freezer containers. To use, partially thaw in refrigerator overnight. Heat through in a covered saucepan, stirring gently; add water if necessary.

1 SANDWICH: 378 cal., 9g fat (1g sat. fat), 50mg chol., 1246mg sod., 48g carb. (4g sugars, 2g fiber), 25g pro.

ITALIAN SLOPPY JOES

✳ ITALIAN SLOPPY JOES

These tasty sloppy joes are perfect for a gathering. If you're taking them to an event, simplify things by cooking the beef mixture and stirring in other ingredients the night before. Cool the meat sauce in shallow bowls in the fridge, then cover and refrigerate them overnight. The next day, transfer the meat mixture to the slow cooker to keep it warm for the party.
—*Hope Wasylenki, Gahanna, OH*

PREP: 30 min. • **COOK:** 4 hours
MAKES: 36 servings

- 2 lbs. lean ground beef (90% lean)
- 2 lbs. bulk Italian sausage
- 2 medium green peppers, chopped
- 1 large onion, chopped
- 4 cups spaghetti sauce
- 1 can (28 oz.) diced tomatoes, undrained
- ½ lb. sliced fresh mushrooms
- 1 can (6 oz.) tomato paste
- 2 garlic cloves, minced
- 2 bay leaves
- 36 hamburger buns, split

1. Cook the beef, sausage, peppers and onion in a Dutch oven over medium heat, breaking meat into crumbles, until meat is no longer pink, 6-8 minutes; drain. Transfer to a 6-qt. slow cooker. Stir in the spaghetti sauce, diced tomatoes, mushrooms, tomato paste, garlic and bay leaves.

2. Cook, covered, on high until flavors are blended, 4-5 hours. Discard bay leaves. Serve on buns, ½ cup on each.

FREEZE OPTION: Freeze cooled meat mixture in freezer containers. To use, partially thaw in refrigerator overnight. Heat through in a saucepan, stirring occasionally; add broth or water if necessary.

1 SANDWICH: 246 cal., 9g fat (3g sat. fat), 29mg chol., 522mg sod., 27g carb. (6g sugars, 2g fiber), 13g pro.
DIABETIC EXCHANGES: 2 starch, 2 lean meat.

"This complete Sloppy Joe recipe makes a delicious pasta sauce—just stir in additional spaghetti sauce!"
JENNIFERNY, TASTEOFHOME.COM

ITALIAN
MEATBALL SUBS

ITALIAN MEATBALL SUBS

This is one of those recipes you always come back to. A flavorful tomato sauce and mildly spiced meatballs make a hearty sandwich filling, or they can be served over pasta. I broil the meatballs first to quickly brown them.
—*Jean Glacken, Elkton, MD*

PREP: 25 min. • **COOK:** 4 hours
MAKES: 6 servings

- 2 large eggs, lightly beaten
- ¼ cup whole milk
- ½ cup dry bread crumbs
- 2 Tbsp. grated Parmesan cheese
- ½ tsp. salt
- ¼ tsp. pepper
- ⅛ tsp. garlic powder
- 1 lb. ground beef
- ½ lb. bulk Italian sausage

SAUCE

- 1 can (15 oz.) tomato sauce
- 1 can (6 oz.) tomato paste
- 1 small onion, chopped
- ½ cup chopped green pepper
- ½ cup dry red wine or beef broth
- ⅓ cup water
- 2 garlic cloves, minced
- 1 tsp. dried oregano
- ½ tsp. sugar
- ½ tsp. salt
- ½ tsp. pepper
- 6 Italian rolls, split
  Shredded Parmesan cheese, optional

1. In a large bowl, combine eggs and milk; add the bread crumbs, cheese, salt, pepper and garlic powder. Add beef and sausage; mix lightly but thoroughly. Shape into 1-in. balls. Preheat broiler. Place meatballs in a 15x10x1-in. baking pan. Broil 4 in. from the heat for 4 minutes; turn and broil 3 minutes longer.
2. Transfer to a 5-qt. slow cooker. Combine the tomato sauce and paste, onion, green pepper, wine, water and seasonings; pour over meatballs. Cook, covered, on low for 4-5 hours. Serve on rolls. Sprinkle with shredded cheese if desired.
1 SANDWICH: 501 cal., 24g fat (8g sat. fat), 137mg chol., 1410mg sod., 39g carb. (6g sugars, 4g fiber), 29g pro.

HOT PINEAPPLE HAM SANDWICHES

HOT PINEAPPLE HAM SANDWICHES

Your trusty slow cooker lets you make these warm, gooey sandwiches without heating up the house on a hot day. Mustard and brown sugar give them a richness everybody loves.
—*Nancy Foust, Stoneboro, PA*

PREP: 25 min. • **COOK:** 3 hours
MAKES: 10 servings

- 2 cans (20 oz. each) unsweetened crushed pineapple, undrained
- 1 medium onion, finely chopped
- ¾ cup packed light brown sugar
- ¼ cup Dijon mustard
- 2½ lbs. thinly sliced deli ham
- 2 Tbsp. cornstarch
- 2 Tbsp. water
- 10 slices Swiss cheese or cheddar cheese, optional
- 10 kaiser rolls, split

1. Mix first 4 ingredients. Place half the mixture in a 5-qt. slow cooker; top with half the ham. Repeat layers. Cook, covered, on low until heated through, 3-4 hours.
2. Using tongs, remove ham from slow cooker, leaving the pineapple mixture behind; keep warm. In a large saucepan, mix cornstarch and water until smooth. Stir in pineapple mixture; bring to a boil. Reduce heat; simmer, uncovered, until mixture is slightly thickened, stirring occasionally. Serve ham, pineapple mixture and, if desired, cheese on rolls.
1 SANDWICH: 468 cal., 8g fat (2g sat. fat), 60mg chol., 1540mg sod., 69g carb. (36g sugars, 2g fiber), 29g pro.

❄

SLOW-COOKED PULLED PORK

Every time I bring this dish to a potluck I am asked, "Where did you get the pork?" People are surprised to hear me say I made it. When I tell them how simple the recipe is, they are doubly surprised.
—*Betsy Rivas, Chesterfield, MO*

PREP: 20 min. + chilling
COOK: 8 hours • **MAKES:** 10 servings

- 2 Tbsp. brown sugar
- 4½ tsp. paprika
- 2 Tbsp. coarsely ground pepper, divided
- 1 Tbsp. kosher salt
- 1 tsp. chili powder
- ½ tsp. cayenne pepper
- 1 boneless pork shoulder butt roast (3 to 4 lbs.), cut in half
- 1 cup cider vinegar
- ¼ cup beef broth
- ¼ cup barbecue sauce
- 2 Tbsp. Worcestershire sauce
- 1½ tsp. hickory liquid smoke, optional
- 10 kaiser rolls, split

1. In a small bowl, combine the brown sugar, paprika, 1 Tbsp. pepper, salt, chili powder and cayenne. Rub over roast; cover and refrigerate for 8 hours or overnight.
2. Place roast in a 4- or 5-qt. slow cooker. Combine the vinegar, broth, barbecue sauce, Worcestershire sauce, liquid smoke (if desired), and remaining 1 Tbsp. pepper; pour over roast. Cook, covered, on low until meat is tender, 8-10 hours.
3. Remove meat from slow cooker; cool slightly. Shred with 2 forks and return to the slow cooker; heat through. Using a slotted spoon, place ½ cup meat on each roll.
FREEZE OPTION: Freeze cooled pork mixture in freezer containers. To use, partially thaw in refrigerator overnight. Heat through in a saucepan, stirring occasionally; add broth if necessary.
1 SANDWICH: 419 cal., 16g fat (5g sat. fat), 81mg chol., 1076mg sod., 36g carb. (5g sugars, 2g fiber), 29g pro.

SHREDDED LAMB SLIDERS

I made about 1,500 of these easy, tasty sliders for the Great American Beer Fest. Everyone—right down to the last customer—thought the bites were delish.
—*Craig Kuczek, Aurora, CO*

PREP: 45 min. • **COOK:** 6 hours
MAKES: 2 dozen

- 1 boneless lamb shoulder roast (3½ to 4¼ lbs.)
- 1½ tsp. salt
- ½ tsp. pepper
- 1 Tbsp. olive oil
- 2 medium carrots, chopped
- 4 shallots, chopped
- 6 garlic cloves
- 2 cups beef stock
PESTO
- ¾ cup fresh mint leaves
- ¾ cup loosely packed basil leaves
- ⅓ cup pine nuts
- ¼ tsp. salt
- ¾ cup olive oil
- ¾ cup shredded Parmesan cheese
- ⅓ cup shredded Asiago cheese
- 24 slider buns
- 1 pkg. (4 oz.) crumbled feta cheese

1. Sprinkle roast with salt and pepper. In a large skillet, heat oil over medium-high heat; brown meat. Transfer to a 6- or 7-qt. slow cooker. In the same skillet, cook and stir carrots, shallots and garlic until crisp-tender, about 4 minutes. Add stock, stirring to loosen browned bits from pan. Pour over lamb. Cook, covered, on low until lamb is tender, 6-8 hours.
2. Meanwhile, for pesto, place mint, basil, pine nuts and salt in a food processor; pulse until chopped. Continue processing while gradually adding oil in a steady stream. Add Parmesan and Asiago cheeses; pulse just until blended.
3. When cool enough to handle, remove meat from bones; discard bones. Shred meat with 2 forks. Strain cooking juices, adding vegetables to shredded meat; skim fat. Return cooking juices and meat to slow cooker. Heat through. Serve on buns with pesto and feta.
1 SLIDER: 339 cal., 22g fat (7g sat. fat), 56mg chol., 459mg sod., 16g carb. (2g sugars, 1g fiber), 18g pro.

SHREDDED
LAMB SLIDERS

CRANBERRY BBQ
PULLED PORK

CRANBERRY BBQ PULLED PORK

Cranberry sauce adds a yummy twist to pulled pork, and my family can't get enough of it! The slow cooker also makes this dish conveniently portable.
—*Carrie Wiegand, Mount Pleasant, IA*

PREP: 20 min. • **COOK:** 9 hours
MAKES: 14 servings

- 1 boneless pork shoulder roast (4 to 6 lbs.)
- 1/3 cup cranberry juice
- 1 tsp. salt

SAUCE
- 1 can (14 oz.) whole-berry cranberry sauce
- 1 cup ketchup
- 1/3 cup cranberry juice
- 3 Tbsp. brown sugar
- 4 1/2 tsp. chili powder
- 2 tsp. garlic powder
- 1 tsp. onion powder
- 1/2 tsp. salt
- 1/4 tsp. ground chipotle pepper
- 1/2 tsp. liquid smoke, optional
- 14 hamburger buns, split

1. Cut roast in half. Place in a 4-qt. slow cooker. Add cranberry juice and salt. Cook, covered, on low 8-10 hours or until meat is tender.
2. Remove roast and set aside. In a small saucepan, combine cranberry sauce, ketchup, cranberry juice, brown sugar, seasonings and liquid smoke if desired. Cook, stirring, over medium heat until slightly thickened, about 5 minutes.
3. Skim fat from cooking juices; set aside 1/2 cup juices. Discard remaining juices. When cool enough to handle, shred pork with 2 forks and return to slow cooker.
4. Stir in sauce mixture and the reserved cooking juices. Cook, covered, on low about 1 hour or until heated through. Serve on buns.

EASY PHILLY CHEESESTEAKS

FREEZE OPTION: Freeze cooled meat mixture in freezer containers. To use, partially thaw in refrigerator overnight. Heat through in a saucepan, stirring occasionally; add a little water if necessary.
1 SANDWICH: 409 cal., 15g fat (5g sat. fat), 77mg chol., 772mg sod., 42g carb. (19g sugars, 2g fiber), 26g pro.

EASY PHILLY CHEESESTEAKS

Since we live in a rural area where there aren't any restaurants to speak of, I thought it would be fun to make this classic sandwich at home. For an extra flavor boost, add a splash of steak sauce.
—*Lenette A. Bennett, Como, CO*

PREP: 20 min. • **COOK:** 6 hours
MAKES: 6 servings

- 2 medium onions, halved and sliced
- 2 medium sweet red or green peppers, halved and sliced
- 1 beef top sirloin steak (1 1/2 lbs.), cut into thin strips
- 1 envelope onion soup mix
- 1 can (14 1/2 oz.) reduced-sodium beef broth
- 6 hoagie buns, split
- 12 slices provolone cheese, halved
  Pickled hot cherry peppers, optional

1. Place onions and red peppers in a 4- or 5-qt. slow cooker. Add beef, soup mix and broth. Cook, covered, on low 6-8 hours or until the meat is tender.
2. Arrange buns on a baking sheet, cut side up. Using tongs, place meat mixture on the bun bottoms; top with cheese.
3. Broil 2-3 in. from heat until the cheese is melted and bun tops are toasted, 30-60 seconds. If desired, serve with cherry peppers.
1 SANDWICH: 539 cal., 21g fat (10g sat. fat), 77mg chol., 1256mg sod., 45g carb. (9g sugars, 3g fiber), 44g pro.

MELT-IN-YOUR-MOUTH SAUSAGES

BBQ BACON PULLED CHICKEN SANDWICHES

This simple recipe tastes amazing. My family prefers putting mayo on the bun and adding cheddar or Muenster cheese, lettuce, tomato and onion. Several of us put ranch dressing on our sandwiches, too.
—*Jennifer Darling, Ventura, CA*

PREP: 20 min. • **COOK:** 3 hours
MAKES: 12 servings

- 1   bottle (18 oz.) barbecue sauce
- ½   cup amber beer or root beer
- ¼   cup cider vinegar
- 2   green onions, chopped
- 2   Tbsp. dried minced onion
- 2   Tbsp. Dijon mustard
- 2   Tbsp. Worcestershire sauce
- 4   garlic cloves, minced
- 1   Tbsp. dried parsley flakes
- 2   lbs. boneless skinless chicken breasts
- 12   hamburger buns, split and toasted
- 24   cooked bacon strips
- 12   lettuce leaves

In a large bowl, combine the first 9 ingredients. Place chicken in a greased 4- or 5-qt. slow cooker; pour sauce over top. Cook, covered, on low, until tender, 3-4 hours.
FREEZE OPTION: Freeze cooled, cooked chicken mixture in freezer containers. To use, partially thaw in refrigerator overnight. Heat through in a saucepan, stirring occasionally and adding a little water if necessary.
1 SANDWICH: 401 cal., 12g fat (4g sat. fat), 65mg chol., 1175mg sod., 43g carb. (19g sugars, 2g fiber), 28g pro.

MELT-IN-YOUR-MOUTH SAUSAGES

My family loves this recipe. It's such a good all-around dish, either for sandwiches such as these or served with hot cooked spaghetti.
—*Ilean Schultheiss, Cohocton, NY*

PREP: 10 min. • **COOK:** 4 hours
MAKES: 8 servings

- 8   Italian sausage links (2 lbs.)
- 1   jar (26 oz.) meatless spaghetti sauce
- ½   cup water
- 1   can (6 oz.) tomato paste
- 1   large green pepper, thinly sliced
- 1   large onion, thinly sliced
- 1   Tbsp. grated Parmesan cheese
- 1   tsp. dried parsley flakes
- 8   brat buns, split Additional Parmesan cheese, optional

1. Place sausages in a large skillet; cover with water. Bring to a boil. Reduce heat. Cover and simmer for 10 minutes or until a thermometer reads 160°; drain well.
2. Meanwhile, in a 3-qt. slow cooker, combine the spaghetti sauce, water, tomato paste, green pepper, onion, cheese and parsley. Add sausages. Cook, covered, on low 4-5 hours or until vegetables are tender. Serve in buns. Sprinkle with additional cheese if desired.
1 SANDWICH: 557 cal., 29g fat (9g sat. fat), 62mg chol., 1510mg sod., 51g carb. (14g sugars, 4g fiber), 24g pro.

**BBQ BACON PULLED
CHICKEN SANDWICHES**

PULLED TURKEY TENDERLOIN

PULLED TURKEY TENDERLOIN

Not your ordinary pulled turkey sandwich, this one shines thanks to its unique yogurt sauce. Serve the turkey by itself or stack on sweet pickle slices and jalapenos to echo the dressing.
—*Shana Conradt, Greenville, WI*

PREP: 15 min. • **COOK:** 6 hours
MAKES: 5 servings

- 1 pkg. (20 oz.) turkey breast tenderloins
- 2 cups water
- ½ cup sweet pickle juice
- 1 envelope onion soup mix
- 2 Tbsp. canned diced jalapeno peppers
- ½ cup fat-free plain Greek yogurt
- 1 Tbsp. yellow mustard
- ⅛ tsp. pepper
- 5 kaiser rolls, split
  Optional: Prepared coleslaw, sliced jalapeno peppers and sweet pickles

1. Place turkey in a 3-qt. slow cooker. In a small bowl, combine the water, pickle juice, soup mix and jalapeno peppers; pour over turkey. Cook, covered, on low for 6-8 hours or until meat is tender. Remove turkey and shred with 2 forks. Transfer to a small bowl.
2. Strain cooking juices, reserving ½ cup juices. In another small bowl, combine yogurt, mustard, pepper and reserved cooking juices. Pour over turkey; toss to coat. Serve on rolls and, if desired, with optional toppings.
NOTE: Wear disposable gloves when cutting hot peppers; the oils can burn skin. Avoid touching your face.
1 SANDWICH: 339 cal., 4g fat (1g sat. fat), 56mg chol., 1074mg sod., 40g carb. (7g sugars, 2g fiber), 36g pro.
DIABETIC EXCHANGES: 4 lean meat, 2 starch.

COFFEE-BRAISED PULLED PORK SANDWICHES

COFFEE-BRAISED PULLED PORK SANDWICHES

Adding coffee to meat adds such a deep flavor. This recipe is so easy—I put it in before work and by the time we all get home, it's ready for us to dig in.
—*Jacquelynn Sanders, Burnsville, MN*

PREP: 30 min. • **COOK:** 8 hours
MAKES: 10 servings

- 1 boneless pork shoulder butt roast (3 to 3½ lbs.)
- ⅓ cup ground coffee beans
- ½ tsp. salt
- ½ tsp. pepper
- 2 Tbsp. canola oil
- 2 celery ribs, chopped
- 1 large carrot, chopped
- 1 medium onion, chopped
- 2 cups chicken stock
- 1½ cups strong brewed coffee
- 2 Tbsp. minced fresh parsley
- 1 tsp. coriander seeds
- 1 tsp. ground cumin
- 1 tsp. whole peppercorns, crushed
- 1 cinnamon stick (3 in.)
- 1 bay leaf
- 10 hoagie or kaiser buns, split
- 10 slices pepper jack cheese

1. Cut roast into thirds. Combine the ground coffee, salt and pepper; rub over roast. In a large skillet, brown meat in oil on all sides; drain.
2. Transfer meat to a 5-qt. slow cooker. Add the celery, carrot, onion, chicken stock, brewed coffee, parsley, coriander seeds, cumin, peppercorns, cinnamon stick and bay leaf; pour over roast.
3. Cook, covered, on low until meat is tender, 8-10 hours. When cool enough to handle, shred the meat. Skim fat from cooking juices. Strain the cooking juices, discarding the vegetables, cinnamon stick and bay leaf.
4. Spoon about ½ cup pork onto each bun; top with cheese. Serve with cooking juices.
1 SANDWICH: 458 cal., 23g fat (8g sat. fat), 85mg chol., 689mg sod., 32g carb. (5g sugars, 1g fiber), 31g pro.

BANDITO CHILI DOGS

These deluxe chili dogs are a surefire hit at family functions. Adults and children alike love the cheesy chili sauce, and the toppings are fun!
—*Marion Lowery, Medford, OR*

PREP: 15 min. • **COOK:** 4 hours
MAKES: 10 servings

- 1 pkg. (1 lb.) hot dogs
- 2 cans (15 oz. each) chili without beans
- 1 can (10¾ oz.) condensed cheddar cheese soup, undiluted
- 1 can (4 oz.) chopped green chiles
- 10 hot dog buns, split
- 1 medium onion, chopped
- 1 to 2 cups corn chips, coarsely crushed
- 1 cup shredded cheddar cheese

1. Place hot dogs in a 3-qt. slow cooker. In a large bowl, combine chili, soup and green chiles; pour over hot dogs. Cook, covered, on low for 4-5 hours.
2. Serve hot dogs in buns; top with the chili mixture, onion, corn chips and cheese.

1 CHILI DOG: 450 cal., 23g fat (10g sat. fat), 53mg chol., 1442mg sod., 43g carb. (6g sugars, 3g fiber), 19g pro.

BANDITO CHILI DOGS

❄ ITALIAN TURKEY SANDWICHES

I hope you enjoy these tasty turkey sandwiches as much as our family does. The recipe makes plenty, so it's fantastic for potlucks. Plus, the leftovers are just as good.
—*Carol Riley, Ossian, IN*

PREP: 10 min. • **COOK:** 5 hours
MAKES: 12 sandwiches

- 1 bone-in turkey breast (6 lbs.), skin removed
- 1 medium onion, chopped
- 1 small green pepper, chopped
- ¼ cup chili sauce
- 3 Tbsp. white vinegar
- 2 Tbsp. dried oregano or Italian seasoning
- 4 tsp. beef bouillon granules
- 12 kaiser or hard rolls, split

1. Place turkey breast in a greased 5-qt. slow cooker. Add onion and green pepper.
2. Combine the chili sauce, vinegar, oregano and bouillon; pour over the turkey and vegetables. Cook, covered, on low until turkey is tender, 5-6 hours.
3. Shred turkey with 2 forks and return to the slow cooker; heat through. Spoon ½ cup turkey onto each roll.
FREEZE OPTION: Place cooled meat and juices in freezer containers. To use, partially thaw in refrigerator overnight. Microwave, covered, on high in a microwave-safe dish until heated through, gently stirring and adding a little water if necessary.
1 SANDWICH: 374 cal., 4g fat (1g sat. fat), 118mg chol., 724mg sod., 34g carb. (3g sugars, 2g fiber), 49g pro.
DIABETIC EXCHANGES: 6 lean meat, 2 starch.

SLOW-COOKED TURKEY SANDWICHES

These sandwiches have been such a hit at office potlucks that I keep copies of the recipe in my desk to hand out.
—*Diane Twait Nelsen, Ringsted, IA*

PREP: 15 min. • **COOK:** 3 hours
MAKES: 18 servings

- 6 cups cubed cooked turkey
- 2 cups cubed Velveeta
- 1 can (10¾ oz.) condensed cream of chicken soup, undiluted
- 1 can (10¾ oz.) condensed cream of mushroom soup, undiluted
- ½ cup finely chopped onion
- ½ cup chopped celery
- 18 wheat sandwich buns, split

In a 4-qt. slow cooker, combine the first 6 ingredients. Cook, covered, on low until vegetables are tender and cheese is melted, 3-4 hours. Stir mixture; spoon ½ cup onto each bun.
1 SANDWICH: 263 cal., 9g fat (3g sat. fat), 62mg chol., 680mg sod., 26g carb. (5g sugars, 4g fiber), 20g pro.

HONEY BUFFALO MEATBALLS SLIDERS

HONEY BUFFALO MEATBALL SLIDERS

These little sliders deliver big Buffalo chicken flavor without the messiness of wings. The spicy-sweet meatballs are a hit with kids and adults alike on game day.
—*Julie Peterson, Crofton, MD*

PREP: 10 min. • **COOK:** 2 hours
MAKES: 6 servings

- ¼ cup packed brown sugar
- ¼ cup Louisiana-style hot sauce
- ¼ cup honey
- ¼ cup apricot preserves
- 2 Tbsp. cornstarch
- 2 Tbsp. reduced-sodium soy sauce
- 1 pkg. (24 oz.) frozen fully cooked Italian turkey meatballs, thawed
  Additional hot sauce, optional
  Bibb lettuce leaves
- 12 mini buns

Crumbled blue cheese
Ranch salad dressing, optional

1. In a 3- or 4-qt. slow cooker, mix the first 6 ingredients until smooth. Stir in meatballs until coated. Cook, covered, on low for 2-3 hours, until meatballs are heated through.
2. If desired, stir in additional hot sauce. Serve the meatballs on lettuce-lined buns; top with cheese and, if desired, dressing.
2 SLIDERS: 524 cal., 21g fat (6g sat. fat), 110mg chol., 1364mg sod., 61g carb. (29g sugars, 1g fiber), 28g pro.

MOJITO PULLED PORK

This fork-tender pulled pork tastes fabulous in a wrap or tortilla or on a bun. My kids like it spooned over rice in its citrus-flavored juices.
—*Mindy Oswalt, Winnetka, CA*

PREP: 20 min. • **COOK:** 7 hours
MAKES: 16 servings

- 1 boneless pork shoulder roast (4 to 5 lbs.)
- 2 tsp. salt
- 2 tsp. each oregano, ground cumin, paprika and pepper
- 1 bunch fresh cilantro, divided
- 2 medium onions, halved and sliced
- ¼ cup canned chopped green chiles
- 4 garlic cloves, minced
- 2 cans (14½ oz. each) reduced-sodium chicken broth
- ⅔ cup orange juice
- ½ cup lime juice
- 16 sandwich buns, split
  Barbecue sauce and pickle chips

1. Cut roast in half. Combine the salt, oregano, cumin, paprika and pepper; rub over pork. Place in a 4- or 5-qt. slow cooker.
2. Mince cilantro to measure ¼ cup; set aside. Trim remaining cilantro, discarding stems. Add the whole cilantro leaves, onions, chiles and garlic to the slow cooker. Combine broth, orange juice and lime juice; pour over roast. Cook, covered, on low until meat is tender, 7-9 hours.
3. Remove roast; cool slightly. Skim fat from cooking juices; set aside 3 cups juices. Discard remaining juices. Shred pork with 2 forks and return to slow cooker. Stir in minced cilantro and the reserved cooking juices; heat through.
4. Spoon ½ cup meat onto each bun. Serve with barbecue sauce and pickle chips.
1 SANDWICH: 418 cal., 16g fat (5g sat. fat), 67mg chol., 916mg sod., 40g carb. (8g sugars, 2g fiber), 29g pro.

OVER-THE-RAINBOW
MINESTRONE P. 156

SOUPS, STEWS & CHILIS

Perhaps no meal is better suited to the slow cooker than a hearty soup, stew or chili. All that long-simmered flavor in one bowl— what could be more satisfying?

MEATY SLOW-COOKED JAMBALAYA

SPICY PORK CHILI

Tender pork adds extra heartiness to this slow-cooked chili. You can use pork tenderloin, boneless pork roast or boneless pork chops.
—Taste of Home *Test Kitchen*

PREP: 10 min. • **COOK:** 6 hours
MAKES: 6 servings (2½ qt.)

- 2 lbs. boneless pork, cut into ½-in. cubes
- 1 Tbsp. canola oil
- 1 can (28 oz.) crushed tomatoes
- 2 cups frozen corn
- 1 can (15 oz.) black beans, rinsed and drained
- 1 cup chopped onion
- 2 cups beef broth
- 1 can (4 oz.) chopped green chiles
- 1 Tbsp. chili powder
- 1 tsp. minced garlic
- ½ tsp. salt
- ½ tsp. cayenne pepper
- ½ tsp. pepper
- ¼ cup minced fresh cilantro
  Shredded cheddar cheese, optional

1. In a large skillet, cook pork in oil over medium-high heat until browned, 5-6 minutes. Transfer pork and drippings to a 5-qt. slow cooker. Stir in the tomatoes, corn, beans, onion, broth, chiles, chili powder, garlic, salt, cayenne and pepper.
2. Cook, covered, on low until pork is tender, 6-7 hours. Stir in cilantro. Serve with cheese if desired.
1¾ CUPS: 395 cal., 12g fat (4g sat. fat), 89mg chol., 1055mg sod., 34g carb. (9g sugars, 8g fiber), 39g pro.

MEATY SLOW-COOKED JAMBALAYA

This recipe makes a big batch of delicious, meaty stew. Stash some away in the freezer for days you don't feel like cooking.
—Diane Atherton, Pine Mountain, GA

PREP: 25 min. • **COOK:** 7¼ hours
MAKES: 12 servings (3 qt.)

- 1 can (28 oz.) diced tomatoes, undrained
- 1 cup reduced-sodium chicken broth
- 1 large green pepper, chopped
- 1 medium onion, chopped
- 2 celery ribs, sliced
- ½ cup white wine or additional reduced-sodium chicken broth
- 4 garlic cloves, minced
- 2 tsp. Cajun seasoning
- 2 tsp. dried parsley flakes
- 1 tsp. dried basil
- 1 tsp. dried oregano
- ¾ tsp. salt
- ½ to 1 tsp. cayenne pepper
- 2 lbs. boneless skinless chicken thighs, cut into 1-in. pieces
- 1 pkg. (12 oz.) fully cooked andouille or other spicy chicken sausage links
- 2 lbs. uncooked medium shrimp, peeled and deveined
- 8 cups hot cooked brown rice

1. In a large bowl, combine the first 13 ingredients. Place chicken and sausage in a 6-qt. slow cooker. Pour the tomato mixture over top. Cook, covered, on low until the chicken is tender, 7-9 hours.
2. Stir in shrimp. Cook, covered, until the shrimp turn pink, 15-20 minutes longer. Serve with rice.
1 CUP JAMBALAYA WITH ⅔ CUP COOKED RICE: 387 cal., 10g fat (3g sat. fat), 164mg chol., 674mg sod., 37g carb. (4g sugars, 4g fiber), 36g pro. **DIABETIC EXCHANGES:** 3 lean meat, 2½ starch.

SPICY
PORK CHILI

SPICED SPLIT PEA SOUP

A hint of curry adds just the right kick to this soup. Just assemble the ingredients in the slow cooker and go about your day while it simmers.
—*Sue Mohre, Mount Gilead, OH*

PREP: 25 min. • **COOK:** 8 hours
MAKES: 10 servings (2½ qt.)

- 1 cup dried green split peas
- 2 medium potatoes, chopped
- 2 medium carrots, halved and thinly sliced
- 1 medium onion, chopped
- 1 celery rib, thinly sliced
- 3 garlic cloves, minced
- 3 bay leaves
- 4 tsp. curry powder
- 1 tsp. ground cumin
- ½ tsp. coarsely ground pepper
- ½ tsp. ground coriander
- 1 carton (32 oz.) reduced-sodium chicken broth
- 1 can (28 oz.) diced tomatoes, undrained

1. In a 4-qt. slow cooker, combine first 12 ingredients. Cook, covered, on low until peas are tender, 8-10 hours.
2. Stir in tomatoes; heat through. Discard bay leaves.
1 CUP: 139 cal., 0 fat (0 sat. fat), 0 chol., 347mg sod., 27g carb. (7g sugars, 8g fiber), 8g pro. **DIABETIC EXCHANGES:** 1 starch, 1 vegetable, 1 lean meat.

VERMICELLI BEEF STEW

I love to try new recipes for my husband and me, and also when we entertain friends and relatives. The vermicelli makes this stew a little different from most.
—*Sharon Delaney-Chronis, South Milwaukee, WI*

PREP: 20 min. • **COOK:** 8½ hours
MAKES: 8 servings (2 qt.)

- 1½ lbs. beef stew meat, cut into 1-in. cubes
- 1 medium onion, chopped
- 2 Tbsp. canola oil
- 3 cups water
- 1 can (14½ oz.) diced tomatoes
- 1 pkg. (16 oz.) frozen mixed vegetables, thawed
- 1 Tbsp. dried basil
- 1 tsp. salt
- 1 tsp. dried oregano
- 6 oz. uncooked vermicelli, broken into 2-in. pieces
- ¼ cup grated Parmesan cheese

1. In a large skillet, brown meat and onion in oil; drain. Transfer to a 5-qt. slow cooker. Stir in the water, tomatoes, vegetables, basil, salt and oregano. Cook, covered, on low until meat and vegetables are tender, 8-10 hours.
2. Stir in vermicelli. Cook, covered, 30 minutes longer or until pasta is tender. Sprinkle with Parmesan cheese.
1 CUP: 294 cal., 10g fat (3g sat. fat), 55mg chol., 455mg sod., 28g carb. (5g sugars, 5g fiber), 22g pro.
DIABETIC EXCHANGES: 2 vegetable, 2 lean meat, 1 starch, 1 fat.

CHICKEN TORTILLA SOUP

CHICKEN TORTILLA SOUP

Don't be shy about loading up the spices and shredded chicken into your slow cooker. Chicken tortilla soup tastes amazing as leftovers the next day.
—*Karen Kelly, Germantown, MD*

PREP: 10 min. • **COOK:** 4 hours
MAKES: 8 servings (2 qt.)

- 1 lb. boneless skinless chicken breasts
- 1 Tbsp. canola oil
- 1 medium onion, chopped
- 3 garlic cloves, minced
- 1 carton (32 oz.) reduced-sodium chicken broth
- 1 can (15 oz.) black beans, rinsed and drained
- 1 can (14 oz.) fire-roasted diced tomatoes
- 1½ cups frozen corn
- 1 Tbsp. chili powder
- 1 Tbsp. ground cumin
- 1 tsp. paprika
- ½ tsp. salt
- ¼ tsp. pepper
- ¼ cup minced fresh cilantro
  Crumbled tortilla chips
  Optional: Chopped avocado, jalapeno peppers and lime wedges

1. In a large skillet, brown chicken in oil. Add onion; cook and stir until tender, 6-8 minutes. Add garlic; cook 1 minute longer. Transfer mixture to a 3-qt. slow cooker.
2. Add the next 10 ingredients. Cook, covered, on low for 4-5 hours.
3. Remove chicken and shred with 2 forks; return meat to slow cooker. Stir in cilantro; sprinkle with chips. Serve with toppings as desired.
NOTE: Wear disposable gloves when cutting hot peppers; the oils can burn skin. Avoid touching your face.
1 CUP: 176 cal., 4g fat (1g sat. fat), 31mg chol., 725mg sod., 19g carb. (3g sugars, 4g fiber), 17g pro.

SLOW-COOKER
BEEF STEW

FRENCH LENTIL &
CARROT SOUP

It's crazy how just a few ingredients can make such a difference. Using finely chopped rotisserie chicken in this recipe makes it perfect for a busy weeknight meal, but you can leave the chicken out if you prefer.
—*Colleen Delawder, Herndon, VA*

PREP: 15 min. • **COOK:** 6¼ hours
MAKES: 6 servings (2¼ qt.)

- 5   large carrots, peeled and sliced
- 1½ cups dried green lentils, rinsed
- 1   shallot, finely chopped
- 2   tsp. herbes de Provence
- ½   tsp. pepper
- ¼   tsp. kosher salt
- 6   cups reduced-sodium chicken broth
- 2   cups cubed rotisserie chicken
- ¼   cup heavy whipping cream

1. Combine the first 7 ingredients in a 5- or 6-qt. slow cooker. Cook, covered, on low 6-8 hours or until lentils are tender.
2. Stir in chicken and cream. Cover; continue cooking until heated through, about 15 minutes.
1½ CUPS: 338 cal., 8g fat (3g sat. fat), 53mg chol., 738mg sod., 39g carb. (5g sugars, 7g fiber), 29g pro.
DIABETIC EXCHANGES: 3 lean meat, 2 starch, 1 vegetable.

TEST KITCHEN TIP

For a creamier soup, puree half of it in a blender and then combine it with the remaining unblended half—or use an immersion blender to partially puree it in the pot.

SLOW-COOKER
BEEF STEW

When there's a chill in the air, I love to make my slow-cooked stew. It's loaded with tender chunks of beef, potatoes and carrots.
—*Earnestine Wilson, Waco, TX*

PREP: 25 min. • **COOK:** 7 hours
MAKES: 8 servings (2 qt.)

- 1½ lbs. potatoes, peeled and cubed
- 6   medium carrots, cut into 1-in. lengths
- 1   medium onion, coarsely chopped
- 3   celery ribs, coarsely chopped
- 3   Tbsp. all-purpose flour
- 1½ lbs. beef stew meat, cut into 1-in. cubes
- 3   Tbsp. canola oil
- 1   can (14½ oz.) diced tomatoes, undrained
- 1   can (14½ oz.) beef broth
- 1   tsp. ground mustard
- ½   tsp. salt
- ½   tsp. pepper
- ½   tsp. dried thyme
- ½   tsp. browning sauce, optional
      Minced fresh thyme, optional

1. Layer the potatoes, carrots, onion and celery in a 5-qt. slow cooker. Place flour in a large shallow dish. Add stew meat; turn to coat evenly. In a large skillet, brown meat in oil in batches. Place over vegetables.
2. Combine the tomatoes, broth, mustard, salt, pepper, thyme and, if desired, browning sauce. Pour over beef. Cook, covered, on low until the meat and vegetables are tender, 7-8 hours. If desired, sprinkle with fresh thyme to serve.
1 CUP: 272 cal., 12g fat (3g sat. fat), 53mg chol., 541mg sod., 23g carb. (6g sugars, 4g fiber), 19g pro.
DIABETIC EXCHANGES: 2 lean meat, 1½ starch, 1 fat.

FRENCH LENTIL
& CARROT SOUP

TEX-MEX CHILI

TEX-MEX CHILI

Need to satisfy big, hearty appetites? Look no further than a chili brimming with beef stew meat, plenty of beans and tasty spices.
—*Eric Hayes, Antioch, CA*

PREP: 20 min. • **COOK:** 6 hours
MAKES: 12 servings (about 4 qt.)

- 3 lbs. beef stew meat
- 1 Tbsp. canola oil
- 3 garlic cloves, minced
- 3 cans (16 oz. each) kidney beans, rinsed and drained
- 3 cans (15 oz. each) tomato sauce
- 1 can (14½ oz.) diced tomatoes, undrained
- 1 cup water
- 1 can (6 oz.) tomato paste
- ¾ cup salsa verde
- 1 envelope chili seasoning
- 2 tsp. dried minced onion
- 1 tsp. chili powder
- ½ tsp. crushed red pepper flakes
- ½ tsp. ground cumin
- ½ tsp. cayenne pepper
  Optional: Shredded cheddar cheese, minced fresh cilantro, sour cream, sliced jalapeno or Fresno peppers and additional salsa verde

1. In a large skillet, brown beef in oil in batches. Add garlic; cook 1 minute longer. Transfer to a 6-qt. slow cooker.
2. Stir in the beans, tomato sauce, tomatoes, water, tomato paste, salsa verde and seasonings. Cook, covered, on low for 6-8 hours or until meat is tender. Garnish each serving with toppings as desired.
FREEZE OPTION: Before adding toppings, cool chili. Freeze chili in freezer containers. To use, partially thaw in refrigerator overnight. Heat through in a saucepan, stirring occasionally; add broth or water if necessary.

LENTIL & CHICKEN SAUSAGE STEW

NOTE: Wear disposable gloves when cutting hot peppers; the oils can burn skin. Avoid touching your face.
1⅓ CUPS: 334 cal., 9g fat (3g sat. fat), 70mg chol., 1030mg sod., 31g carb. (7g sugars, 8g fiber), 32g pro.
DIABETIC EXCHANGES: 3 lean meat, 1 starch, 1 vegetable.

LENTIL & CHICKEN SAUSAGE STEW

This hearty and healthy stew will warm your family right down to their toes! Serve with cornbread or rolls to soak up every last morsel.
—*Jan Valdez, Chicago, IL*

PREP: 15 min. • **COOK:** 8 hours
MAKES: 6 servings. (2¼ qt.)

- 1 carton (32 oz.) reduced-sodium chicken broth
- 1 can (28 oz.) diced tomatoes, undrained
- 3 fully cooked spicy chicken sausage links (3 oz. each), cut into ½-in. slices
- 1 cup dried lentils, rinsed
- 1 medium onion, chopped
- 1 medium carrot, chopped
- 1 celery rib, chopped
- 2 garlic cloves, minced
- ½ tsp. dried thyme

Combine all ingredients in a 4- or 5-qt. slow cooker. Cook, covered, on low for 8-10 hours or until lentils are tender.
1½ CUPS: 231 cal., 4g fat (1g sat. fat), 33mg chol., 803mg sod., 31g carb. (8g sugars, 13g fiber), 19g pro.
DIABETIC EXCHANGES: 2 vegetable, 2 lean meat, 1 starch.

ZESTY BEEF STEW

ZESTY BEEF STEW

Preparation couldn't be simpler for this hearty stew. I created the dish when I didn't have some of my usual ingredients for vegetable beef soup. My husband says it's the best I have ever made!
—Margaret Turza, South Bend, IN

PREP: 10 min. • **COOK:** 3½ hours
MAKES: 6 servings

- 1 lb. beef stew meat, cut into 1-in. cubes
- 1 pkg. (16 oz.) frozen mixed vegetables, thawed
- 1 can (15 oz.) pinto beans, rinsed and drained
- 1½ cups water
- 1 can (8 oz.) pizza sauce
- 2 Tbsp. medium pearl barley
- 1 Tbsp. dried minced onion
- 2 tsp. beef bouillon granules
- ¼ tsp. crushed red pepper flakes

In a 3-qt. slow cooker, combine all ingredients. Cook, covered, on low 3½-4½ hours or until stew meat is tender.
1 CUP: 251 cal., 6g fat (2g sat. fat), 47mg chol., 526mg sod., 28g carb. (5g sugars, 8g fiber), 21g pro.
DIABETIC EXCHANGES: 3 lean meat, 2 starch.

"Delicious! The beef comes out very tender and the pizza sauce provides extra kick. I added ¼ teaspoon of granulated garlic."
MYTHYAGAIN, TASTEOFHOME.COM

LOUISIANA RED BEANS & RICE

Smoked turkey sausage and red pepper flakes add zip to this slow-cooked version of the New Orleans classic. For extra heat, add red pepper sauce.
—Julia Bushree, Menifee, CA

PREP: 20 min. • **COOK:** 3 hours
MAKES: 8 servings (2 qt.)

- 4 cans (16 oz. each) kidney beans, rinsed and drained
- 1 can (14½ oz.) diced tomatoes, undrained
- 1 pkg. (14 oz.) smoked turkey sausage, sliced
- 3 celery ribs, chopped
- 1 large onion, chopped
- 1 cup chicken broth
- 1 medium green pepper, chopped
- 1 small sweet red pepper, chopped
- 6 garlic cloves, minced
- 1 bay leaf
- ½ tsp. crushed red pepper flakes
- 2 green onions, chopped
  Hot cooked rice

1. In a 4- or 5-qt. slow cooker, combine the first 11 ingredients. Cook, covered, on low until the vegetables are tender, 3-4 hours.
2. Stir before serving. Remove bay leaf. Serve with green onions and rice.

FREEZE OPTION: Discard bay leaf; freeze cooled bean mixture in freezer containers. To use, partially thaw in refrigerator overnight. Heat through in a saucepan, stirring occasionally; add broth or water if necessary. Serve as directed.
1 CUP: 291 cal., 3g fat (1g sat. fat), 32mg chol., 1070mg sod., 44g carb. (8g sugars, 13g fiber), 24g pro.

LOUISIANA
RED BEANS & RICE

SPICY SEAFOOD STEW

To speed up assembly of this flavorful recipe, you can peel and dice the potatoes the night before. Just place the spuds in water and refrigerate them overnight.
—*Bonnie Marlow, Ottoville, OH*

PREP: 30 min. • **COOK:** 4¾ hours
MAKES: 9 servings (2¼ qt.)

- 2 lbs. potatoes, peeled and diced
- 1 lb. carrots, sliced
- 1 jar (24 oz.) pasta sauce
- 2 jars (6 oz. each) sliced mushrooms, drained
- 1½ tsp. ground turmeric
- 1½ tsp. minced garlic
- 1 tsp. cayenne pepper
- ¼ tsp. salt
- 1½ cups water
- 1 lb. sea scallops
- 1 lb. uncooked shrimp (31-40 per lb.), peeled and deveined

1. In a 5-qt. slow cooker, combine first 8 ingredients. Cook, covered, on low until potatoes are tender, 4½-5 hours.
2. Stir in water, scallops and shrimp. Cook, covered, until the scallops are opaque and shrimp turn pink, 15-20 minutes longer.
1 CUP: 229 cal., 2g fat (0 sat. fat), 73mg chol., 803mg sod., 34g carb. (10g sugars, 6g fiber), 19g pro.

VIETNAMESE CHICKEN MEATBALL SOUP WITH BOK CHOY

 ## VIETNAMESE CHICKEN MEATBALL SOUP WITH BOK CHOY

Throughout Vietnam there are many kinds of soups *(canh)* served all year long. I particularly love enjoying this warm, flavorful bowl of Vietnamese chicken soup on laid-back weekends, but it's also terrific packed in a Thermos for lunch. It's the perfect bok choy soup too!
—*Brenda Watts, Gaffney, SC*

PREP: 45 min. • **COOK:** 6 hours
MAKES: 8 servings (about 2½ qt.)

- ¼ cup panko bread crumbs
- ¼ cup finely chopped onion
- 1 large egg, lightly beaten
- 2 serrano peppers, seeded and minced
- 1 garlic clove, minced
- ½ lb. ground chicken
- 2 Tbsp. peanut oil

SOUP
- 6 cups chicken or vegetable stock
- 1 can (14½ oz.) fire-roasted diced tomatoes, undrained
- 1 small onion, cut into thin strips
- 1 cup bok choy leaves, cut into 1-in. strips
- 1 cup fresh baby carrots, julienned
- 1 cup julienned roasted sweet red peppers
- 3 serrano peppers, julienned
- 2 garlic cloves, minced
- ½ tsp. salt
- ¼ cup panko bread crumbs, optional
- 1 large egg, beaten

1. Combine panko bread crumbs, onion, egg, minced peppers and garlic. Add chicken; mix lightly but thoroughly. Shape into ¾-in. balls. In a large skillet, heat oil over medium heat. Brown the meatballs in batches, then drain and transfer to a 4- or 5-qt. slow cooker.

2. Add stock, tomatoes, onion, bok choy, carrots, red peppers, julienned serrano peppers, garlic and salt. Cook, covered, on low for 6-8 hours or until meatballs are cooked through and vegetables are tender.

3. If desired, stir in panko. Without stirring, drizzle beaten egg into slow cooker. Let stand until egg is set, 2-3 minutes.

FREEZE OPTION: Before adding egg, cool the soup. Freeze in freezer containers. To use, partially thaw in refrigerator overnight. Heat through in a saucepan, stirring occasionally; add broth or water if necessary. Without stirring, drizzle beaten egg into soup. Let stand until egg is set, 2-3 minutes.

NOTE: Wear disposable gloves when cutting hot peppers; the oils can burn skin. Avoid touching your face.

1⅓ CUPS: 147 cal., 7g fat (2g sat. fat), 65mg chol., 836mg sod., 9g carb. (5g sugars, 1g fiber), 10g pro.

CORN CHOWDER

CORN CHOWDER

I combine and refrigerate the ingredients for this easy chowder the night before. In the morning, I start the slow cooker before I leave for work. When I come home, a hot, satisfying meal awaits.
—*Mary Hogue, Rochester, PA*

PREP: 10 min. • **COOK:** 6 hours
MAKES: 8 servings (2 qt.)

- 2½ cups 2% milk
- 1 can (14¾ oz.) cream-style corn
- 1 can (10¾ oz.) condensed cream of mushroom soup, undiluted
- 1¾ cups frozen corn
- 1 cup frozen shredded hash brown potatoes
- 1 cup cubed fully cooked ham
- 1 large onion, chopped
- 2 tsp. dried parsley flakes
- 2 Tbsp. butter
  Salt and pepper to taste
  Optional: Crumbled cooked bacon and minced parsley

In a 3-qt. slow cooker, combine all ingredients. Cover and cook on low for 6 hours.
1 CUP: 196 cal., 8g fat (3g sat. fat), 26mg chol., 687mg sod., 26g carb. (7g sugars, 2g fiber), 9g pro.

TEST KITCHEN TIP

You can store this chowder in an airtight container in the refrigerator for 3-4 days. Unfortunately, dairy-based soups such as this one do not freeze well.

BONNIE'S CHILI

BONNIE'S CHILI

This incredibly easy chili has a surprising depth of flavor—it tastes like chilis that take all day! I can make this for people who like it hot or mild just by changing the salsa.
—*Bonnie Altig, North Pole, AK*

PREP: 25 min. • **COOK:** 5 hours
MAKES: 8 servings (2½ qt.)

- 2 lbs. lean ground beef (90% lean)
- 2 cans (16 oz. each) kidney beans, rinsed and drained
- 2 cans (15 oz. each) tomato sauce
- 1½ cups salsa
- ½ cup water or reduced-sodium beef broth
- 4½ tsp. chili powder
- ½ tsp. garlic powder
- ½ tsp. pepper
- ¼ tsp. salt

Optional toppings: Corn chips, sliced jalapeno peppers and shredded cheddar cheese

In a Dutch oven, cook ground beef over medium heat until no longer pink, 8-10 minutes, breaking into crumbles; drain. Transfer to a 4- or 5-qt. slow cooker. Stir in the next 8 ingredients. Cook, covered, on low 5-6 hours or until heated through. Serve with toppings as desired.
FREEZE OPTION: Freeze cooled chili in freezer containers. To use, partially thaw in refrigerator overnight. Heat through in a saucepan, stirring occasionally; add broth or water if necessary.
NOTE: Wear disposable gloves when cutting hot peppers; the oils can burn skin. Avoid touching your face.
1¼ CUPS: 323 cal., 10g fat (4g sat. fat), 71mg chol., 1027mg sod., 27g carb. (5g sugars, 8g fiber), 31g pro.

COUNTRY CASSOULET: Instead of cubed ham, add 1½ pounds smoked ham hocks or pork neck bones or a meaty ham bone to slow cooker. Omit onion soup mix; add ¼ tsp. each dried thyme and rosemary. Remove ham bones at end of cooking; stir 2 cups shredded cooked chicken or turkey and ½ lb. sliced smoked fully cooked sausage into soup. Heat through. Cut meat from ham bones; add to soup.

✱ NAVY BEAN VEGETABLE SOUP

My family really likes bean soup, so I came up with this enticing version. The leftovers are, dare I say, even better the next day!
—*Eleanor Mielke, Mitchell, SD*

PREP: 15 min. • **COOK:** 9 hours
MAKES: 12 servings (3 qt.)

- 4   medium carrots, thinly sliced
- 2   celery ribs, chopped
- 1   medium onion, chopped
- 2   cups cubed fully cooked ham
- 1½ cups dried navy beans
- 1   envelope vegetable recipe mix (Knorr)
- 1   envelope onion soup mix
- 1   bay leaf
- ½   tsp. pepper
- 8   cups water

In a 5-qt. slow cooker, combine the first 9 ingredients. Stir in water. Cover and cook on low until beans are tender, 9-10 hours. Discard bay leaf.
FREEZE OPTION: Freeze cooled soup in freezer containers. To use, partially thaw in refrigerator overnight. Heat through in a saucepan, stirring occasionally; add water or broth if necessary.
1 CUP: 157 cal., 2g fat (1g sat. fat), 12mg chol., 763mg sod., 24g carb. (4g sugars, 8g fiber), 11g pro.

✱ FAMILY-PLEASING TURKEY CHILI

My children really love this recipe—it's one of their favorite comfort foods. It's relatively inexpensive, and the leftovers are wonderful!
—*Sheila Christensen, San Marcos, CA*

PREP: 25 min. • **COOK:** 4 hours
MAKES: 6 servings (2¼ qt.)

- 1   lb. lean ground turkey
- 1   medium green pepper, finely chopped
- 1   small red onion, finely chopped
- 2   garlic cloves, minced
- 1   can (28 oz.) diced tomatoes, undrained
- 1   can (16 oz.) kidney beans, rinsed and drained
- 1   can (15 oz.) black beans, rinsed and drained
- 1   can (14½ oz.) reduced-sodium chicken broth
- 1¾ cups frozen corn, thawed
- 1   can (6 oz.) tomato paste
- 1   Tbsp. chili powder
- ½   tsp. pepper
- ¼   tsp. ground cumin
- ¼   tsp. garlic powder
     Optional toppings: Reduced-fat sour cream and minced fresh cilantro

1. In a large nonstick skillet, cook ground turkey, green pepper and onion over medium heat until meat is no longer pink, breaking it into crumbles. Add the garlic; cook 1 minute longer. Drain.
2. Transfer to a 4-qt. slow cooker. Stir in the tomatoes, kidney beans, black beans, broth, corn, tomato paste, chili powder, pepper, cumin and garlic powder.
3. Cover and cook on low until heated through, 4-5 hours. If desired, serve with sour cream and cilantro.
FREEZE OPTION: Freeze cooled chili in freezer containers. To use, partially thaw in refrigerator overnight. Heat through in a saucepan, stirring occasionally; add broth or water if necessary.
1½ CUPS: 349 cal., 7g fat (2g sat. fat), 60mg chol., 725mg sod., 47g carb. (11g sugars, 12g fiber), 27g pro.
DIABETIC EXCHANGES: 3 lean meat, 2 starch, 2 vegetable.

TEST KITCHEN TIPS

- Browning the turkey before adding it to the slow cooker creates a rich flavor that adds depth to the dish. If you like, you can use ground beef instead of the turkey.
- In addition to sour cream and cilantro, serve this slow-cooker turkey chili with crushed corn chips, cheddar cheese or jalapeno slices.

FAMILY-PLEASING
TURKEY CHILI

OVER-THE-RAINBOW MINESTRONE

This vegetarian soup features a rainbow of vegetables. You can use any multicolored pasta in place of the spirals.
—*Crystal Schlueter, Northglenn, CO*

PREP: 20 min.
COOK: 6 hours 20 min.
MAKES: 10 servings (3¾ qt.)

- 4 large stems Swiss chard (about ½ lb.) or fresh baby spinach
- 2 Tbsp. olive oil
- 1 medium red onion, finely chopped
- 6 cups vegetable broth
- 2 cans (14½ oz. each) fire-roasted diced tomatoes, undrained
- 1 can (16 oz.) kidney beans, rinsed and drained
- 1 can (15 oz.) garbanzo beans or chickpeas, rinsed and drained
- 1 medium yellow summer squash or zucchini, halved and cut into ¼-in. slices
- 1 medium sweet red or yellow pepper, finely chopped
- 1 medium carrot, finely chopped
- 2 garlic cloves, minced
- 1½ cups uncooked spiral pasta or small pasta shells
- ¼ cup prepared pesto
  Optional toppings: Additional prepared pesto, shredded Parmesan cheese, crushed red pepper flakes and minced fresh basil

1. Cut stems from chard; chop stems and leaves separately. Reserve leaves for adding later. In a large skillet, heat oil over medium heat. Add red onion and chard stems; cook and stir 3-5 minutes or until tender. Transfer to a 6-qt. slow cooker.
2. Stir in broth, tomatoes, kidney beans, garbanzo beans, squash, pepper, carrot and garlic. Cook, covered, on low until vegetables are tender, 6-8 hours.
3. Stir in pasta and reserved chard leaves. Cook, covered, on low until pasta is tender, 20-25 minutes longer; stir in pesto. If desired, serve with additional pesto, Parmesan cheese, red pepper flakes and fresh basil.

1½ CUPS: 231 cal., 7g fat (1g sat. fat), 2mg chol., 1015mg sod., 34g carb. (7g sugars, 6g fiber), 9g pro.

BLACK BEAN SOUP

BLACK BEAN SOUP

Life can get really crazy with young children, but I never want to compromise when it comes to cooking. This recipe is healthy and so easy, thanks to the slow cooker!
—*Angela Lemoine, Howell, NJ*

PREP: 15 min. • **COOK:** 6 hours
MAKES: 8 servings

- 2 cans (15 oz. each) black beans, rinsed and drained
- 1 medium onion, finely chopped
- 1 medium sweet red pepper, finely chopped
- 4 garlic cloves, minced
- 2 tsp. ground cumin
- 2 cans (14½ oz. each) vegetable broth
- 1 tsp. olive oil
  Dash pepper
- 1 cup fresh or frozen corn
  Minced fresh cilantro

1. In a 3-qt. slow cooker, combine the first 6 ingredients. Cook, covered, on low 6-8 hours or until vegetables are softened.
2. Puree soup using an immersion blender, or cool slightly and puree in batches in a blender. Return to slow cooker and heat through.
3. In a small skillet, heat oil over medium heat. Add corn; cook and stir 4-6 minutes or until golden brown. Sprinkle soup with pepper. Garnish with corn and cilantro.

¾ CUP: 117 cal., 1g fat (0 sat. fat), 0 chol., 616mg sod., 21g carb. (3g sugars, 5g fiber), 6g pro. **DIABETIC EXCHANGES:** 1½ starch.

TEST KITCHEN TIP

This version of black bean soup is thinner than most. It's a first-rate base for different mix-ins such as shredded chicken.

MINT LAMB STEW

SOUTHWEST CHICKEN CHILI

Chicken thighs are a nice change of pace in this easy chili. I also add a smoked ham hock and some fresh cilantro to add flavor and keep the dish interesting.
—*Phyllis Beatty, Chandler, AZ*

PREP: 15 min. • **COOK:** 6 hours
MAKES: 5 servings

1½ lbs. boneless skinless chicken
    thighs, cut into 1-in. cubes
1 Tbsp. olive oil
1 smoked ham hock
1 can (15½ oz.) great northern
    beans, rinsed and drained
1 can (14½ oz.) chicken broth
1 can (4 oz.) chopped
    green chiles
¼ cup chopped onion
2 Tbsp. minced fresh cilantro
1 tsp. garlic powder
1 tsp. ground cumin
½ tsp. dried oregano
⅛ to ¼ tsp. crushed red
    pepper flakes
    Optional: Sour cream and
    sliced jalapeno peppers

1. In a large skillet, brown chicken thighs in oil over medium-high heat. Transfer to a 3-qt. slow cooker. Add the ham hock, beans, broth, chiles, onion and seasonings. Cover and cook on low until ham is tender, 6-8 hours.
2. Remove ham bone. When cool enough to handle, remove meat from bone; discard bone. Cut meat into bite-sized pieces and return to slow cooker. If desired, serve with sour cream and sliced jalapenos.
NOTE: Wear disposable gloves when cutting hot peppers; the oils can burn skin. Avoid touching your face.
1 CUP: 343 cal., 16g fat (4g sat. fat), 104mg chol., 735mg sod., 16g carb. (1g sugars, 5g fiber), 33g pro.

MINT LAMB STEW

The lamb here isn't just tender—it melts in your mouth! This recipe is an adaptation of a stew my mother used to make while I was growing up in England. Now I round it out with local root vegetables.
—*Maureen Evans,*
Rancho Cucamonga, CA

PREP: 40 min. • **COOK:** 6 hours
MAKES: 6 servings (2¼ qt.)

½ cup all-purpose flour
½ tsp. salt
¼ tsp. pepper
1½ lbs. lamb stew meat, cubed
2 shallots, sliced
2 Tbsp. olive oil
½ cup red wine
2 cans (14½ oz. each) beef broth
2 medium potatoes, cubed
1 large sweet potato,
    peeled and cubed
2 large carrots, cut
    into 1-in. pieces
2 medium parsnips,
    peeled and cubed

1 garlic clove, minced
1 Tbsp. mint jelly
4 bacon strips, cooked
    and crumbled
    Minced fresh mint, optional

1. In a large shallow dish, combine the flour, salt and pepper. Add the meat, a few pieces at a time, and turn to coat. In a large skillet, brown meat and shallots in oil in batches.
2. Transfer to a 5- or 6-qt. slow cooker. Add wine to the skillet, stirring to loosen browned bits from pan. Bring to a boil. Reduce heat; simmer, uncovered, for 1-2 minutes. Add to slow cooker.
3. Stir in the broth, potatoes, sweet potato, carrots, parsnips and garlic. Cover and cook on low for 6-8 hours or until meat is tender. Stir in jelly; sprinkle with bacon. If desired, sprinkle with fresh mint before serving.
1½ CUPS: 442 cal., 13g fat (4g sat. fat), 79mg chol., 1016mg sod., 46g carb. (11g sugars, 5g fiber), 31g pro.

SOUTHWEST
CHICKEN CHILI

CUBED BEEF & BARLEY SOUP

GENERAL TSO'S STEW

I love Asian food and wanted a stew with the flavors of General Tso's chicken. The slow cooker makes this super easy, and you can use any meat you like. It's wonderful with turkey, ground meats or pork.
—*Lori McLain, Denton, TX*

PREP: 10 min. • **COOK:** 2 hours
MAKES: 6 servings

- 1 cup tomato juice
- ½ cup pickled cherry peppers, chopped
- 2 Tbsp. soy sauce
- 2 Tbsp. hoisin sauce
- 1 Tbsp. peanut oil
- 1 to 2 tsp. crushed red pepper flakes
- 1 lb. shredded cooked chicken
- 1½ cups chopped onion
- 1 cup chopped fresh broccoli
- ¼ cup chopped green onions
- 1 tsp. sesame seeds, toasted

In a 4- or 5-qt. slow cooker, combine first 6 ingredients. Stir in chicken, onion and broccoli. Cook, covered, on low 2 hours or until vegetables are tender. Top with green onions and sesame seeds to serve.
1 CUP: 222 cal., 9g fat (2g sat. fat), 67mg chol., 791mg sod., 10g carb. (5g sugars, 2g fiber), 25g pro.
DIABETIC EXCHANGES: 3 lean meat, 2 vegetable, ½ fat.

CUBED BEEF & BARLEY SOUP

This hearty soup will really stick to your ribs! I've also used a chuck roast, rump roast and London broil that's been cut into bite-sized pieces with tremendous success.
—*Jane Whittaker, Pensacola, FL*

PREP: 20 min. • **COOK:** 8½ hours
MAKES: 8 servings (2 qt.)

1½ lbs. beef stew meat,
    cut into ½-in. cubes
1 Tbsp. canola oil
1 carton (32 oz.) beef broth
1 bottle (12 oz.) beer or
    nonalcoholic beer
1 small onion, chopped
½ cup medium pearl barley
3 garlic cloves, minced
1 tsp. dried oregano
1 tsp. dried parsley flakes
1 tsp. Worcestershire sauce
½ tsp. crushed red pepper flakes
½ tsp. pepper
¼ tsp. salt
1 bay leaf
2 cups frozen mixed
    vegetables, thawed

1. In a large skillet, brown beef in oil; drain. Transfer to a 3-qt. slow cooker.

2. Add the beef broth, beer, onion, barley, garlic, oregano, parsley, Worcestershire sauce, pepper flakes, pepper, salt and bay leaf. Cover and cook on low 8-10 hours.

3. Stir in vegetables; cover and cook 30 minutes longer or until meat is tender and vegetables are heated through. Discard bay leaf.

FREEZE OPTION: Cool soup; freeze in freezer containers. To use, partially thaw in refrigerator overnight. Heat through in a saucepan, stirring occasionally; add broth or water if necessary.

1 CUP: 233 cal., 8g fat (2g sat. fat), 53mg chol., 644mg sod., 18g carb. (3g sugars, 4g fiber), 20g pro.
DIABETIC EXCHANGES: 3 lean meat, 1 starch

CHICKEN STEW
OVER BISCUITS

CHICKEN STEW OVER BISCUITS

Rich gravy makes this a classic comfort food, with chicken slow-cooked to tender perfection and served over hot biscuits. My family can't get enough of this meal.
—*Kathy Garrett, Browns Mills, NJ*

PREP: 5 min. • **COOK:** 4 hours
MAKES: 5 servings

- 2   envelopes chicken gravy mix
- 2   cups water
- ¾   cup white wine
- 1   Tbsp. minced fresh parsley
- 1   to 2 tsp. chicken bouillon granules
- 1   tsp. minced garlic
- ½   tsp. pepper
- 5   medium carrots, cut into 1-in. chunks
- 1   large onion, cut into 8 wedges
- 1   broiler/fryer chicken (3 to 4 lbs.), cut up and skin removed
- 3   Tbsp. all-purpose flour
- ⅓   cup cold water
- 1   tube (6 oz.) refrigerated buttermilk biscuits

1. In a 5-qt. slow cooker, combine the gravy mix, water, wine, parsley, bouillon, garlic and pepper. Add the carrots, onion and chicken. Cook, covered, on low until chicken is tender, 3-4 hours.
2. Remove chicken to cutting board. When cool enough to handle, remove meat from bones; discard bones. Cut meat into bite-sized pieces; return to slow cooker.
3. Combine flour and cold water until smooth; gradually stir into slow cooker. Cook, covered, on high for 1 hour or until thickened.
4. Meanwhile, bake biscuits according to package directions. Place biscuits in soup bowls; top with stew.

VEGETARIAN CHILI OLE!

1½ CUPS WITH 1 BISCUIT: 429 cal., 11g fat (2g sat. fat), 88mg chol., 1288mg sod., 42g carb. (6g sugars, 3g fiber), 34g pro

VEGETARIAN CHILI OLE!

I combine ingredients for this hearty chili the night before, start my trusty slow cooker in the morning and come home to a rich, spicy meal at night!
—*Marjorie Au, Honolulu, HI*

PREP: 35 min. • **COOK:** 6 hours
MAKES: 7 servings

- 1   can (16 oz.) kidney beans, rinsed and drained
- 1   can (15 oz.) black beans, rinsed and drained
- 1   can (14½ oz.) diced tomatoes, undrained
- 1½   cups frozen corn
- 1   large onion, chopped
- 1   medium zucchini, chopped
- 1   medium sweet red pepper, chopped
- 1   can (4 oz.) chopped green chiles
- 1   oz. Mexican chocolate, chopped
- 1   cup water
- 1   can (6 oz.) tomato paste
- 1   Tbsp. cornmeal
- 1   Tbsp. chili powder
- ½   tsp. salt
- ½   tsp. dried oregano
- ½   tsp. ground cumin
- ¼   tsp. hot pepper sauce, optional
      Optional: Diced tomatoes and chopped green onions

In a 4-qt. slow cooker, combine the first 9 ingredients. Combine water, tomato paste, cornmeal, chili powder, salt, oregano, cumin and, if desired, pepper sauce until smooth; stir into slow cooker. Cook, covered, on low until vegetables are tender, 6-8 hours. Serve with tomatoes and green onions if desired.
FREEZE OPTION: Freeze chili in freezer containers. To use, partially thaw in refrigerator overnight. Heat through in a saucepan, stirring occasionally; add water or broth if necessary.
1 CUP : 216 cal., 1g fat (0 sat. fat), 0 chol., 559mg sod., 43g carb. (11g sugars, 10g fiber), 11g pro. **DIABETIC EXCHANGES:** 2½ starch, 1 lean meat.

CHICKEN WILD RICE SOUP WITH SPINACH

I stir together this creamy soup whenever we're craving something warm and comforting. Reduced-fat and reduced-sodium ingredients make it a healthier option.
—*Deborah Williams, Peoria, AZ*

PREP: 10 min. • **COOK:** 5¼ hours
MAKES: 6 servings (about 2 qt.)

- 3 cups water
- 1 can (14½ oz.) reduced-sodium chicken broth
- 1 can (10¾ oz.) reduced-fat reduced-sodium condensed cream of chicken soup, undiluted
- ⅔ cup uncooked wild rice
- 1 garlic clove, minced
- ½ tsp. dried thyme
- ½ tsp. pepper
- ¼ tsp. salt
- 3 cups cubed cooked chicken breast
- 2 cups fresh baby spinach

In a 3-qt. slow cooker, mix the first 8 ingredients until blended. Cook, covered, on low until rice is tender, 5-7 hours. Stir in cubed chicken and spinach. Cook, covered, on low until heated through, about 15 minutes longer.

1¼ CUPS: 212 cal., 3g fat (1g sat. fat), 56mg chol., 523mg sod., 19g carb. (4g sugars, 2g fiber), 25g pro. starch.

GRANDMA'S OXTAIL STEW

GRANDMA'S OXTAIL STEW

This wonderfully rich meal will warm your soul and your taste buds. Oxtail stew is a favorite family heirloom recipe. Don't let the name of this dish turn you off. Oxtail describes the meaty part of the tail of an ox (now commonly cow). The meat is delicious but requires long and slow cooking.
—*Bobbie Keefer, Byers, CO*

PREP: 20 min. • **COOK:** 10 hours
MAKES: 8 servings (3 qt.)

2 lbs. oxtails, trimmed
2 Tbsp. olive oil
4 medium carrots, sliced (about 2 cups)
1 medium onion, chopped
2 garlic cloves, minced
2 cans (14½ oz. each) diced tomatoes, undrained
1 can (15 oz.) beef broth
3 bay leaves
1 tsp. salt
1 tsp. dried oregano
½ tsp. dried thyme
½ tsp. pepper
6 cups chopped cabbage

1. In a large skillet, brown oxtails in oil over medium heat. Remove from pan; place in a 5-qt. slow cooker.
2. Add carrots and chopped onion to drippings; cook and stir until just softened, 3-5 minutes. Add garlic, cook 1 minute longer. Transfer vegetable mixture to slow cooker. Add tomatoes, broth, bay leaves, salt, oregano, thyme and pepper; stir to combine.
3. Cook, covered, on low 8 hours. Add cabbage; cook until cabbage is tender and meat pulls away easily from bones, about 2 hours longer. Remove oxtails; set aside until cool enough to handle. Remove meat from bones; discard bones and shred meat. Return meat to soup. Discard bay leaves.
FREEZE OPTION: Freeze cooled stew in freezer containers. To use, partially thaw in refrigerator overnight. Heat through in a saucepan, stirring occasionally; add broth or water if necessary.
1½ CUPS: 204 cal., 10g fat (3g sat. fat), 34mg chol., 705mg sod., 14g carb. (8g sugars, 5g fiber), 16g pro.

TEST KITCHEN TIP

Oxtails can be tough to cut so it's best to ask the butcher to slice them into pieces, if they aren't already. Trimming the thick pieces of excess fat off the oxtails before cooking will make a less oily stew that's flavorful with a velvety mouthfeel. After cooking, skim off excess fat from the surface with a shallow ladle or large serving spoon.

HEARTY PORK BEAN SOUP

It's wonderful to come home to this pork bean soup dinner simmering away in a slow cooker, especially on a busy weeknight. This soup uses dried beans and is simple to throw together in the morning before work. When you get home, just add a few more ingredients, and in half an hour dinner is ready! Do not put the tomatoes in until the last step of cooking, or the beans will not become soft.
—*Colleen Delawder, Herndon, VA*

PREP: 20 min. + soaking
COOK: 6 hours 20 min.
MAKES: 12 servings (about 4 qt.)

- 1   pkg. (16 oz.) dried great northern beans, rinsed and drained
- 1   large sweet onion, chopped
- 3   medium carrots, chopped
- 3   celery ribs, chopped
- 1   pork tenderloin (1 lb.)
- 1   tsp. garlic powder
- 1   Tbsp. fresh minced chives or 1 tsp. dried chives
- 1   tsp. dried oregano
- ½   tsp. dried thyme
- 1   tsp. pepper
- 1   carton (32 oz.) reduced-sodium chicken broth
- 1   can (14½ oz.) reduced-sodium chicken broth
- 1   bottle (12 oz.) extra pale ale
- 1   can (14½ oz.) diced tomatoes, drained
- 5   oz. fresh spinach
- 1½ to 2 tsp. salt

1. Place beans in a large bowl; add cool water to cover. Soak 5 hours or overnight. Drain beans, discarding water; rinse with cool water.
2. In a 6-qt. slow cooker, layer beans, onion, carrots, celery and pork. Add seasonings, broth and ale. Cook, covered, on low 6-8 hours or until beans and pork are tender.
3. Remove pork; shred with 2 forks. Stir in tomatoes, spinach and salt. Return pork to slow cooker. Cook, covered, on low for 15-20 minutes or until heated through.

1⅓ CUPS: 207 cal., 2g fat (1g sat. fat), 21mg chol., 695mg sod., 30g carb. (5g sugars, 9g fiber), 18g pro.
DIABETIC EXCHANGES: 2 starch, 2 lean meat.

VEGETABLE CURRY

I love the fuss-free nature of the slow cooker, but I don't want to sacrifice flavor for convenience. This cozy, spiced-up dish has both.
—*Susan Smith, Mead, WA*

PREP: 35 min. • **COOK:** 5 hours
MAKES: 6 servings (about 2½ qt.)

- 1   Tbsp. canola oil
- 1   medium onion, finely chopped
- 4   garlic cloves, minced
- 3   tsp. ground coriander
- 1½ tsp. ground cinnamon
- 1   tsp. ground ginger
- 1   tsp. ground turmeric
- ½   tsp. cayenne pepper
- 2   Tbsp. tomato paste
- 2   cans (15 oz. each) garbanzo beans or chickpeas, rinsed and drained
- 3   cups cubed peeled sweet potatoes (about 1 lb.)
- 3   cups fresh cauliflower florets (about 8 oz.)
- 4   medium carrots, cut into ¾-in. pieces (about 2 cups)
- 2   medium tomatoes, seeded and chopped
- 2   cups chicken broth
- 1   cup light coconut milk
- ½   tsp. pepper
- ¼   tsp. salt
     Minced fresh cilantro
     Hot cooked brown rice
     Lime wedges
     Plain yogurt, optional

1. In a large skillet, heat oil over medium heat; saute onion until soft and lightly browned, 5-7 minutes. Add garlic and spices; cook and stir 1 minute. Stir in tomato paste; cook 1 minute. Transfer to a 5- or 6-qt. slow cooker.
2. Mash 1 can of garbanzo beans until smooth; add to the slow cooker. Stir in remaining beans, vegetables, broth, coconut milk, pepper and salt.
3. Cook, covered, on low until vegetables are tender, 5-6 hours. Sprinkle with cilantro. Serve with rice, lime wedges and, if desired, yogurt.

1⅔ CUPS CURRY: 304 cal., 8g fat (2g sat. fat), 2mg chol., 696mg sod., 49g carb. (12g sugars, 12g fiber), 9g pro.

TEST KITCHEN TIPS

- Garbanzo beans are a smart way to add a dose of protein to a meatless main. They are also a good source of fiber, folate and vitamin B6.
- There's no curry powder in the ingredients because curry is actually a blend of spices like those used here. The curry powder you see in grocery stores is a premixed spice blend.

VEGETABLE CURRY

THAI BUTTERNUT SQUASH PEANUT SOUP

This seemingly exotic dish is simple, vegan, healthy and hearty. The peanut butter blends with the sweetness of the squash and Thai seasonings. You can also serve this soup without pureeing it first.
—*Kayla Capper, Ojai, CA*

PREP: 25 min. • **COOK:** 5 hours
MAKES: 8 servings (1½ qt.)

- 3 cups cubed peeled butternut squash
- 1 can (13.66 oz.) light coconut milk
- 1 medium sweet red pepper, finely chopped
- 1 medium onion, finely chopped
- 1 cup vegetable stock
- ½ cup chunky peanut butter
- 3 Tbsp. lime juice
- 2 Tbsp. red curry paste
- 4 garlic cloves, minced
- 1 Tbsp. reduced-sodium soy sauce
- 1 tsp. minced fresh gingerroot
- ½ tsp. salt
- ¼ tsp. pepper
  Optional: Chopped fresh cilantro and chopped salted peanuts

1. In a 4- or 5-qt. slow cooker, combine the first 13 ingredients. Cook, covered, on low until squash is tender, 5-6 hours.
2. Puree soup using an immersion blender, or cool slightly and puree soup in batches in a blender, then return to slow cooker and heat through. If desired, garnish with cilantro and peanuts.

¾ CUP: 181 cal., 12g fat (4g sat. fat), 0 chol., 470mg sod., 16g carb. (5g sugars, 3g fiber), 5g pro. **DIABETIC EXCHANGES:** 1 starch, 1 high-fat meat, 1 fat.

THAI BUTTERNUT SQUASH PEANUT SOUP

HEARTY BEEF VEGGIE SOUP

Here's a slow-cooked meal perfect for chilly winter nights. It's nice to come home to dinner that's ready to eat. This hearty soup goes well with a fruit salad and bread.
—*Colleen Jubl, Dayton, OH*

PREP: 10 min. • **COOK:** 3 hours
MAKES: 9 servings (2¼ qt.)

- 1 lb. lean ground beef (90% lean)
- 1 medium onion, chopped
- 2 garlic cloves, minced
- 4 cups spicy hot V8 juice
- 2 cups coleslaw mix
- 1 can (14½ oz.) Italian stewed tomatoes
- 2 Tbsp. Worcestershire sauce
- 1 tsp. dried basil
- ¼ tsp. pepper
- 1 pkg. (10 oz.) frozen corn
- 1 pkg. (9 oz.) frozen cut green beans

1. In a large nonstick skillet, cook beef and onion over medium heat until the meat is no longer pink, crumbling beef. Add garlic; cook 1 minute longer. Drain.
2. Transfer to a 5-qt. slow cooker. Stir in V8 juice, coleslaw mix, tomatoes, Worcestershire sauce, basil and pepper. Cook, covered, on low for 3-4 hours or until heated through. Add corn and green beans during last 30 minutes of cooking.
1 CUP: 162 cal., 4g fat (2g sat. fat), 31mg chol., 380mg sod., 18g carb. (8g sugars, 3g fiber), 13g pro.
DIABETIC EXCHANGES: 1 starch, 1 vegetable. 1 lean meat.

SAUSAGE SAUERKRAUT SOUP

I've taken this satisfying soup to church gatherings and family reunions, and it always receives great compliments. Everyone loves it!
—*Elizabeth Goetzinger, Lewiston, ID*

PREP: 25 min. • **COOK:** 8 hours
MAKES: 6 servings

- 6 small red potatoes, quartered
- 3 medium carrots, cut into ¼-in. slices
- 1 medium onion, cut into thin wedges
- 1 can (14 oz.) sauerkraut, rinsed and well drained
- 1 Tbsp. brown sugar
- 1 Tbsp. spicy brown mustard
- 1 tsp. caraway seeds
- 1 lb. smoked kielbasa or Polish sausage, cut into 1-in. slices
- 2 cans (14½ oz. each) reduced-sodium chicken broth

In a 3- or 4-qt. slow cooker, combine the potatoes, carrots and onion. Combine the sauerkraut, brown sugar, mustard and caraway seeds; spoon over vegetables. Top with sausage and broth. Cook, covered, on low until the vegetables are tender, 8-9 hours.
1¼ CUPS: 373 cal., 21g fat (8g sat. fat), 51mg chol., 1707mg sod., 31g carb. (8g sugars, 5g fiber), 16g pro.

MANCHESTER STEW

MANCHESTER STEW

While in college, I studied abroad at the University of Manchester in England. I was pleasantly surprised at how delicious and diverse vegetarian food in Britain could be. My favorite meal, served at my favorite restaurant, was Beans Burgundy; after returning to the States, I created this version. As it simmers in the slow cooker and the enticing aroma fills the kitchen, I'm reminded of my time in England!
—*Kimberly Hammond, Kingwood, TX*

PREP: 25 min. • **COOK:** 8 hours
MAKES: 6 servings (2½ qt.)

- 2 Tbsp. olive oil
- 2 medium onions, chopped
- 2 garlic cloves, minced
- 1 tsp. dried oregano
- 1 cup dry red wine
- 1 lb. small red potatoes, quartered
- 1 can (16 oz.) kidney beans, rinsed and drained
- ½ lb. sliced fresh mushrooms
- 2 medium leeks (white portions only), sliced
- 1 cup fresh baby carrots
- 2½ cups water
- 1 can (14½ oz.) no-salt-added diced tomatoes
- 1 tsp. dried thyme
- ½ tsp. salt
- ¼ tsp. pepper
   Fresh basil leaves

1. In a large skillet, heat oil over medium-high heat. Add onions; cook and stir 2-3 minutes or until tender. Add garlic and oregano; cook and stir 1 minute longer. Stir in red wine. Bring to a boil; cook 3-4 minutes or until the liquid is reduced by half.
2. Transfer to a 5- or 6-qt. slow cooker. Add the potatoes, beans, mushrooms, leeks and carrots. Stir in water, tomatoes, thyme, salt and pepper. Cook, covered, on low until potatoes are tender, 8-10 hours. Top with basil.
1⅔ CUPS: 221 cal., 5g fat (1g sat. fat), 0 chol., 354mg sod., 38g carb. (8g sugars, 8g fiber), 8g pro. **DIABETIC EXCHANGES:** 2 starch, 1 vegetable, 1 fat.

CHICKEN CASSOULET SOUP

CHICKEN CASSOULET SOUP

After my sister spent a year in France as an au pair, I created this lighter, easier version of traditional French cassoulet for her. It uses chicken instead of the usual duck.
—*Bridget Klusman, Otsego, MI*

PREP: 35 min. • **COOK:** 6 hours
MAKES: 7 servings (about 2¾ qt.)

- ½ lb. bulk pork sausage
- 5 cups water
- ½ lb. cubed cooked chicken
- 1 can (16 oz.) kidney beans, rinsed and drained
- 1 can (15 oz.) black beans, rinsed and drained
- 1 can (15 oz.) garbanzo beans or chickpeas, rinsed and drained
- 2 medium carrots, shredded
- 1 medium onion, chopped
- ¼ cup dry vermouth or chicken broth
- 5 tsp. chicken bouillon granules
- 4 garlic cloves, minced
- 1½ tsp. minced fresh thyme or ½ tsp. dried thyme
- ¼ tsp. fennel seed, crushed
- 1 tsp. dried lavender flowers, optional
- ½ lb. bacon strips, cooked and crumbled
   Additional fresh thyme, optional

1. In a large skillet, cook sausage over medium heat until no longer pink, breaking into crumbles; drain.
2. Transfer to a 4- or 5-qt. slow cooker. Add water, chicken, beans, carrots, onion, vermouth, bouillon, garlic, thyme, fennel and, if desired, lavender. Cook, covered, on low for 6-8 hours or until heated through.
3. Divide among bowls; sprinkle with bacon. If desired, top with additional fresh thyme.
1½ CUPS: 494 cal., 23g fat (7g sat. fat), 77mg chol., 1821mg sod., 34g carb. (6g sugars, 9g fiber), 34g pro.

HEARTY HOMEMADE CHICKEN NOODLE SOUP

This satisfying soup with a hint of cayenne brims with vegetables, chicken and noodles. The recipe came from my father-in-law, but I made some adjustments to give it my own spin.
—*Norma Reynolds, Overland Park, KS*

PREP: 20 min. • **COOK:** 5½ hours
MAKES: 12 servings (3 qt.)

- 12 fresh baby carrots, cut into ½-in. pieces
- 4 celery ribs, cut into ½-in. pieces
- ¾ cup finely chopped onion
- 1 Tbsp. minced fresh parsley
- ½ tsp. pepper
- ¼ tsp. cayenne pepper
- 1½ tsp. mustard seed
- 2 garlic cloves, peeled and halved
- 1¼ lbs. boneless skinless chicken breast halves
- 1¼ lbs. boneless skinless chicken thighs
- 4 cans (14½ oz. each) chicken broth
- 1 pkg. (9 oz.) refrigerated linguine
  Optional: Coarsely ground pepper and additional minced fresh parsley

1. In a 5-qt. slow cooker, combine the first 6 ingredients. Place mustard seed and garlic on a double thickness of cheesecloth; bring up corners of cloth and tie with kitchen string to form a bag. Place in slow cooker. Add chicken and broth. Cook, covered, on low until meat is tender, 5-6 hours.
2. Discard the spice bag. Remove chicken; set aside. Stir linguine into soup; cook, covered, on high until pasta is tender, about 30 minutes longer.
3. Cut the chicken into pieces and return to soup; heat through. Sprinkle with coarsely ground pepper and additional parsley if desired.

1 CUP: 199 cal., 6g fat (2g sat. fat), 73mg chol., 663mg sod., 14g carb. (2g sugars, 1g fiber), 22g pro.
DIABETIC EXCHANGES: 3 lean meat, 1 starch.

"This is the best chicken soup that I have ever made! You need to make this soup. I wouldn't change a thing."
AMYDOO, TASTEOFHOME.COM

CHORIZO CHILI

CHORIZO CHILI

I modified a bean soup recipe and came up with this wonderful chili. I make it mild, since that's how my family likes it, then just add Tabasco sauce to spice up my bowl. You can make it vegetarian by using soy chorizo and vegetable broth.
—*Jenne Delkus, Des Peres, MO*

PREP: 20 min. • **COOK:** 5 hours
MAKES: 8 servings (2 qt.)

- 2 cans (15 oz. each) black beans, rinsed and drained
- 1 can (16 oz.) kidney beans, rinsed and drained
- 1 jar (16 oz.) chunky salsa
- 1 can (15 oz.) whole kernel corn, drained
- 1 pkg. (12 oz.) fully cooked Spanish chorizo links, chopped
- 1 can (10 oz.) diced tomatoes and green chiles, undrained
- 1 cup reduced-sodium chicken broth
- 2 Tbsp. ground cumin
- 1 to 2 tsp. hot pepper sauce
- 1 medium ripe avocado, peeled and cubed
- 6 Tbsp. sour cream
- ¼ cup fresh cilantro leaves

Combine first 9 ingredients in a 4- or 5-qt. slow cooker. Cook, covered, on low 5-6 hours or until flavors are blended. Serve with avocado, sour cream and cilantro.
1 CUP: 366 cal., 17g fat (6g sat. fat), 30mg chol., 1262mg sod., 37g carb. (8g sugars, 10g fiber), 18g pro.

CHICKEN
MUSHROOM STEW

CHICKEN MUSHROOM STEW

The flavors blend beautifully in this dish of chicken, vegetables and herbs as it simmers in a slow cooker. Folks with busy schedules will love this convenient recipe.
—*Kenny Van Rheenen, Mendota, IL*

PREP: 20 min. • **COOK:** 4 hours
MAKES: 6 servings (2 qt.)

- 6 boneless skinless chicken breast halves (4 oz. each)
- 2 Tbsp. canola oil, divided
- 8 oz. fresh mushrooms, sliced
- 1 medium onion, diced
- 3 cups diced zucchini
- 1 cup chopped green pepper
- 4 garlic cloves, minced
- 3 medium tomatoes, chopped
- 1 can (6 oz.) tomato paste
- ¾ cup water
- 2 tsp. each dried thyme, oregano, marjoram, and basil
  Chopped fresh thyme, optional

1. Cut chicken into 1-in. cubes; brown in 1 Tbsp. oil in a large skillet. Transfer to a 3-qt. slow cooker.
2. In the same skillet, saute the mushrooms, onion, zucchini and green pepper in remaining 1 Tbsp. oil until crisp-tender; add garlic; cook 1 minute longer. Place in the slow cooker.
3. Add the tomatoes, tomato paste, water and seasonings. Cook, covered, on low for 4-5 hours or until the meat is no longer pink and vegetables are tender. If desired, top with chopped fresh thyme.
1⅓ CUPS: 237 cal., 8g fat (1g sat. fat), 63mg chol., 82mg sod., 15g carb. (7g sugars, 3g fiber), 27g pro. **DIABETIC EXCHANGES:** 3 lean meat, 1 starch, 1 fat.

HOLY MOLY POTATO SOUP

❄ HOLY MOLY POTATO SOUP

We eat this spiced-up version of cheesy potato soup often, especially on cold winter evenings. It would also be a lovely addition to family get-togethers or potlucks during the holidays! Crushed red pepper flakes turn up the heat.
—*Angela Sheridan, Opdyke, IL*

PREP: 20 min. • **COOK:** 4 hours
MAKES: 10 servings (3¾ qt.)

- 4 cans (14½ oz. each) diced new potatoes, undrained
- 2 cans (10¾ oz. each) condensed cream of mushroom soup, undiluted
- 2½ cups water
- 1 can (11 oz.) whole kernel corn, drained
- 1 can (10 oz.) diced tomatoes and green chiles, undrained
- 6 green onions, chopped
- 1 medium sweet red pepper, chopped
- 1 Tbsp. dried minced onion
- 1 tsp. cayenne pepper
- ¼ tsp. pepper
- 1 lb. bulk spicy pork sausage
- 2 cups (8 oz.) shredded sharp cheddar cheese
- 1 carton (8 oz.) French onion dip
  Tortilla chips

1. In a 6-qt. slow cooker, combine the first 10 ingredients. In a large skillet, cook sausage over medium heat 6-8 minutes or until no longer pink, breaking it into crumbles; drain. Add to slow cooker.
2. Cook, covered, on low to allow flavors to blend, 4-5 hours.
3. Add cheese and dip in the last 30 minutes of cooking. Stir before serving. Serve with tortilla chips.
FREEZE OPTION: Cool soup; freeze in freezer containers. To use, partially thaw in refrigerator overnight. Heat through in a saucepan, stirring occasionally; add broth or water if necessary.
1½ CUPS: 529 cal., 30g fat (13g sat. fat), 62mg chol., 1981mg sod., 43g carb. (5g sugars, 8g fiber), 18g pro.

SPICY GOULASH

Ground cumin, chili powder and a can of Mexican diced tomatoes jazz up my goulash recipe. Even the elbow macaroni is prepared in the slow cooker.
—*Melissa Polk, West Lafayette, IN*

PREP: 25 min. • **COOK:** 5½ hours
MAKES: 12 servings (3 qt.)

- 1   lb. lean ground beef (90% lean)
- 4   cans (14½ oz. each) Mexican diced tomatoes, undrained
- 2   cans (16 oz. each) kidney beans, rinsed and drained
- 2   cups water
- 1   medium onion, chopped
- 1   medium green pepper, chopped
- ¼   cup red wine vinegar
- 2   Tbsp. chili powder
- 1   Tbsp. Worcestershire sauce
- 2   tsp. beef bouillon granules
- 1   tsp. dried basil
- 1   tsp. dried parsley flakes
- 1   tsp. ground cumin
- ¼   tsp. pepper
- 2   cups uncooked elbow macaroni

1. In a large skillet over medium heat, cook ground beef until no longer pink, 6-8 minutes, breaking into crumbles; drain. Transfer to a 5-qt. slow cooker.
2. Stir in tomatoes, beans, water, onion, green pepper, vinegar, chili powder, Worcestershire sauce, bouillon and seasonings. Cook, covered, on low for 5-6 hours or until heated through.
3. Stir in macaroni; cover and cook 30 minutes longer or until macaroni is tender.

1 CUP: 222 cal., 5g fat (2g sat. fat), 23mg chol., 585mg sod., 30g carb. (7g sugars, 6g fiber), 15g pro.
DIABETIC EXCHANGES: 2 lean meat, 1½ starch, 1 vegetable.

TOMATO BASIL TORTELLINI SOUP

The first time my family tried this soup, they all had to have seconds; my husband is happy any time I put it on the table. Sometimes I include cooked, crumbled bacon and serve it with mozzarella cheese.
—*Christy Addison, Clarksville, OH*

PREP: 25 min. • **COOK:** 6¼ hours
MAKES: 18 servings (4½ qt.)

- 2   Tbsp. olive oil
- 1   medium onion, chopped
- 3   medium carrots, chopped
- 5   garlic cloves, minced
- 3   cans (28 oz. each) crushed tomatoes, undrained
- 1   carton (32 oz.) vegetable broth
- 1   Tbsp. sugar
- 1   tsp. dried basil
- 1   bay leaf
- 3   pkg. (9 oz. each) refrigerated cheese tortellini
- ¾   cup half-and-half cream
     Shredded Parmesan cheese
     Minced fresh basil

1. In a large skillet, heat oil over medium-high heat. Add onion and carrots; cook and stir until crisp-tender, 5-6 minutes. Add garlic; cook 1 minute longer.
2. Transfer to a 6- or 7-qt. slow cooker. Add the tomatoes, broth, sugar, basil and bay leaf. Cook, covered, on low until vegetables are tender, 6-7 hours.
3. Stir in tortellini. Cook, covered, on high 15 minutes longer. Reduce heat to low; stir in cream until heated through. Discard bay leaf. Serve topped with Parmesan cheese and minced basil.

FREEZE OPTION: Before stirring in cream, cool soup and freeze in freezer containers. To use, partially thaw in refrigerator overnight. Heat through in a saucepan, stirring occasionally; add cream as directed.

1 CUP: 214 cal., 7g fat (3g sat. fat), 23mg chol., 569mg sod., 32g carb. (9g sugars, 4g fiber), 9g pro.
DIABETIC EXCHANGES: 2 starch, 1 fat.

"We greatly enjoyed this recipe. I prepared 1 cup frozen tortellini as it is more budget friendly. I didn't have fresh basil so I used a small amount of prepared pesto in each serving. Definitely a keeper!"

ANNRMS, TASTEOFHOME.COM

TOMATO BASIL
TORTELLINI SOUP

GERMAN-STYLE
SHORT RIBS P. 190

ENTREES

Loads of flavor and ultra-convenience—the
slow cooker delivers dinners that hit the
right spot, even on the busiest nights.

POT ROAST
WITH GRAVY

POT ROAST WITH GRAVY

My family loves this tangy slow-cooked roast with its rich onion and mushroom gravy.
—*Deborah Dailey, Vancouver, WA*

PREP: 30 min. • **COOK:** 6½ hours
MAKES: 10 servings

- 1 beef rump roast or bottom round roast (5 lbs.)
- 6 Tbsp. balsamic vinegar, divided
- 1 tsp. salt
- ½ tsp. garlic powder
- ¼ tsp. pepper
- 2 Tbsp. canola oil
- 3 garlic cloves, minced
- 4 bay leaves
- 1 large onion, thinly sliced
- 3 tsp. beef bouillon granules
- ½ cup boiling water
- 1 can (10¾ oz.) condensed cream of mushroom soup, undiluted
- 4 to 5 Tbsp. cornstarch
- ¼ cup cold water

1. Cut roast in half; rub with 2 Tbsp. vinegar. Combine the salt, garlic powder and pepper; rub over meat. In a large skillet, brown roast in oil on all sides. Transfer to a 5-qt. slow cooker. Place garlic, bay leaves and onion on roast.
2. Dissolve bouillon granules in boiling water; stir in soup and the remaining 4 Tbsp. vinegar. Slowly pour over roast. Cook, covered, on low until meat is tender, 6-8 hours.
3. Remove beef roast; keep warm. Discard the bay leaves. Whisk cornstarch and cold water until smooth; stir into the cooking juices. Cook, covered, on high until gravy is thickened, about 30 minutes.
4. Slice roast; return to slow cooker and heat through.
5 OZ. COOKED BEEF WITH ⅓ CUP GRAVY: 306 cal., 13g fat (3g sat. fat), 114mg chol., 638mg sod., 8g carb. (3g sugars, 1g fiber), 38g pro.

STUFFED SWEET PEPPERS

STUFFED SWEET PEPPERS

Italian sausage and feta cheese give zest to the rice filling in these tender peppers I've prepared often over the years. When I was married in 1970, slow cookers were all the rage. In our home, it's one appliance that's never gone out of style.
—*Judy Earl, Sarasota, FL*

PREP: 15 min. • **COOK:** 4 hours
MAKES: 5 servings

- 3 medium sweet red peppers
- 2 medium sweet yellow peppers
- 1 jar (14 oz.) spaghetti sauce, divided
- ¾ lb. Italian turkey sausage links, casings removed
- ¾ cup uncooked instant rice
- ½ cup crumbled feta cheese
- ½ cup chopped onion
- ¼ cup chopped tomato
- ¼ cup minced fresh parsley
- 2 Tbsp. sliced ripe olives
- ¼ to ½ tsp. garlic powder
- ½ tsp. salt
- ½ tsp. Italian seasoning
- ½ tsp. crushed red pepper flakes

1. Cut tops off peppers; chop tops and set aside. Discard stems and seeds; set pepper cups aside. Set aside ¾ cup spaghetti sauce; pour the remaining sauce into a 5-qt. slow cooker.
2. In a large bowl, combine the sausage, rice, cheese, onion, tomato, parsley, olives, garlic powder, salt, Italian seasoning, pepper flakes and reserved chopped peppers and spaghetti sauce. Spoon into peppers.
3. Transfer peppers to slow cooker. Cover and cook on low for 4-5 hours or until sausage is no longer pink and peppers are tender.
1 STUFFED PEPPER: 292 cal., 12g fat (3g sat. fat), 48mg chol., 1182mg sod., 30g carb. (10g sugars, 4g fiber), 17g pro.

CHEDDAR-TOPPED BARBECUE MEAT LOAF

My family loves the bold barbecue flavor of this meat loaf. I love that it's such an easy recipe to prepare in the slow cooker.
—*David Snodgrass, Columbia, MO*

PREP: 20 min. • **COOK:** 3¼ hours
MAKES: 8 servings

- 3 large eggs, lightly beaten
- ¾ cup old-fashioned oats
- 1 large green or sweet red pepper, chopped (about 1½ cups)
- 1 small onion, finely chopped
- 1 envelope onion soup mix
- 3 garlic cloves, minced
- ½ tsp. salt
- ¼ tsp. pepper
- 2 lbs. lean ground beef (90% lean)
- 1 cup ketchup
- 2 Tbsp. brown sugar
- 1 Tbsp. barbecue seasoning
- 1 tsp. ground mustard
- 1 cup shredded cheddar cheese

1. Cut three 18x3-in. strips of heavy-duty foil; crisscross them so they resemble spokes of a wheel. Place strips on bottom and up side of a 3-qt. slow cooker. Coat strips with cooking spray.
2. In a large bowl, combine eggs, oats, chopped peppers, onion, soup mix, garlic, salt and pepper. Add beef; mix lightly but thoroughly. Shape into a 7-in. round loaf. Place loaf in center of foil strips in slow cooker. Cook, covered, on low for 3-4 hours or until a thermometer reads at least 160°.
3. In a small bowl, mix ketchup, brown sugar, barbecue seasoning and mustard; pour over meat loaf and sprinkle with cheese. Cook, covered, on low until cheese is melted, about 15 minutes longer. Let stand 5 minutes. Using foil strips as handles, remove meat loaf to a platter.

1 PIECE: 356 cal., 17g fat (7g sat. fat), 154mg chol., 1358mg sod., 22g carb. (13g sugars, 2g fiber), 29g pro.

❄️

STEAK FAJITAS

We enjoy the flavors of Mexican food, so I was glad when I found a fajita recipe loaded with vegetables. The beef comes out nice and tender.
—*Twila Burkholder, Middleburg, PA*

PREP: 10 min. • **COOK:** 8 hours
MAKES: 6 servings

- 1 beef flank steak (1½ lbs.)
- 1 can (14½ oz.) diced tomatoes with garlic and onion, undrained
- 1 jalapeno pepper, seeded and chopped
- 2 garlic cloves, minced
- 1 tsp. ground coriander
- 1 tsp. ground cumin
- 1 tsp. chili powder
- ½ tsp. salt
- 1 medium onion, sliced
- 1 medium green pepper, julienned
- 1 medium sweet red pepper, julienned
- 1 Tbsp. minced fresh cilantro
- 12 flour tortillas (6 in.), warmed
  Optional: Sour cream, salsa, fresh cilantro leaves and lime wedges

1. Thinly slice steak across the grain into strips; place in a 5-qt. slow cooker. Add the tomatoes, jalapeno, garlic, coriander, cumin, chili powder and salt. Cook, covered, on low for 7 hours.
2. Add onion, peppers and cilantro. Cook, covered, until meat is tender, 1-2 hours longer.
3. Using a slotted spoon, place about ½ cup meat mixture down the center of each tortilla. Fold the bottom of tortilla over the filling and roll up. Serve with toppings as desired.

NOTE: Wear disposable gloves when cutting hot peppers; the oils can burn skin. Avoid touching your face.
FREEZE OPTION: Freeze cooled meat mixture and juices in freezer containers. To use, partially thaw in refrigerator overnight. Heat through in a saucepan, stirring occasionally; add broth or water if necessary.
2 FAJITAS: 435 cal., 15g fat (6g sat. fat), 54mg chol., 897mg sod., 42g carb. (5g sugars, 6g fiber), 28g pro.

TEST KITCHEN TIP

Poblano, Anaheim, or banana peppers would also be delicious in these fajitas. For flavorful additions (or substitutions), try broccoli, mushrooms or jicama, or grilled or sauteed strips of zucchini, summer squash or eggplant.

STEAK FAJITAS

❄

BEEF BARBACOA

I love this beef barbacoa because the meat is fall-apart tender and the sauce is smoky, slightly spicy and so flavorful. It's an amazing alternative to ground beef tacos or even pulled pork carnitas. It's also versatile. You can have a soft taco bar and let people make their own—or offer mouthwatering Mexican pizzas or rice bowls.
—*Holly Sander, Lake Mary, FL*

PREP: 20 min. • **COOK:** 6 hours
MAKES: 8 servings

- 1 beef rump or bottom round roast (3 lbs.)
- ½ cup minced fresh cilantro
- ⅓ cup tomato paste
- 8 garlic cloves, minced
- 2 Tbsp. chipotle peppers in adobo sauce plus 1 Tbsp. sauce
- 2 Tbsp. cider vinegar
- 4 tsp. ground cumin
- 1 Tbsp. brown sugar
- 1½ tsp. salt
- 1 tsp. pepper
- 1 cup beef stock
- 1 cup beer or additional stock
- 16 corn tortillas (6 in.)
  Pico de gallo
  Optional: Lime wedges, queso fresco and additional cilantro

1. Cut roast in half. Mix the next 9 ingredients; rub over roast. Place in a 5-qt. slow cooker. Add stock and beer. Cook, covered, until meat is tender, 6-8 hours.
2. Remove roast; shred with 2 forks. Reserve 3 cups cooking juices; discard remaining juices. Skim fat from reserved juices. Return beef and reserved juices to slow cooker; heat through.
3. Serve with tortillas and pico de gallo. If desired, serve with lime wedges, queso fresco and additional cilantro.
FREEZE OPTION: Place shredded beef in freezer containers. Cool and freeze. To use, partially thaw in refrigerator overnight. Heat through in a covered saucepan, stirring gently; add broth if necessary.
2 FILLED TORTILLAS: 361 cal., 10g fat (3g sat. fat), 101mg chol., 652mg sod., 28g carb. (4g sugars, 4g fiber), 38g pro. **DIABETIC EXCHANGES:** 5 lean meat, 2 starch.

"I used a sirloin tri-tip roast that I had in the freezer, but other than that I followed the recipe exactly. I've made beef barbacoa before, but I will keep this as my favorite. The seasonings were just right and the meat was very tender and tasty."
BONNIETURNER, TASTEOFHOME.COM

BUTTER & HERB TURKEY

BUTTER & HERB TURKEY

My kids love turkey for dinner, and this easy recipe lets me make it whenever I want—no special occasion required! The meat is so tender it comes right off the bone.
—*Rochelle Popovic, South Bend, IN*

PREP: 10 min. • **COOK:** 5 hours
MAKES: 12 servings (3 cups gravy)

- 1 bone-in turkey breast (6 to 7 lbs.)
- 2 Tbsp. butter, softened
- ½ tsp. dried rosemary, crushed
- ½ tsp. dried thyme
- ¼ tsp. garlic powder
- ¼ tsp. pepper
- 1 can (14½ oz.) chicken broth
- 3 Tbsp. cornstarch
- 2 Tbsp. cold water

1. Rub turkey with butter. Combine the rosemary, thyme, garlic powder and pepper; sprinkle over turkey. Place in a 6-qt. slow cooker. Pour broth over top. Cook, covered, on low until tender, 5-6 hours.
2. Remove turkey to a serving platter; keep warm. Skim fat from cooking juices; transfer juices to a small saucepan. Bring to a boil. Combine cornstarch and water until smooth. Gradually stir into the pan. Bring to a boil; cook and stir until thickened, about 2 minutes. Serve with turkey.

5 OZ. COOKED TURKEY WITH ¼ CUP GRAVY: 339 cal., 14g fat (5g sat. fat), 128mg chol., 266mg sod., 2g carb. (0 sugars, 0 fiber), 48g pro.

CHICKEN MARBELLA

COUNTRY CASSOULET

This bean stew is great with fresh dinner rolls and your favorite green salad. It's a hearty and satisfying meal that's perfect after a long day in the garden.
—*Suzanne McKinley, Lyons, GA*

PREP: 20 min. + soaking
COOK: 6 hours • **MAKES:** 10 servings

- 1 lb. dried great northern beans
- 2 uncooked garlic-flavored pork sausage links
- 3 bacon strips, diced
- 1½ lbs. boneless pork, cut into 1-in. cubes
- 1 lb. boneless lamb, cut into 1-in. cubes
- 1½ cups chopped onion
- 3 garlic cloves, minced
- 2 tsp. salt
- 1 tsp. dried thyme
- 4 whole cloves
- 2 bay leaves
- 2½ cups chicken broth
- 1 can (8 oz.) tomato sauce

1. Rinse and sort beans; soak according to package directions. Drain and rinse, discarding liquid.
2. In a large skillet over medium-high heat, brown sausage links; transfer to a 5-qt. slow cooker. Add bacon to the skillet; cook until crisp. Use a slotted spoon to transfer bacon to the slow cooker; leave drippings in the pan.
3. In bacon drippings, brown pork and lamb on all sides. Place in slow cooker. Stir in beans and the remaining ingredients.
4. Cook, covered, on low until the beans are tender, 6-8 hours. Discard cloves and bay leaves. Remove sausage and cut into ¼-in. slices; return to slow cooker and stir gently.
1 CUP: 375 cal., 12g fat (4g sat. fat), 74mg chol., 950mg sod., 32g carb. (5g sugars, 10g fiber), 35g pro.

CHICKEN MARBELLA

This sweet, briny, savory and herbal recipe packs a big punch of garlic. The Mediterranean flavors make me think of dinner on the patio with family or friends.
—*Beth Jacobson, Milwaukee, WI*

PREP: 30 min. • **COOK:** 4 hours
MAKES: 6 servings

- 1 cup pitted green olives, divided
- 1 cup pitted dried plums (prunes), divided
- 2 Tbsp. dried oregano
- 2 Tbsp. brown sugar
- 2 Tbsp. capers, drained
- 2 Tbsp. olive oil
- 4 garlic cloves, minced
- ½ tsp. salt
- ½ tsp. pepper
- 6 bone-in chicken thighs (about 2 lbs.), skin removed
- ¼ cup reduced-sodium chicken broth
- 1 Tbsp. minced fresh parsley
- 1 Tbsp. white wine
- 1 Tbsp. lemon juice
  Hot cooked couscous

1. Place ½ cup olives, ½ cup dried plums, oregano, brown sugar, capers, oil, garlic, salt and pepper in a food processor; process until smooth. Transfer mixture to a 4-qt. slow cooker. Place chicken in slow cooker. Cook, covered, on low until chicken is tender, 4-5 hours.
2. Chop remaining ½ cup olives and ½ cup dried plums. Remove chicken from slow cooker; keep warm. Stir chicken broth, parsley, wine, lemon juice and chopped olives and dried plums into olive mixture. Serve with chicken and couscous.
1 SERVING: 372 cal., 18g fat (3g sat. fat), 87mg chol., 845mg sod., 26g carb. (13g sugars, 2g fiber), 25g pro.

COUNTRY
CASSOULET

SLOW-COOKER
BAKED ZITI

SLOW-COOKER BAKED ZITI

I don't know one family that doesn't have some crazy, hectic evenings. This recipe is an easy fix for a busy weeknight dinner.
—*Christy Addison, Clarksville, OH*

PREP: 10 min. • **COOK:** 2 hours
MAKES: 6 servings

- 1 container (15 oz.) whole-milk ricotta cheese
- 1 large egg, beaten
- 1 tsp. dried basil
- ½ tsp. crushed red pepper flakes, optional
- 1 jar (24 oz.) meatless pasta sauce
- 2 cups uncooked ziti
- ¼ cup water
- 2 cups shredded mozzarella cheese
- ¼ cup minced fresh basil
  Grated Parmesan cheese, optional

1. In a small bowl, stir together ricotta cheese, egg, basil and, if desired, red pepper flakes. Pour the pasta sauce into a 5-qt. slow cooker. Evenly top sauce with pasta; pour water over top. Drop heaping tablespoons of ricotta cheese mixture over the pasta. Sprinkle with mozzarella cheese.
2. Cook, covered, on high until heated through and the pasta is tender, 2-2½ hours.
3. Top with fresh basil and, if desired, Parmesan cheese and additional red pepper flakes; serve immediately.

1½ CUPS: 379 cal., 17g fat (10g sat. fat), 89mg chol., 886mg sod., 36g carb. (13g sugars, 3g fiber), 23g pro.

COUNTRY-STYLE PORK LOIN

❄ COUNTRY-STYLE PORK LOIN

This pork roast is so moist and tender, it melts in your mouth. My son puts it at the top of his list of favorite foods. We like it served with mashed potatoes.
—*Corina Flansberg, Carson City, NV*

PREP: 20 min.
COOK: 5 hours + standing
MAKES: 8 servings

- 1 boneless pork loin roast (3 lbs.)
- ½ cup all-purpose flour
- 1 tsp. onion powder
- 1 tsp. ground mustard
- 2 Tbsp. canola oil
- 2 cups reduced-sodium chicken broth
- ¼ cup cornstarch
- ¼ cup cold water

1. Cut roast in half. In a large shallow dish, combine the flour, onion powder and mustard. Add pork, 1 portion at a time, and turn to coat. In a large skillet, brown pork in oil on all sides.
2. Transfer to a 5-qt. slow cooker. Pour broth over the pork. Cook, covered, on low for 5-6 hours or until tender. Remove pork and keep warm. Let pork stand 10-15 minutes before slicing.
3. For gravy, strain cooking juices, reserving 2½ cups juices; skim fat from reserved juices. Transfer liquid to a small saucepan. Bring to a boil. Combine cornstarch and water until smooth; gradually stir into the pan. Bring to a boil; cook and stir gravy for 2 minutes or until thickened.

FREEZE OPTION: Cool pork and gravy. Freeze sliced pork and gravy in freezer containers. To use, partially thaw in refrigerator overnight. Heat through slowly in a covered skillet, stirring occasionally; add broth or water if necessary.

5 OZ. COOKED MEAT WITH ¼ CUP GRAVY: 291 cal., 11g fat (3g sat. fat), 85mg chol., 204mg sod., 10g carb. (0 sugars, 0 fiber), 34g pro. **DIABETIC EXCHANGES:** 5 lean meat, ½ starch, ½ fat.

BUSY-DAY
CHICKEN FAJITAS

GERMAN-STYLE SHORT RIBS

Our whole family gets excited when I plug in the slow cooker to make these amazing ribs. We like them served over rice or egg noodles.
—*Bregitte Rugman, Shanty Bay, ON*

PREP: 15 min. • **COOK:** 8 hours
MAKES: 8 servings

- ¾ cup dry red wine or beef broth
- ½ cup mango chutney
- 3 Tbsp. quick-cooking tapioca
- ¼ cup water
- 3 Tbsp. brown sugar
- 3 Tbsp. cider vinegar
- 1 Tbsp. Worcestershire sauce
- ½ tsp. salt
- ½ tsp. ground mustard
- ½ tsp. chili powder
- ½ tsp. pepper
- 4 lbs. bone-in beef short ribs
- 2 medium onions, sliced
  Optional: Egg noodles or spaetzle and minced fresh parsley

1. In a 5-qt. slow cooker, combine the first 11 ingredients. Add ribs and turn to coat. Top with onions. Cook, covered, on low until meat is tender, 8-10 hours.
2. Remove ribs from slow cooker. Skim fat from cooking juices; serve juices with ribs. If desired, serve ribs with noodles or spaetzle and parsley.
3 OZ. COOKED BEEF: 302 cal., 11g fat (5g sat. fat), 55mg chol., 378mg sod., 28g carb. (17g sugars, 1g fiber), 19g pro.

BUSY-DAY CHICKEN FAJITAS

When I don't have much time to cook supper, chicken fajitas from the slow cooker are a flavorful way to keep my family satisfied. If you aren't cooking for youngsters, try spicing things up with medium or hot picante sauce.
—*Michele Furry, Plains, MT*

PREP: 20 min. • **COOK:** 4 hours
MAKES: 6 servings

- 1 lb. boneless skinless chicken breasts
- 1 can (15 oz.) black beans, rinsed and drained
- 1 medium green pepper, cut into strips
- 1 large onion, sliced
- 1½ cups picante sauce
- ½ tsp. garlic powder
- ½ tsp. ground cumin
- 12 flour tortillas (6 in.), warmed
- 2 cups shredded cheddar cheese
  Optional: Thinly sliced green onions, sliced ripe olives, chopped tomatoes and sour cream

1. Place chicken in a 4-qt. slow cooker; add black beans, pepper and onion. In a small bowl, mix picante sauce, garlic powder and cumin; pour over top. Cook, covered, on low until chicken is tender, 4-5 hours.
2. Remove chicken and cool slightly. Shred meat with 2 forks and return to slow cooker; heat through. Serve with tortillas, cheese and toppings of your choice.
2 FAJITAS: 508 cal., 20g fat (10g sat. fat), 79mg chol., 1192mg sod., 46g carb. (5g sugars, 6g fiber), 32g pro.

GERMAN-STYLE
SHORT RIBS

CHUCK ROAST DINNER

A tasty tomato sauce nicely coats this comforting combination of beef, potatoes and carrots. My father gave me the recipe. It was one of our favorites when we used to hike all day and takes only minutes to throw together!
—*Cindy Miller, Estes Park, CO*

PREP: 10 min. • **COOK:** 6 hours
MAKES: 10 servings

- 1 boneless beef chuck roast (3 lbs.), cut into serving-size pieces
- 3 medium potatoes, peeled and cut into chunks
- 4 medium carrots, cut into chunks
- 2 cans (11½ oz. each) tomato juice
- ¼ cup Worcestershire sauce
- 3 Tbsp. quick-cooking tapioca
   Chopped fresh parsley, optional

In a 5-qt. slow cooker, combine all ingredients. Cook, covered, on high until meat is tender, 6-8 hours. If desired, top with parsley.

1 CUP: 300 cal., 13g fat (5g sat. fat), 88mg chol., 250mg sod., 17g carb. (3g sugars, 1g fiber), 28g pro.

CHUCK ROAST DINNER

NORTH AFRICAN CHICKEN & RICE

I'm always looking to try recipes from different cultures and this one is a huge favorite. We love the combination of spices. This dish cooks equally well in a slow cooker or pressure cooker.
—*Courtney Stultz, Weir, KS*

PREP: 10 min. • **COOK:** 4 hours
MAKES: 8 servings

- 1 medium onion, diced
- 1 Tbsp. olive oil
- 8 boneless skinless chicken thighs (about 2 lbs.)
- 1 Tbsp. minced fresh cilantro
- 1 tsp. ground turmeric
- 1 tsp. paprika
- 1 tsp. sea salt
- ½ tsp. pepper
- ½ tsp. ground cinnamon
- ½ tsp. chili powder
- 1 cup golden raisins
- ½ to 1 cup chopped pitted green olives
- 1 medium lemon, sliced
- 2 garlic cloves, minced
- ½ cup chicken broth or water
- 4 cups hot cooked brown rice

In a 3- or 4-qt. slow cooker, combine onion and oil. Place chicken thighs on top of onion; sprinkle with next 7 ingredients. Top with the raisins, olives, lemon and garlic. Add broth. Cook, covered, on low until chicken is tender, 4-5 hours. Serve with hot cooked rice.
1 SERVING: 386 cal., 13g fat (3g sat. fat), 76mg chol., 556mg sod., 44g carb. (12g sugars, 3g fiber), 25g pro.

TEST KITCHEN TIP

If olives aren't your favorite, don't leave them out entirely, but go with ½ cup. They add a nice underlying flavor as well as a little saltiness to the dish.

ASIAN SHORT RIBS

After a long day of sledding, the aroma of these beautiful short ribs says, "Welcome home!" Warm and comforting, they make a worthy low-maintenance dinner.
—*Amy Chase, Vanderhoof, BC*

PREP: 10 min. • **COOK:** 6 hours
MAKES: 4 servings

- 1 can (28 oz.) stewed tomatoes
- 1 medium onion, chopped
- 4 garlic cloves, minced
- 2 Tbsp. honey
- 2 Tbsp. soy sauce
- 1 Tbsp. Worcestershire sauce
- 1 Tbsp. chili garlic sauce
- 2 bay leaves
- 1 tsp. pepper
- ½ tsp. salt
- 8 bone-in beef short ribs (about 4 lbs.)
  Hot cooked rice, optional

In a 4- or 5-qt. slow cooker, combine the first 10 ingredients. Add short ribs; cook, covered, on low until meat is tender, 6-8 hours. Discard bay leaves. If desired, serve with rice.
1 SERVING: 466 cal., 21g fat (9g sat. fat), 110mg chol., 1338mg sod., 29g carb. (21g sugars, 2g fiber), 39g pro.

LAZY MAN'S RIBS

I'll have to admit these ribs are finger-lickin' good and fall-off-the-bone tender! I've made them for a lot of my buddies—including my preacher—and some have even suggested that I try bottling my sauce and selling it to the public!
—Allan Stackhouse Jr., Jennings, LA

PREP: 20 min. • **COOK:** 5 hours
MAKES: 4 servings

- 2½ lbs. pork baby back ribs, cut into 8 pieces
- 2 tsp. Cajun seasoning
- 1 medium onion, sliced
- 1 cup ketchup
- ½ cup packed brown sugar
- ⅓ cup orange juice
- ⅓ cup cider vinegar
- ¼ cup molasses
- 2 Tbsp. Worcestershire sauce
- 1 Tbsp. barbecue sauce
- 1 tsp. stone-ground mustard
- 1 tsp. paprika
- ½ tsp. garlic powder
- ½ tsp. liquid smoke, optional
  Dash salt
- 5 tsp. cornstarch
- 1 Tbsp. cold water

1. Rub ribs with Cajun seasoning. Layer the ribs and onion in a 5-qt. slow cooker. Combine the ketchup, brown sugar, orange juice, vinegar, molasses, Worcestershire sauce, barbecue sauce, mustard, paprika, garlic powder, liquid smoke (if desired), and salt. Pour over ribs. Cook, covered, on low until meat is tender, 5-6 hours.
2. Remove ribs and keep warm. Strain cooking juices and skim fat; transfer juices to a small saucepan. Combine cornstarch and water until smooth; stir into juices. Bring to a boil; cook and stir until thickened, about 2 minutes. Serve with ribs.
1 SERVING: 753 cal., 39g fat (14g sat. fat), 153mg chol., 1335mg sod., 70g carb. (52g sugars, 2g fiber), 33g pro.

❄ HEARTY CHICKEN ENCHILADAS

My husband, Nathan, and I really like Mexican food, and this is our favorite dish. You can modify it to suit your taste by adding corn, rice or refried beans.
—Jenny Miller, Raleigh, NC

PREP: 6 hours • **BAKE:** 25 min.
MAKES: 2 casseroles
(2 servings each)

- 1 lb. boneless skinless chicken breasts
- 2 cans (15 oz. each) enchilada sauce
- 1 can (4 oz.) chopped green chiles
- 1 can (15 oz.) black beans, rinsed and drained
- 8 flour tortillas (6 in.)
- 1 cup shredded Mexican cheese blend
  Optional: Sour cream, shredded lettuce, pico de gallo and sliced avocado

1. In a 3-qt. slow cooker, combine the chicken, enchilada sauce and chiles. Cook, covered, on low until meat is tender, 6-8 hours.
2. Remove chicken and shred with 2 forks. Reserve 1⅔ cups cooking juices. Pour the remaining cooking juices into a large bowl; add the beans and shredded chicken. Coat 2 freezer-safe 8-in. square baking dishes with cooking spray; add ½ cup reserved juices to each.
3. Place about ⅓ cup chicken mixture down the center of each tortilla. Roll up and place seam side down in prepared dishes. Pour the remaining reserved juices over top; sprinkle with cheese.
4. Cover 1 dish and freeze for up to 3 months. Cover second dish and bake at 350° for 20 minutes. Uncover; bake until cheese is lightly browned, about 5 minutes longer. Serve with toppings as desired.
FREEZE OPTION: To use frozen enchiladas: Thaw in the refrigerator overnight. Remove from the refrigerator 30 minutes before baking. Bake as directed.
2 ENCHILADAS: 577 cal., 20g fat (4g sat. fat), 83mg chol., 1541mg sod., 57g carb. (8g sugars, 8g fiber), 46g pro.

TEST KITCHEN TIP

Try serving your chicken enchiladas with a side of Spanish rice or homemade guacamole and tortilla chips!

HEARTY CHICKEN ENCHILADAS

TEXAS CHILI FRIES

The delicious chili goes together in minutes and then cooks while you run errands. The only way I could think to make it even better was to pour it over crisp french fries and sprinkle it with cheese.
—*Joan Hallford,*
North Richland Hills, TX

PREP: 20 min. • **COOK:** 6 hours
MAKES: 16 servings

- 1 medium onion, chopped
- 1 medium carrot, finely chopped
- 2 lbs. beef stew meat (cut into ½-in. pieces)
- 3 Tbsp. all-purpose flour, divided
- 2 Tbsp. canola oil
- 1 can (14½ oz.) Mexican diced tomatoes
- 1 envelope (1.25 oz.) chili seasoning mix
- 1 can (15 oz.) pinto beans, rinsed and drained
- 1 medium green pepper, chopped
- 1 jalapeno pepper, seeded and finely chopped
- 2 pkg. (32 oz. each) frozen french-fried potatoes
- 2 cups shredded sharp cheddar cheese
  Optional: Sour cream and sliced jalapeno peppers

1. Place onion and carrot in a 5-qt. slow cooker. Toss beef with 2 Tbsp. flour. In a Dutch oven, heat oil over medium heat; brown beef in batches. Transfer meat to the slow cooker.

2. Drain tomatoes, reserving liquid. In a small bowl, whisk reserved liquid, chili seasoning and the remaining 1 Tbsp. flour until blended; pour over beef. Stir in tomatoes, beans and peppers. Cook, covered, on low until meat is tender, about 6 hours.

3. Prepare fries according to package directions. Serve chili over fries; sprinkle with cheese. If desired, top with sour cream and jalapeno slices.

NOTE: Wear disposable gloves when cutting hot peppers; the oils can burn skin. Avoid touching your face.

1 SERVING: 374 cal., 16g fat (6g sat. fat), 49mg chol., 824mg sod., 32g carb. (4g sugars, 5g fiber), 19g pro.

TEST KITCHEN TIP

You can use whatever frozen potatoes you have on hand— waffle fries, curly fries, or tater tots would do nicely. You can even make your french fries from scratch rather than using frozen.

TEXAS CHILI FRIES

MUSHROOM PORK TENDERLOIN

This juicy pork tenderloin in a savory gravy is the best you'll ever taste. Prepared with canned soups, it couldn't be easier to make.
—*Donna Hughes, Rochester, NH*

PREP: 5 min. • **COOK:** 4 hours
MAKES: 6 servings

- 2 pork tenderloins (1 lb. each)
- 1 can (10¾ oz.) condensed cream of mushroom soup, undiluted
- 1 can (10¾ oz.) condensed golden mushroom soup, undiluted
- 1 can (10½ oz.) condensed French onion soup, undiluted
  Hot mashed potatoes, optional

Place pork in a 3-qt. slow cooker. In a small bowl, combine soups; stir until smooth. Pour over pork. Cook, covered, on low until the pork is tender, 4-5 hours. If desired, serve with mashed potatoes.

4 OZ. COOKED PORK WITH ⅔ CUP SAUCE: 269 cal., 10g fat (3g sat. fat), 89mg chol., 951mg sod., 10g carb. (2g sugars, 2g fiber), 32g pro.

SLOW-COOKED
CORNED BEEF

SLOW-COOKED CORNED BEEF

It's not luck; it's just an amazing Irish recipe. With this in the slow cooker by sunrise, you can definitely fill the seats at the dinner table by sundown.
—*Heather Parraz, Rochester, WA*

PREP 20 MIN. • COOK: 9 hours
MAKES: 6 servings (plus about 14 oz. cooked corned beef leftovers)

- 6   medium red potatoes, quartered
- 2   medium carrots, cut into chunks
- 1   large onion, sliced
- 2   corned beef briskets with spice packets (3 lbs. each)
- ¼   cup packed brown sugar
- 2   Tbsp. sugar
- 2   Tbsp. coriander seeds
- 2   Tbsp. whole peppercorns
- 4   cups water

1. In a 6-qt. slow cooker, combine the potatoes, carrots and onion. Add the briskets (discard spice packets from the corned beef or save for another use). Sprinkle the brown sugar, sugar, coriander and peppercorns over meat. Pour water over top.
2. Cook, covered, on low until the meat and vegetables are tender, 9-11 hours.
3. Remove meat and vegetables to a serving platter. Thinly slice 1 brisket across the grain and serve with vegetables. Save remaining brisket for another use.
4 OZ. COOKED CORNED BEEF WITH ¾ CUP VEGETABLES: 557 cal., 31g fat (10g sat. fat), 156mg chol., 1825mg sod., 38g carb. (16g sugars, 4g fiber), 32g pro.

SAUSAGE LASAGNA

SAUSAGE LASAGNA

On especially cold winter days, my family loves this stick-to-your-ribs lasagna. If you prefer, use spicy Italian sausage to give it more zing.
—*Cindi DeClue, Anchorage, AK*

PREP: 40 min.
COOK: 3½ hours + standing
MAKES: 8 servings

- 1   lb. ground beef
- 1   lb. ground mild Italian sausage
- 1   medium onion, finely chopped
- 1   garlic clove, minced
- 1   jar (24 oz.) spaghetti sauce
- 1   can (14½ oz.) diced tomatoes in sauce, undrained
- ½   cup water
- 1   tsp. dried basil
- 1   tsp. dried oregano
- 1   carton (15 oz.) whole-milk ricotta cheese
- 2   large eggs, lightly beaten
- ½   cup grated Parmesan cheese
- 9   uncooked lasagna noodles
- 4   cups shredded part-skim mozzarella cheese
    Minced fresh basil, optional

1. Line side of an oval 6-qt. slow cooker with heavy-duty foil; coat foil with cooking spray. In a Dutch oven, cook beef, sausage, onion and garlic over medium heat until meat is no longer pink, 8-10 minutes, breaking up beef and sausage into crumbles; drain. Stir in spaghetti sauce, tomatoes, water and herbs; heat through.
2. In a small bowl, mix ricotta cheese, eggs and Parmesan cheese. Spread 1½ cups meat sauce onto bottom of prepared slow cooker. Layer with 3 noodles (breaking to fit), ¾ cup ricotta mixture, 1 cup mozzarella cheese and 2 cups meat sauce. Repeat the layers twice. Sprinkle with remaining 1 cup mozzarella cheese.
3. Cook, covered, on low until noodles are tender, 3½-4 hours. Turn off slow cooker; remove insert. Let stand 15 minutes. If desired, sprinkle with fresh basil.
1 SERVING: 667 cal., 37g fat (17g sat. fat), 164mg chol., 1310mg sod., 41g carb. (14g sugars, 4g fiber), 42g pro.

JERKED SHORT RIBS

Sweet and spicy jerk seasonings give these saucy ribs an incredible taste! They're great to make in the summer because they don't heat up the kitchen.
—*Susan Hein, Burlington, WI*

PREP: 15 min. • **COOK:** 6 hours
MAKES: 10 servings

- 1 Tbsp. ground coriander
- 2 tsp. ground ginger
- 2 tsp. onion powder
- 2 tsp. garlic powder
- 1 tsp. salt
- 1 tsp. pepper
- 1 tsp. dried thyme
- ¾ tsp. ground allspice
- ¾ tsp. ground nutmeg
- ½ tsp. ground cinnamon
- 10 bone-in beef short ribs (about 5 lbs.)
- 1 large sweet onion, chopped
- ½ cup beef broth
- 1 jar (10 oz.) apricot preserves
- 3 Tbsp. cider vinegar
- 3 garlic cloves, minced

1. Combine first 10 ingredients. Reserve 2 Tbsp.; rub remaining seasoning mixture over ribs. Place onion and broth in a 6-qt. slow cooker; cover with ribs. Cook, covered, on low until ribs are tender, 6-8 hours.

2. Meanwhile, combine preserves, vinegar, garlic and reserved seasoning mixture. Serve with ribs.
1 SHORT RIB WITH 3 TBSP. SAUCE: 265 cal., 11g fat (5g sat. fat), 55mg chol., 330mg sod., 23g carb. (14g sugars, 1g fiber), 19g pro.

HONEY-GLAZED HAM

Here's an easy solution for feeding a large group. The simple ham is perfect for family dinners where time in the kitchen is as valuable as space in the oven.
—*Jacquie Stolz, Little Sioux, IA*

PREP: 10 min. • **COOK:** 4½ hours
MAKES: 14 servings

- 1 boneless fully cooked ham (4 lbs.)
- 1½ cups ginger ale
- ¼ cup honey
- ½ tsp. ground mustard
- ½ tsp. ground cloves
- ¼ tsp. ground cinnamon

1. Cut ham in half; place in a 5-qt. slow cooker. Pour ginger ale over ham. Cook, covered, on low until heated through, 4-5 hours.
2. Combine the honey, mustard, cloves and cinnamon; stir until smooth. Spread over ham; cook 30 minutes longer.
3 OZ. COOKED HAM: 165 cal., 5g fat (2g sat. fat), 66mg chol., 1348mg sod., 8g carb. (7g sugars, 0 fiber), 24g pro.

SESAME PORK ROAST

My trick to making a roast that's pull-apart tender is marinating a boneless cut of pork in a tangy sauce overnight before cooking it slowly the next day. It's unbeatable.
—*Sue Brown, San Miguel, CA*

PREP: 10 min. + marinating
COOK: 9 hours • **MAKES:** 8 servings

- 1 boneless pork shoulder butt roast (4 lbs.)
- 2 cups water
- ½ cup soy sauce
- ¼ cup sesame seeds, toasted
- ¼ cup molasses
- ¼ cup cider or white wine vinegar
- 4 green onions, sliced
- 2 tsp. garlic powder
- ¼ tsp. cayenne pepper
- 3 Tbsp. cornstarch
- ¼ cup cold water

1. Cut roast in half and place in a bowl. In a separate bowl or shallow dish, combine the water, soy sauce, sesame seeds, molasses, vinegar, onions, garlic powder and cayenne. Pour half over the roast. Turn to coat. Cover and refrigerate roast overnight. Cover and refrigerate remaining marinade.
2. Drain roast, discarding marinade. Place roast in a 5-qt. slow cooker; add the reserved marinade. Cook, covered, on high for 1 hour. Reduce temperature to low; cook until meat is tender, 8-9 hours longer.
3. Remove the meat to a serving platter; keep warm. Skim fat from cooking juices; transfer juices to a small saucepan. Bring to a boil. Combine cornstarch and cold water until smooth. Gradually stir into the pan. Return to a boil; cook and stir until thickened, about 2 minutes. Serve with meat. If desired, sprinkle with additional sesame seeds.
6 OZ. COOKED PORK: 433 cal., 24g fat (8g sat. fat), 135mg chol., 835mg sod., 10g carb. (6g sugars, 1g fiber), 41g pro.

SEASAME PORK
ROAST

BARBECUE PORK
COBB SALAD

BARBECUE PORK COBB SALAD

My lunchtime salad gets way more interesting topped with barbecue pork, cheddar cheese and creamy avocado. It's as satisfying as it is scrumptious.
—Shawn Carleton, San Diego, CA

PREP: 30 min. • **COOK:** 4 hours
MAKES: 6 servings

- 1¼ cups barbecue sauce
- ½ tsp. garlic powder
- ¼ tsp. paprika
- 1½ lbs. pork tenderloin
- 12 cups chopped romaine
- 3 plum tomatoes, chopped
- 2 avocados, peeled and chopped
- 2 small carrots, thinly sliced
- 1 medium sweet red or green pepper, chopped
- 3 hard-boiled large eggs, chopped
- 1½ cups shredded cheddar cheese
  Salad dressing of your choice

1. In a greased 3-qt. slow cooker, mix barbecue sauce, garlic powder and paprika. Add pork; turn to coat. Cook, covered, on low until pork is tender, 4-5 hours.
2. Remove pork from slow cooker; shred into bite-sized pieces. In a bowl, toss pork with 1 cup barbecue sauce mixture. Place romaine on a large serving platter; arrange the pork, tomatoes, avocado, carrots, chopped pepper, eggs and cheese over romaine. Drizzle with dressing.
1 SERVING: 492 cal., 24g fat (9g sat. fat), 185mg chol., 868mg sod., 35g carb. (23g sugars, 7g fiber), 35g pro.

MEATY SPAGHETTI SAUCE

MEATY SPAGHETTI SAUCE

My homemade spaghetti sauce got rave reviews, but it was so time-consuming to make on the stovetop. My family loves this rich, flavorful slow-cooker version.
—Arlene Sommers, Redmond, WA

PREP: 20 min. • **COOK:** 8 hours
MAKES: 12 servings

- 1 lb. lean ground beef (90% lean)
- 1 lb. bulk Italian sausage
- 1 medium green pepper, chopped
- 1 medium onion, chopped
- 8 garlic cloves, minced
- 3 cans (14½ oz. each) Italian diced tomatoes, drained
- 2 cans (15 oz. each) tomato sauce
- 2 cans (6 oz. each) tomato paste
- ⅓ cup sugar
- 2 Tbsp. Italian seasoning
- 1 Tbsp. dried basil
- 2 tsp. dried marjoram
- 1 tsp. salt
- ½ tsp. pepper
  Hot cooked spaghetti
  Shredded Parmesan cheese, optional

1. In a large skillet over medium heat, cook beef and sausage until no longer pink, 10-12 minutes, crumbling meat; drain. Transfer to a 5-qt. slow cooker. Stir in the green pepper, onion, garlic, tomatoes, tomato sauce, paste, sugar and seasonings.
2. Cook, covered, on low until bubbly, about 8 hours. Serve with spaghetti. If desired, top with shredded Parmesan cheese.
½ CUP: 264 cal., 12g fat (4g sat. fat), 44mg chol., 1119mg sod., 26g carb. (17g sugars, 3g fiber), 15g pro.

BUTTER CHICKEN

I spent several years in Malaysia eating a variety of Middle Eastern and Southeast Asian food—and this was one of my favorites! There are many versions of butter chicken, but this is similar to the Middle Eastern version I had.
—*Shannon Copley, Upper Arlington, OH*

PREP: 10 min. • **COOK:** 3 hours
MAKES: 8 servings

- 2 Tbsp. butter
- 1 medium onion, chopped
- 4 garlic cloves, peeled, thinly sliced
- 2 tsp. garam masala
- 2 tsp. red curry powder
- ½ tsp. chili powder
- 1 tsp. ground ginger
- 2 Tbsp. whole wheat flour
- 1 Tbsp. olive oil
- 1 can (14 oz.) coconut milk
- ¼ cup tomato paste
- 1 tsp. salt
- ¼ tsp. pepper
- 3 lbs. boneless skinless chicken breasts, cut into 1-in. pieces
  Hot cooked rice
  Optional: Fresh cilantro leaves and naan bread

1. Heat a large saucepan over medium-high heat; add the butter and onion. Cook and stir until onions are tender, 2-3 minutes. Add garlic and cook 1 minute or until fragrant. Add garam masala, curry powder, chili powder and ginger; cook and stir 1 minute longer. Add flour. Drizzle in olive oil until a paste is formed. Whisk in coconut milk and tomato paste; cook and stir until mixture is combined and slightly thickened, 1-2 minutes. Season with salt and pepper.
2. Using an immersion blender, carefully puree spice mixture. Transfer mixture to a 5-qt. slow cooker. Add chicken; gently stir to combine.
3. Cook, covered, on low until the chicken is no longer pink, 3-4 hours. Serve with rice. If desired, sprinkle with cilantro and serve with naan bread.

1 CUP: 242 cal., 9g fat (3g sat. fat), 102mg chol., 407mg sod., 4g carb. (1g sugars, 1g fiber), 35g pro.
DIABETIC EXCHANGES: 5 lean meat, 1 fat.

TEXAS-STYLE BEEF BRISKET

A friend had success with this recipe, so I tried it. When my husband told me how much he loved it, I knew I'd make it often.
—*Vivian Warner, Elkhart, KS*

PREP: 25 min. + marinating
COOK: 6½ hours
MAKES: 12 servings

- 3 Tbsp. Worcestershire sauce
- 1 Tbsp. chili powder
- 2 garlic cloves, minced
- 1 tsp. celery salt
- 1 tsp. pepper
- 1 tsp. liquid smoke, optional
- 1 fresh beef brisket (6 lbs.)
- ½ cup beef broth
- 2 bay leaves
BARBECUE SAUCE
- 1 medium onion, chopped
- 2 Tbsp. canola oil
- 2 garlic cloves, minced
- 1 cup ketchup
- ½ cup molasses
- ¼ cup cider vinegar
- 2 tsp. chili powder
- ½ tsp. ground mustard

1. In a large bowl or shallow dish, combine the Worcestershire sauce, chili powder, garlic, celery salt, pepper and, if desired, liquid smoke. Cut brisket in half; add to bowl and turn to coat. Cover and refrigerate overnight.
2. Transfer beef to a 5- or 6-qt. slow cooker; add broth and bay leaves. Cook, covered on low until meat is tender, 6-8 hours.
3. For sauce, in a small saucepan, saute onion in oil until tender. Add garlic; cook 1 minute longer. Stir in the remaining ingredients; heat through.
4. Remove brisket from the slow cooker; discard bay leaves. Place 1 cup cooking juices in a measuring cup; skim fat. Discard remaining juices. Add reserved juices to the barbecue sauce.
5. Return brisket to the slow cooker; top with the sauce mixture. Cook, covered, on high for 30 minutes to allow the flavors to blend. Thinly slice beef across the grain; serve with sauce.

FREEZE OPTION: Place individual portions of sliced brisket in freezer containers; top with barbecue sauce. Let cool and then freeze. To use, partially thaw in refrigerator overnight. Heat through in a covered saucepan, gently stirring; add broth or water if necessary.

6 OZ. COOKED BEEF WITH ¼ CUP SAUCE: 381 cal., 12g fat (4g sat. fat), 96mg chol., 548mg sod., 18g carb. (14g sugars, 1g fiber), 47g pro.

TEXAS-STYLE
BEEF BRISKET

HERBED SLOW-COOKER CHICKEN

I use my slow cooker to prepare these well-seasoned chicken breasts that cook up moist and tender. My daughter, who has two young sons to keep up with, shared this recipe with me several years ago. I've since made it repeatedly.
—*Sundra Hauck, Bogalusa, LA*

PREP: 5 min. • **COOK:** 4 hours
MAKES: 4 servings

- 1 Tbsp. olive oil
- 1 tsp. paprika
- ½ tsp. garlic powder
- ½ tsp. seasoned salt
- ½ tsp. dried thyme
- ½ tsp. dried basil
- ½ tsp. pepper
- ½ tsp. browning sauce, optional
- 4 bone-in chicken breast halves (8 oz. each)
- ½ cup chicken broth

In a small bowl, combine the first 7 ingredients and, if desired, browning sauce; rub over chicken. Place in a 5-qt. slow cooker; add broth. Cook, covered, on low until chicken is tender, 4-5 hours.
1 CHICKEN BREAST HALF: 211 cal., 7g fat (2g sat. fat), 91mg chol., 392mg sod., 1g carb. (0 sugars, 0 fiber), 33g pro. **DIABETIC EXCHANGES:** 5 lean meat, 1 fat.

BEEF OSSO BUCO

BEEF OSSO BUCO

Our beef *osso buco* boasts a thick, savory sauce complemented by the addition of gremolata, a chopped herb condiment made of lemon zest, garlic and parsley.
—Taste of Home *Test Kitchen*

PREP: 30 min. • **COOK:** 7 hours
MAKES: 6 servings

- ½ cup all-purpose flour
- ¾ tsp. salt, divided
- ½ tsp. pepper
- 6 beef shanks (14 oz. each)
- 2 Tbsp. butter
- 1 Tbsp. olive oil
- ½ cup white wine or beef broth
- 1 can (14½ oz.) diced tomatoes, undrained
- 1½ cups beef broth
- 2 medium carrots, chopped
- 1 medium onion, chopped
- 1 celery rib, sliced
- 1 Tbsp. dried thyme
- 1 Tbsp. dried oregano
- 2 bay leaves
- 3 Tbsp. cornstarch
- ¼ cup cold water

GREMOLATA

- ⅓ cup minced fresh parsley
- 1 Tbsp. grated lemon zest
- 1 Tbsp. grated orange zest
- 2 garlic cloves, minced

1. In a large resealable container, combine the flour, ½ tsp. salt and the pepper. Add beef, a few pieces at a time, and shake to coat.

2. In a large skillet, brown beef in butter and oil. Transfer meat and drippings to a 6-qt. slow cooker. Add white wine to skillet, stirring to loosen browned bits from pan; pour over the meat. Add the tomatoes, broth, carrots, onion, celery, thyme, oregano, bay leaves and remaining ¼ tsp. salt.

3. Cook, covered, on low until the meat is tender, 7-9 hours. Discard bay leaves.

4. Skim fat from cooking juices; transfer juices to a large saucepan. Bring to a boil. Combine cornstarch and water until smooth; gradually stir into the pan. Bring to a boil; cook and stir for 2 minutes or until thickened.

5. In a small bowl, combine the gremolata ingredients. Serve beef with sauce and gremolata.

1 SHANK WITH 1 CUP SAUCE AND 4 TSP. GREMOLATA: 398 cal., 15g fat (6g sat. fat), 112mg chol., 640mg sod., 17g carb. (5g sugars, 4g fiber), 47g pro.

TEST KITCHEN TIP

This dish goes beautifully with something to help soak up the sauce. Our favorite pairing is polenta, but French bread, mashed potatoes or pasta would also be good choices.

CAJUN CHICKEN
LASAGNA

CAJUN CHICKEN LASAGNA

Destined to be a new favorite with everyone at the table, this zesty take on traditional Italian lasagna nods to the Gulf Coast. Increase the amount of Cajun seasoning if you like spicier fare.
—Mary Lou Cook, Welches, OR

PREP: 20 min. • **COOK:** 3 hours
MAKES: 8 servings

- 2 lbs. ground chicken
- 2 celery ribs with leaves, chopped
- 1 medium green pepper, chopped
- 1 medium onion, chopped
- 1 can (28 oz.) crushed tomatoes, undrained
- 1 cup water
- 1 can (6 oz.) tomato paste
- 3 tsp. Cajun seasoning
- 1 tsp. sugar
- 2 cups shredded part-skim mozzarella cheese
- 1 carton (15 oz.) ricotta cheese
- 9 uncooked lasagna noodles

1. In a large skillet, cook chicken over medium heat until no longer pink. Add the celery, green pepper and onion; cook and stir 5 minutes longer or until tender. Stir in the tomatoes, water, tomato paste, Cajun seasoning and sugar. In a small bowl, combine the cheeses.
2. Spread 1 cup meat sauce in a greased oval 5- or 6-qt. slow cooker. Layer with 3 noodles (breaking noodles if necessary to fit), a third of the remaining meat sauce and a third of the cheese mixture. Repeat layers twice. Cook, covered, on low until noodles are tender, 3-4 hours.
1 PIECE: 466 cal., 19g fat (9g sat. fat), 113mg chol., 618mg sod., 39g carb. (9g sugars, 4g fiber), 38g pro.

BEEF & RICE STUFFED CABBAGE ROLLS

BEEF & RICE STUFFED CABBAGE ROLLS

My family is quick to come to the table when I serve my cabbage rolls. These savory bundles come together fast and really satisfy without being too heavy.
—Lynn Bowen, Geraldine, AL

PREP: 20 min. • **COOK:** 6 hours
MAKES: 6 servings

- 12 cabbage leaves
- 1 cup cooked brown rice
- ¼ cup finely chopped onion
- 1 large egg, lightly beaten
- ¼ cup fat-free milk
- ½ tsp. salt
- ¼ tsp. pepper
- 1 lb. lean ground beef (90% lean)

SAUCE
- 1 can (8 oz.) tomato sauce
- 1 Tbsp. brown sugar
- 1 Tbsp. lemon juice
- 1 tsp. Worcestershire sauce

1. In batches, cook cabbage in boiling water until crisp-tender, 3-5 minutes. Drain; cool slightly. Trim the thick vein from the bottom of each leaf, making a V-shaped cut.
2. Combine rice, onion, egg, milk, salt and pepper. Add beef; mix lightly but thoroughly. Place about ¼ cup beef mixture on each cabbage leaf. Pull together cut edges of leaf to overlap; fold over filling. Fold in sides and roll up.
3. Place 6 rolls in a 4- or 5-qt. slow cooker, seam side down. In a bowl, mix sauce ingredients; pour half of the sauce over cabbage rolls. Top with remaining rolls and sauce. Cook, covered, on low until a thermometer inserted in the beef reads 160° and the cabbage is tender, 6-8 hours.
2 CABBAGE ROLLS: 204 cal., 7g fat (3g sat. fat), 83mg chol., 446mg sod., 16g carb. (5g sugars, 2g fiber), 18g pro. **DIABETIC EXCHANGES:** 2 lean meat, 1 starch.

APPLE-DIJON PORK ROAST

This cold-weather favorite takes just minutes to assemble and is incredibly delicious. I like to serve the roast with rice, then use the tangy sauce as a gravy for both.
—*Cindy Steffen, Cedarburg, WI*

PREP: 15 min. • **COOK:** 4 hours
MAKES: 8 servings

- 1 boneless pork loin roast (2 to 3 lbs.)
- 1 can (14½ oz.) chicken broth
- 1 cup unsweetened apple juice
- ½ cup Dijon mustard
- 6 Tbsp. cornstarch
- 6 Tbsp. cold water
  Coarsely ground pepper, optional

1. Place roast in a 5-qt. slow cooker. In a small bowl, combine the broth, apple juice and mustard; pour over roast. Cook, covered, on low until tender, 4-5 hours. Remove roast and keep warm.

2. For gravy, strain cooking juices and skim the fat. Pour juices into a small saucepan. Combine the cornstarch and water until smooth; gradually stir into juices. Bring to a boil; cook and stir until thickened, about 2 minutes.

3. Serve pork with gravy. If desired, top with coarsely ground pepper.

3 OZ. COOKED PORK WITH ABOUT 2 TBSP. GRAVY: 197 cal., 7g fat (2g sat. fat), 56mg chol., 413mg sod., 11g carb. (3g sugars, 0 fiber), 23g pro.
DIABETIC EXCHANGES: 3 lean meat, ½ starch.

APPLE-DIJON PORK ROAST

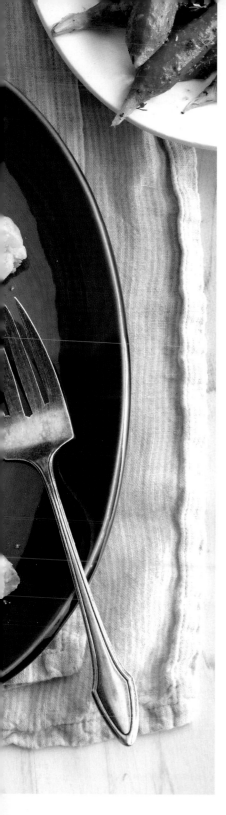

OLD-FASHIONED POOR MAN'S STEAK

These flavorful beef steaks fit into everybody's budget. A special friend shared the recipe, and I think of her each time I make this.
—*Susan Wright, Mineral Wells, WV*

PREP: 25 min. + chilling
COOK: 4 hours • **MAKES:** 9 servings

- 1   cup crushed saltine crackers (about 30 crackers)
- ⅓   cup water
      Salt and pepper to taste
- 2   lbs. ground beef
- ¼   cup all-purpose flour
- 2   Tbsp. canola oil
- 2   cans (10¾ oz. each) condensed cream of mushroom soup, undiluted
      Hot mashed potatoes or noodles
      Minced fresh parsley, optional

1. In a large bowl, combine cracker crumbs, water, salt and pepper. Crumble beef over cracker mixture and mix lightly but thoroughly. Press into an ungreased 9-in. square pan. Refrigerate, covered, at least 3 hours.
2. Cut into 3-in. squares; dredge in flour. In a large skillet, heat oil over medium heat; add beef and cook until browned on both sides, 2-3 minutes per side.
3. Transfer to a 3-qt. slow cooker with a slotted spatula or spoon. Add soup.
4. Cook, covered, on high until meat is no longer pink, about 4 hours. Serve with mashed potatoes or noodles. If desired, top with minced fresh parsley.
1 SERVING: 292 cal., 18g fat (6g sat. fat), 68mg chol., 372mg sod., 10g carb. (1g sugars, 1g fiber), 22g pro.

PORK CHOPS WITH SAUERKRAUT

I pair tender pork chops with tangy sauerkraut for this filling main dish. It's quick and easy to put together, and it leaves everyone satisfied.
—*Stephanie Miller, Omaha, NE*

PREP: 15 min. • **COOK:** 3 hours
MAKES: 4 servings

- 2   Tbsp. canola oil
- 4   bone-in center-cut pork loin chops (8 oz. each)
- 1   jar (32 oz.) sauerkraut, undrained
- ¾   cup packed brown sugar
- 1   medium green pepper, sliced
- 1   medium onion, sliced

1. Heat oil in a large skillet over medium heat; cook until pork chops are browned on each side, 3-4 minutes. Drain.
2. In a 5-qt. slow cooker, combine sauerkraut and brown sugar. Top with the pork chops, green pepper and onion.
3. Cook, covered, on low until meat is tender, 3-4 hours. Serve with a slotted spoon.
1 SERVING: 361 cal., 12g fat (3g sat. fat), 28mg chol., 1536mg sod., 55g carb. (45g sugars, 7g fiber), 12g pro.

MOROCCAN
APRICOT CHICKEN

MOROCCAN APRICOT CHICKEN

Chili sauce, apricots and Moroccan seasoning create an incredible sauce for slow-cooked chicken thighs. Traditional Moroccan apricot chicken typically includes chili pepper paste, but I use chili sauce in my version. Serve alone or with couscous for a heartier meal.
—*Arlene Erlbach, Morton Grove, IL*

PREP: 25 min. • **COOK:** 4¼ hours
MAKES: 6 servings

- 1 tsp. olive oil
- ½ cup slivered almonds
- 6 bone-in chicken thighs (about 2¼ lbs.)
- ¾ cup chili sauce
- ½ cup apricot preserves
- ½ cup dried apricots, quartered
- 4 tsp. Moroccan seasoning (ras el hanout)
- 1 Tbsp. vanilla extract
- 1½ tsp. garlic powder
- 1 can (15 oz.) garbanzo beans or chickpeas, rinsed and drained
- ¼ cup orange juice
  Chopped fresh parsley, optional

1. In a large skillet, heat oil over medium heat. Add the almonds; cook and stir until lightly browned, 2-3 minutes. Remove with a slotted spoon; drain on paper towels.
2. In the same skillet, brown the chicken on both sides. Transfer to a 4- or 5-qt. slow cooker. Stir the chili sauce, preserves, apricots, Moroccan seasoning, vanilla and garlic powder into pan drippings; pour over chicken.
3. Cook, covered, on low until a thermometer inserted in chicken reads 170°-175°, 4-4½ hours.
4. Stir in the garbanzo beans and orange juice. Cook, covered, on low until heated through, 15-30 minutes longer. Serve with the almonds. If desired, sprinkle with parsley.

1 CHICKEN THIGH WITH ¾ CUP GARBANZO BEAN MIXTURE: 482 cal., 21g fat (4g sat. fat), 81mg chol., 633mg sod., 47g carb. (27g sugars, 5g fiber), 28g pro.

CHILI MAC

This recipe has regularly appeared on my family menus for more than 40 years, and it's never failed to please at potlucks and bring-a-dish gatherings. Sometimes I turn it into soup by adding a can of beef broth.
—*Marie Posavec, Berwyn, IL*

PREP: 15 min. • **COOK:** 6 hours
MAKES: 6 servings

- 1 lb. lean ground beef (90% lean), cooked and drained
- 2 cans (16 oz. each) hot chili beans, undrained
- 2 large green peppers, chopped
- 1 large onion, chopped
- 4 celery ribs, chopped
- 1 can (8 oz.) no-salt-added tomato sauce
- 2 Tbsp. chili seasoning mix
- 2 garlic cloves, minced
- 1 pkg. (7 oz.) elbow macaroni, cooked and drained
  Salt and pepper to taste
  Optional: Shredded pepper jack cheese and sliced jalapeno pepper

1. In a 5-qt. slow cooker, combine first 8 ingredients. Cook, covered, on low until heated through, about 6 hours.
2. Stir in macaroni. Season with salt and pepper. If desired, top servings with cheese and sliced jalapenos.
NOTE: Wear disposable gloves when cutting hot peppers; the oils can burn skin. Avoid touching your face.
1 SERVING: 348 cal., 8g fat (3g sat. fat), 47mg chol., 713mg sod., 49g carb. (8g sugars, 12g fiber), 27g pro.
DIABETIC EXCHANGES: 3 starch, 3 lean meat.

CHILI MAC

THAI CHICKEN THIGHS

THAI CHICKEN THIGHS

Thanks to the slow cooker, a traditional Thai dish with peanut butter, jalapeno peppers and chili sauce becomes incredibly easy to make. To crank up the spice a bit, use more jalapeno peppers.
—*Taste of Home* Test Kitchen

PREP: 25 min. • **COOK:** 5 hours
MAKES: 8 servings

- 8   bone-in chicken thighs (about 3 lbs.), skin removed
- ½   cup salsa
- ¼   cup creamy peanut butter
- 2   Tbsp. lemon juice
- 2   Tbsp. reduced-sodium soy sauce
- 1   Tbsp. chopped seeded jalapeno pepper
- 2   tsp. Thai chili sauce
- 1   garlic clove, minced
- 1   tsp. minced fresh gingerroot
- 2   green onions, sliced
- 2   Tbsp. sesame seeds, toasted Hot cooked basmati rice, optional

1. Place chicken in a 3-qt. slow cooker. In a small bowl, combine the salsa, peanut butter, lemon juice, soy sauce, jalapeno, Thai chili sauce, garlic and ginger; pour over the chicken.
2. Cook, covered, on low until chicken is tender, 5-6 hours. Sprinkle with green onions and sesame seeds. Serve with rice if desired.
NOTE: Wear disposable gloves when cutting hot peppers; the oils can burn skin. Avoid touching your face.
1 CHICKEN THIGH WITH ¼ CUP SAUCE: 261 cal., 15g fat (4g sat. fat), 87mg chol., 350mg sod., 5g carb. (2g sugars, 1g fiber), 27g pro. **DIABETIC EXCHANGES:** 4 lean meat, 1 fat, ½ starch.

SALSA ROAST

SALSA ROAST

This is so easy and fast to put together on your way out the door in the morning—and so good when you come home! Try it with rice or on soft tacos, or pile it on hamburger buns.
—*Lavonne Peden, Olympia, WA*

PREP: 15 min.
COOK: 6 hours + standing
MAKES: 8 servings (2 cups sauce)

- 1   boneless beef chuck roast (3½ to 4 lbs.)
- ¼   tsp. garlic salt
- ¼   tsp. pepper
- 1   Tbsp. canola oil
- 1   jar (24 oz.) salsa
- 1   cup water
- 1   small onion, chopped
- 1   jalapeno pepper, seeded and finely chopped
- 1   envelope taco seasoning
- 1   Tbsp. cornstarch
- 1   Tbsp. cold water

1. Sprinkle roast with garlic salt and pepper. In a large skillet, heat oil over medium heat; brown roast on all sides. Transfer to a 5-qt. slow cooker. Combine salsa, water, onion, jalapeno and taco seasoning; pour over roast. Cook, covered, on low until meat is tender, 6-7 hours.
2. Remove roast from slow cooker; tent with foil. Let stand 15 minutes before slicing. Reserve 2 cups cooking juices from slow cooker; discard remaining juices.
3. Skim fat from reserved juices; transfer juices to a small saucepan; bring to a boil. Mix cornstarch and water until smooth; stir into pan. Return to a boil, stirring constantly; cook and stir 1-2 minutes or until thickened. Serve with roast.
NOTE: Wear disposable gloves when cutting hot peppers; the oils can burn skin. Avoid touching your face.
5 OZ. COOKED BEEF WITH ¼ CUP SAUCE: 402 cal., 21g fat (7g sat. fat), 129mg chol., 884mg sod., 11g carb. (3g sugars, 0 fiber), 39g pro.

❄

PAD THAI

I love pad thai, but I hate standing over a hot stir-fry—especially in the summer. This slow-cooker version lets me keep my cool and enjoy pad thai too.
—*Shawn Barto, Palmetto, FL*

PREP: 20 min. • **COOK:** 4 hours
MAKES: 4 servings

- 3 boneless skinless chicken breast halves (5 to 6 oz. each)
- ¼ cup packed brown sugar
- ¼ cup lime juice
- 2 Tbsp. soy sauce
- 2 garlic cloves, minced
- 1 tsp. fish sauce or additional soy sauce
- ¼ tsp. crushed red pepper flakes
- 8 oz. uncooked Asian lo mein noodles
- 2 tsp. butter
- 2 large eggs, beaten
- 3 green onions, thinly sliced
- ¼ cup chopped salted peanuts
- ¼ cup chopped fresh cilantro

1. Place chicken in a 1½- or 3-qt. slow cooker. In a small bowl, combine the next 6 ingredients; pour over chicken. Cook, covered, on low until a thermometer inserted in the chicken reads 165°, about 4 hours. Remove chicken; cool slightly. Shred with 2 forks and return to slow cooker.

2. In a large saucepan, cook noodles according to package directions. In a small nonstick skillet, heat butter over medium heat. Pour in eggs; cook and stir until the eggs are thickened and no liquid egg remains.

3. Drain noodles. Stir eggs and noodles into slow cooker. Top with green onions, peanuts and cilantro.

FREEZE OPTION: Freeze the cooled chicken mixture in freezer-safe containers. To use, partially thaw in refrigerator overnight. Heat through in a saucepan, stirring occasionally; add broth or water if necessary. Prepare the noodles and eggs as directed; stir into chicken mixture. Garnish as directed.

1 SERVING: 482 cal., 12g fat (3g sat. fat), 157mg chol., 891mg sod., 59g carb. (14g sugars, 2g fiber), 34g pro.

TEST KITCHEN TIP

You can easily substitute chicken thighs for breasts in this recipe.

CHICKEN PARMESAN

I love this satisfying dish—it's easy and elegant, and the slow cooker minimizes my time in the kitchen. I make this during football season too. For game days, I skip the pasta and serve the chicken on sub rolls with a bit of the sauce and some chopped lettuce. It's also good cut in half and served on smaller buns as sliders.
—*Bonnie Hawkins, Elkhorn, WI*

PREP: 25 min.
COOK: 4 hours 10 min.
MAKES: 4 servings

- ½ cup seasoned bread crumbs
- ½ cup grated Parmesan cheese
- ½ tsp. Italian seasoning
- ½ tsp. pepper
- ¼ tsp. salt
- 1 large egg, lightly beaten
- 1 Tbsp. water
- 4 (6 oz. each) boneless skinless chicken breast halves
- 1 jar (24 oz.) marinara sauce
- 4 slices part-skim mozzarella cheese
  Hot cooked pasta, optional

1. In a shallow bowl, combine bread crumbs, Parmesan cheese, Italian seasoning, pepper and salt. In another bowl, combine egg and water. Dip chicken in the egg mixture, then in crumb mixture to coat both sides, patting to help the coating adhere.
2. Transfer chicken to a 4- or 5-qt. slow cooker. Pour sauce over chicken. Cook, covered, on low for 4-6 hours or until a thermometer inserted in chicken reads 165°. Top with cheese, recover, and cook until cheese is melted, 10-15 minutes longer. If desired, serve with hot cooked pasta.
1 SERVING: 475 cal., 17g fat (7g sat. fat), 171mg chol., 1689mg sod., 27g carb. (11g sugars, 4g fiber), 50g pro.

GREEN CHILE CHICKEN ENCHILADA PIE

slow cooker insert one-half turn midway through cooking, lifting carefully with oven mitts.

3. Turn off slow cooker; let stand, uncovered, 15 minutes before serving. Using foil strips as handles, remove pie to a platter. Cut into wedges. If desired, serve with additional cilantro and lime wedges, salsa and sour cream.

1 SERVING: 541 cal., 27g fat (15g sat. fat), 116mg chol., 1202mg sod., 36g carb. (2g sugars, 6g fiber), 39g pro.

SLOW-COOKER SPIRAL HAM

My family loves when I make this ham. I'm not sure which they love more, though: eating it straight away or as leftovers on sandwiches.
—*Angela Lively, Conroe, TX*

PREP: 10 min. • **COOK:** 4 hours
MAKES: 15 servings

- 1   spiral-sliced fully cooked bone-in ham (5 lbs.)
- 1   cup unsweetened pineapple juice
- ½   cup packed brown sugar
- ¼   cup butter, melted
- 2   Tbsp. cider vinegar
- 1   garlic clove, minced
- ½   tsp. crushed red pepper flakes
- 1   medium onion, sliced

1. Place ham in a 5-qt. slow cooker. In a small bowl, combine pineapple juice, brown sugar, butter, vinegar, garlic and red pepper flakes; pour over ham. Top with onion slices.
2. Cook, covered, on low 4-5 hours or until a thermometer reads 140°. Serve warm.

3 OZ. HAM: 194 cal., 7g fat (3g sat. fat), 75mg chol., 821mg sod., 11g carb. (10g sugars, 0 fiber), 22g pro.

GREEN CHILE CHICKEN ENCHILADA PIE

My husband likes some heat in our meals, but our children—not so much. This is the best of both worlds. Serve with additional chopped cilantro and a dollop of sour cream if you like.
—*Dana Beery, Ione, WA*

PREP: 30 min.
COOK: 4 hours + standing
MAKES: 6 servings

- 3   cups shredded cooked chicken
- 1   can (15 oz.) black beans, rinsed and drained
- 1   can (10½ oz.) condensed cream of chicken soup, undiluted
- 1   can (10 oz.) mild green enchilada sauce
- 1   can (4 to 4½ oz.) chopped green chiles
- ¼   cup minced fresh cilantro
- 1   Tbsp. lime juice
- 9   corn tortillas (6 in.)
- 3   cups shredded Colby-Monterey Jack cheese
    Optional: Minced fresh cilantro, lime wedges, salsa and sour cream

1. In a large bowl, combine the first 7 ingredients. Cut three 30x6-in. strips of heavy-duty foil; crisscross so they resemble spokes of a wheel. Place strips on bottom and up side of a round 4- or 5-qt. slow cooker. Coat strips with cooking spray. Spread ¼ cup chicken mixture over bottom of slow cooker. Top with 3 tortillas, overlapping and tearing them to fit, a third of the chicken mixture and a third of the cheese. Repeat layers twice.
2. Cook, covered, on low until a thermometer reads 165°, about 4 hours. To avoid scorching, rotate

SLOW-COOKER
SPIRAL HAM

TURKEY LEG POT ROAST

TURKEY LEG POT ROAST

Well-seasoned turkey legs and tender veggies make an ideal dinner for a crisp fall day. And the recipe couldn't be easier!
—*Rick and Vegas Pearson, Cadillac, MI*

PREP: 15 min. • **COOK:** 5 hours
MAKES: 3 servings

- 3 medium potatoes, quartered
- 2 cups fresh baby carrots
- 2 celery ribs, cut into
     2½-in. pieces
- 1 medium onion, peeled and
     quartered
- 3 garlic cloves, peeled and
     quartered
- ½ cup chicken broth
- 3 turkey drumsticks
     (12 oz. each), skin removed
- 2 tsp. seasoned salt
- 1 tsp. dried thyme
- 1 tsp. dried parsley flakes
- ¼ tsp. pepper
     Chopped fresh parsley,
     optional

1. In a greased 5-qt. slow cooker, combine the first 6 ingredients. Place drumsticks over vegetables. Sprinkle with the seasoned salt, thyme, parsley and pepper.
2. Cook, covered, on low until turkey is tender, 5-5½ hours. If desired, top with chopped fresh parsley just before serving.
1 SERVING: 460 cal., 7g fat (2g sat. fat), 202mg chol., 1416mg sod., 44g carb. (10g sugars, 6g fiber), 54g pro.

DEVILED SWISS STEAK

DEVILED SWISS STEAK

This main dish is satisfying all by itself, but you can also serve it over hot mashed potatoes.
—*Melissa Gerken, Zumbrota, MN*

PREP: 20 min. • **COOK:** 6 hours
MAKES: 8 servings

- ½ cup all-purpose flour
- 1 Tbsp. ground mustard
- ½ tsp. salt
- ⅛ tsp. pepper
- 2 beef flank steaks (1 lb. each),
     halved
- 2 Tbsp. butter
- 1 cup thinly sliced onion
- 1 can (28 oz.) stewed tomatoes
- 2 Tbsp. Worcestershire sauce
- 1 Tbsp. brown sugar

1. In a bowl or shallow dish, combine the flour, mustard, salt and pepper. Add steaks and turn to coat. In a large nonstick skillet, brown steaks on both sides in butter. Transfer to a 5-qt. slow cooker. Top with onion.
2. In a bowl, combine the tomatoes, Worcestershire sauce and brown sugar; pour over meat and onion. Cook, covered, on low until beef is tender, 6-8 hours.
1½ CUPS: 177 cal., 5g fat (2g sat. fat), 35mg chol., 675mg sod., 19g carb. (8g sugars, 5g fiber), 15g pro.
DIABETIC EXCHANGES: 2 meat, 1 starch.

TROPICAL COMPOTE
DESSERT P. 233

DESSERTS

Custards, cakes, puddings, crumbles and more—
you won't believe the variety of sweet treats
you can make in your slow cooker!

BERRY COBBLER

APPLE BETTY WITH ALMOND CREAM

I love making this treat for friends during the peak of apple season. I plan a quick soup and bread meal so we can get right to the dessert!
—*Elizabeth Godecke, Chicago, IL*

PREP: 15 min. • **COOK:** 3 hours
MAKES: 8 servings

- 3 lbs. tart apples, peeled and sliced
- 10 slices cinnamon-raisin bread, cubed
- ¾ cup packed brown sugar
- ½ cup butter, melted
- 1 tsp. almond extract
- ½ tsp. ground cinnamon
- ¼ tsp. ground cardamom
- ⅛ tsp. salt

ALMOND CREAM
- 1 cup heavy whipping cream
- 2 Tbsp. sugar
- 1 tsp. grated lemon zest
- ½ tsp. almond extract

1. Place apples in an ungreased 4- or 5-qt. slow cooker. In a large bowl, combine the bread, brown sugar, butter, extract, cinnamon, cardamom and salt; spoon over apples. Cook, covered, on low until apples are tender, 3-4 hours.
2. In a small bowl, beat cream until it begins to thicken. Add the sugar, lemon zest and extract; beat until soft peaks form. Serve with the apple mixture. If desired, sprinkle with additional cinnamon.
1 CUP WITH ¼ CUP ALMOND CREAM: 468 cal., 23g fat (14g sat. fat), 71mg chol., 224mg sod., 65g carb. (45g sugars, 5g fiber), 5g pro.

BERRY COBBLER

Cobbler is the perfect dessert to take advantage of summer fruit— here's a way to enjoy it without heating up the kitchen!
—*Karen Jarocki, Yuma, AZ*

PREP: 15 min. • **COOK:** 1¾ hours
MAKES: 8 servings

- 1¼ cups all-purpose flour, divided
- 2 Tbsp. plus 1 cup sugar, divided
- 1 tsp. baking powder
- ¼ tsp. ground cinnamon
- 1 large egg
- ¼ cup fat-free milk
- 2 Tbsp. canola oil
- ⅛ tsp. salt
- 2 cups fresh or frozen raspberries, thawed
- 2 cups fresh or frozen blueberries, thawed
  Low-fat vanilla frozen yogurt, optional

1. Whisk 1 cup flour, 2 Tbsp. sugar, baking powder and cinnamon. In another bowl, whisk together egg, milk and oil; add to dry ingredients, stirring just until moistened (batter will be thick). Spread onto bottom of a 5-qt. slow cooker coated with cooking spray.
2. Mix salt and remaining ¼ cup flour and 1 cup sugar; toss with berries. Spoon over batter. Cook, covered, on high until berry mixture is bubbly, 1¾-2 hours. If desired, serve with frozen yogurt.
1 SERVING: 260 cal., 5g fat (1g sat. fat), 23mg chol., 110mg sod., 53g carb. (34g sugars, 3g fiber), 4g pro.

APPLE BETTY WITH
ALMOND CREAM

STRAWBERRY-BANANA
PUDDING CAKE

STRAWBERRY-BANANA PUDDING CAKE

This luscious pink pudding cake is so easy to put together. Top it with ice cream and fresh fruit, and you'll have one very happy family.
—*Nadine Mesch, Mount Healthy, OH*

PREP: 15 min.
COOK: 3½ hours + standing
MAKES: 10 servings

- 1 pkg. strawberry cake mix (regular size)
- 1 pkg. (3.4 oz.) instant banana cream pudding mix
- 2 cups plain Greek yogurt
- 4 large eggs
- 1 cup water
- ¾ cup canola oil
- 2 Tbsp. minced fresh basil
- 1 cup white baking chips
  Optional: Vanilla ice cream, sliced bananas, sliced strawberries and fresh basil

1. In a large bowl, combine first 6 ingredients; beat on low speed for 30 seconds. Beat on medium 2 minutes; stir in basil. Transfer to a greased 5-qt. slow cooker. Cook, covered, on low until edges of cake are golden brown (center will be moist), 3½-4 hours.
2. Remove slow-cooker insert; sprinkle cake with baking chips. Let cake stand, uncovered, for 10 minutes before serving. Serve with toppings as desired.
1 SERVING: 373 cal., 29g fat (8g sat. fat), 90mg chol., 239mg sod., 23g carb. (21g sugars, 0 fiber), 5g pro.

HOT FUDGE CAKE

HOT FUDGE CAKE

A cake baked in a slow cooker may seem unusual. But smiles around the dinner table prove how tasty it is. Sometimes, for a change of pace, I use butterscotch chips instead.
—*Marleen Adkins, Placentia, CA*

PREP: 20 min. • **COOK:** 4 hours
MAKES: 8 servings

- 1¾ cups packed brown sugar, divided
- 1 cup all-purpose flour
- 6 Tbsp. baking cocoa, divided
- 2 tsp. baking powder
- ½ tsp. salt
- ½ cup 2% milk
- 2 Tbsp. butter, melted
- ½ tsp. vanilla extract
- 1½ cups semisweet chocolate chips
- 1¾ cups boiling water
  Vanilla ice cream

1. In a small bowl, combine 1 cup brown sugar, flour, 3 Tbsp. cocoa, baking powder and salt. In a second bowl, combine the milk, butter and vanilla; stir into the dry ingredients just until combined.
2. Spread into a 3-qt. slow cooker coated with cooking spray. Sprinkle with chocolate chips. In another bowl, combine the remaining ¾ cup brown sugar and 3 Tbsp. cocoa; stir in boiling water. Pour over batter (do not stir).
3. Cook, covered, on high until a toothpick inserted in the center comes out clean, 4-4½ hours. Serve warm, with ice cream.
1 SERVING: 435 cal., 13g fat (8g sat. fat), 10mg chol., 306mg sod., 82g carb. (66g sugars, 3g fiber), 4g pro.

SLOW-COOKER BAKED APPLES

On a cool fall day, coming home to the scent of this apple dessert cooking and then eating it is a double dose of just plain wonderful.
—*Evangeline Bradford, Covington, KY*

PREP: 25 min. • **COOK:** 4 hours
MAKES: 6 servings

- 6 medium tart apples
- ½ cup raisins
- ⅓ cup packed brown sugar
- 1 Tbsp. grated orange zest
- 1 cup water
- 3 Tbsp. thawed orange juice concentrate
- 2 Tbsp. butter

1. Core apples; peel the top third of each if desired. Combine the raisins, brown sugar and orange zest; spoon into apples. Place in a 5-qt. slow cooker.

2. Pour water around apples. Drizzle with the orange juice concentrate. Dot with butter. Cook, covered, on low until the apples are tender, 4-5 hours.

1 STUFFED APPLE: 203 cal., 4g fat (2g sat. fat), 10mg chol., 35mg sod., 44g carb. (37g sugars, 4g fiber), 1g pro.

TEST KITCHEN TIP

You can experiment with the filling for these apples; try adding dried cranberries with the raisins, and chopped walnuts or pecans for texture.

SLOW-COOKER BAKED APPLES

CRANBERRY-ALMOND CORNMEAL CAKE

This warm, comforting slow-cooker dessert is guaranteed to ward off the wintertime blues. Top with a scoop of simple vanilla ice cream for an extra layer of flavor.
—*Shannon Kohn, Simpsonville, SC*

PREP: 15 min. • **COOK:** 2 hours
MAKES: 10 servings

- 1 pkg. (8½ oz.) cornbread/ muffin mix
- 1 cup all-purpose flour
- ⅔ cup sugar
- 1 tsp. baking powder
- 3 large eggs, room temperature, lightly beaten
- 1 cup buttermilk
- ½ cup butter, melted
- 1½ cups dried cranberries
- 1 can (12½ oz.) almond cake and pastry filling
  Optional: Confectioners' sugar and whipped cream

1. In large bowl, whisk together cornbread mix, flour, sugar and baking powder. Stir in eggs, buttermilk and melted butter until combined. Pour batter into a 5-qt. slow cooker coated with cooking spray. Sprinkle batter with dried cranberries; drop almond filling by heaping tablespoonfuls evenly over cranberries and batter.
2. Cook, covered, on high until a toothpick inserted in center comes out clean, about 2 hours. If desired, sprinkle with confectioners' sugar and serve with whipped cream.
1 SERVING: 506 cal., 17g fat (8g sat. fat), 82mg chol., 433mg sod., 84g carb. (50g sugars, 3g fiber), 7g pro.

KEY LIME FONDUE

Love fondue but want something other than milk chocolate? Dip into this white chocolate Key lime fondue with graham crackers, fresh fruit and cubed pound cake.
—*Elisabeth Larsen, Pleasant Grove, UT*

PREP: 5 min. • **COOK:** 50 min.
MAKES: 3 cups

- 1 can (14 oz.) sweetened condensed milk
- 12 oz. white baking chocolate, finely chopped
- ½ cup Key lime or regular lime juice
- 1 Tbsp. grated lime zest
  Graham crackers, macaroon cookies, fresh strawberries and sliced ripe bananas

1. In a 1½-qt. slow cooker, combine the milk, white chocolate and lime juice. Cook, covered, on low until chocolate is melted, 50-60 minutes.
2. Stir in lime zest. Serve with graham crackers, cookies and fruit.
¼ CUP: 251 cal., 11g fat (8g sat. fat), 11mg chol., 62mg sod., 37g carb. (36g sugars, 0 fiber), 5g pro.

CARAMEL PECAN PUMPKIN CAKE

CARAMEL PECAN PUMPKIN CAKE

Use your slow cooker as a cake-maker for a seriously yummy dessert that is easy enough for any weekday and tasty enough for a holiday meal—and frees up oven space too.
—*Julie Peterson, Crofton, MD*

PREP: 15 min.
COOK: 2 hours + standing
MAKES: 10 servings

 1 cup butter, softened
1¼ cups sugar
 4 large eggs, room temperature
 2 cups all-purpose flour
 2 tsp. baking powder
 1 tsp. baking soda
 1 tsp. pumpkin pie spice or ground cinnamon
 ½ tsp. salt
 1 can (15 oz.) pumpkin
 ½ cup caramel sundae syrup
 ½ cup chopped pecans

1. In large bowl, cream butter and sugar until light and fluffy, 5-7 minutes. Add eggs, 1 at a time, beating well after each addition. In a second bowl, whisk together the next 5 ingredients; add to creamed mixture alternately with pumpkin, beating well after each addition.
2. Line a 5-qt. round slow cooker with heavy-duty foil extending over sides; spray with cooking spray. Spread batter evenly into slow cooker. Cook, covered, on high until a toothpick inserted in center comes out clean, about 2 hours. To avoid scorching, rotate the slow-cooker insert a half turn midway through cooking, lifting carefully with oven mitts.
3. Turn off slow cooker; let stand, uncovered, 10 minutes. Using foil, carefully lift cake out of slow cooker and invert onto a serving plate.
4. Drizzle caramel syrup over cake; top with pecans. Serve warm.
1 PIECE: 473 cal., 25g fat (13g sat. fat), 123mg chol., 561mg sod., 59g carb. (35g sugars, 2g fiber), 7g pro.

APPLE PUDDING CAKE

A satisfying dessert like this is a superb treat on a chilly night. It has three separate layers—apples, cake and sauce—and I like to serve it in a bowl.
—*Ellen Schroeder, Reedsburg, WI*

PREP: 15 min. • **COOK:** 2 hours
MAKES: 10 servings

 2 cups all-purpose flour
 ⅔ cup plus ¼ cup sugar, divided
 3 tsp. baking powder
 1 tsp. salt
 ½ cup cold butter
 1 cup 2% milk
 2 medium tart apples, peeled and chopped
1½ cups orange juice
 ½ cup honey
 2 Tbsp. butter, melted
 1 tsp. ground cinnamon
1⅓ cups sour cream
 ¼ cup confectioners' sugar

1. In a small bowl, combine the flour, ⅔ cup sugar, baking powder and salt. Cut in butter until mixture resembles coarse crumbs. Stir in milk just until moistened. Spread into the bottom of a greased 4- or 5-qt. slow cooker; sprinkle apples over batter.
2. In a small bowl, combine the orange juice, honey, melted butter, cinnamon and the remaining ¼ cup sugar; pour over apples. Cook, covered, on high until apples are tender, 2-3 hours.
3. In a small bowl, combine sour cream and confectioners' sugar. Serve with warm pudding cake.
1 CUP WITH 2 TBSP. SOUR CREAM MIXTURE: 431 cal., 17g fat (11g sat. fat), 53mg chol., 461mg sod., 64g carb. (44g sugars, 1g fiber), 5g pro.

APPLE PUDDING
CAKE

APPLE PIE OATMEAL DESSERT

APPLE PIE OATMEAL DESSERT

This warm and comforting dessert brings back memories of times spent with my family around the kitchen table. I serve the dish with sweetened whipped cream or vanilla ice cream as a topper.
—*Carol Greer, Earlville, IL*

PREP: 15 min. • **COOK:** 4 hours
MAKES: 6 servings

- 1 cup quick-cooking oats
- ½ cup all-purpose flour
- ⅓ cup packed brown sugar
- 2 tsp. baking powder
- 1½ tsp. apple pie spice
- ¼ tsp. salt
- 3 large eggs
- 1⅔ cups 2% milk, divided
- 1½ tsp. vanilla extract
- 3 medium apples, peeled and finely chopped
  Vanilla ice cream, optional

1. In a large bowl, whisk oats, flour, brown sugar, baking powder, pie spice and salt. In a small bowl, whisk eggs, 1 cup milk and vanilla until blended. Add to oat mixture, stirring just until moistened. Fold in apples.
2. Transfer to a greased 3-qt. slow cooker. Cook, covered, on low until apples are tender and top is set, 4-5 hours.
3. Stir in remaining ⅔ cup milk. Serve warm or cold, with ice cream if desired.
¾ CUP: 238 cal., 5g fat (2g sat. fat), 111mg chol., 306mg sod., 41g carb. (22g sugars, 3g fiber), 8g pro.

TROPICAL COMPOTE DESSERT

TROPICAL COMPOTE DESSERT

Have the taste of summer throughout the year! To make a more adult version of this recipe, use brandy instead of the extra tropical fruit juice.
—*Taste of Home Test Kitchen*

PREP: 15 min. • **COOK:** 2¼ hours
MAKES: 6 servings

- 1 jar (23½ oz.) mixed tropical fruit
- 1 jalapeno pepper, seeded and chopped
- ¼ cup sugar
- 1 Tbsp. chopped crystallized ginger
- ¼ tsp. ground cinnamon
- 1 can (15 oz.) mandarin oranges, drained
- 1 jar (6 oz.) maraschino cherries, drained
- 1 medium firm banana, sliced
- 6 individual round sponge cakes
- 6 Tbsp. sweetened shredded coconut, toasted

1. Drain tropical fruit, reserving ¼ cup liquid. Combine fruit and jalapeno in a 1½-qt. slow cooker. Combine sugar, ginger, cinnamon and reserved juice; pour over fruit. Cook, covered, on low for 2 hours.
2. Stir in the mandarin oranges, maraschino cherries and banana; cook 15 minutes longer.
3. Place cakes on plates; top with compote. Sprinkle with coconut.
NOTE: Wear disposable gloves when cutting hot peppers; the oils can burn skin. Avoid touching your face.
1 SPONGE CAKE WITH ⅔ CUP COMPOTE AND 1 TBSP. COCONUT: 257 cal., 3g fat (2g sat. fat), 0 chol., 28mg sod., 62g carb. (31g sugars, 3g fiber), 1g pro.

CHOCOLATE-COVERED CHERRY PUDDING CAKE

I remember how much my grandfather cherished the chocolate-covered cherries we brought him each Christmas. After he passed away, I came up with this rich recipe in his honor. It's delicious served with whipped topping.
—*Meredith Coe, Charlottesville, VA*

PREP: 20 min.
COOK: 2 hours + standing
MAKES: 8 servings

- ½ cup reduced-fat sour cream
- 2 Tbsp. canola oil
- 1 Tbsp. butter, melted
- 2 tsp. vanilla extract
- 1 cup all-purpose flour
- ¼ cup sugar
- ¼ cup packed brown sugar
- 3 Tbsp. baking cocoa
- 2 tsp. baking powder
- ½ tsp. ground cinnamon
- ⅛ tsp. salt
- 1 cup fresh or frozen pitted dark sweet cherries, thawed
- 1 cup fresh or frozen pitted tart cherries, thawed
- ⅓ cup 60% cacao bittersweet chocolate baking chips

PUDDING
- ½ cup packed brown sugar
- 2 Tbsp. baking cocoa
- 1¼ cups hot water
  Confectioners' sugar, optional

1. In a large bowl, beat the sour cream, oil, butter and vanilla until blended. Combine the flour, sugars, cocoa, baking powder, cinnamon and salt. Add to the sour cream mixture just until combined. Stir in cherries and chips. Pour into a 3-qt. slow cooker coated with cooking spray.
2. For the pudding, in a small bowl, combine brown sugar and cocoa. Stir in hot water until blended. Pour over the batter (do not stir). Cook, covered, on high 2-2½ hours or until cake is set. Let stand for 15 minutes. If desired, dust each serving with confectioners' sugar.
1 SERVING: 291 cal., 9g fat (3g sat. fat), 9mg chol., 167mg sod., 51g carb. (35g sugars, 2g fiber), 4g pro.

TEST KITCHEN TIP

You can adjust the proportions of sweet to tart cherries, if you like—or use all of just one kind!

CHOCOLATE-COVERED CHERRY PUDDING CAKE

SPICED SWEET POTATO PUDDING

One of my favorite fall desserts, this treat is full of rich flavors that are well-suited to the chillier months. I like to serve it over a slice of pound cake or with a scoop of vanilla ice cream.
—Aysha Schurman, Ammon, ID

PREP: 15 min. • **COOK:** 3 hours
MAKES: 7 servings

- 2 cans (15¾ oz. each) sweet potatoes, drained and mashed
- 3 large eggs
- 1 can (12 oz.) evaporated milk
- ⅔ cup biscuit/baking mix
- ½ cup packed brown sugar
- ½ cup apple butter
- 2 Tbsp. butter, softened
- 2 tsp. vanilla extract
- ⅓ cup finely chopped pecans
  Pound cake, optional

In a large bowl, beat the first 8 ingredients until well-blended. Pour into a greased 3-qt. slow cooker. Sprinkle with the pecans. Cook, covered, on low for 3-4 hours or until a thermometer reads 160°. Serve with pound cake if desired.
¾ CUP: 418 cal., 15g fat (6g sat. fat), 115mg chol., 309mg sod., 64g carb. (45g sugars, 4g fiber), 8g pro.

BLUEBERRY GRUNT

BLUEBERRY GRUNT

If you love blueberries, then you can't go wrong with this easy slow-cooked dessert. For a special treat, serve it while it's still warm, with a scoop of vanilla ice cream melting on top.
—Cleo Gonske, Redding, CA

PREP: 20 min. • **COOK:** 2½ hours
MAKES: 6 servings

- 4 cups fresh or frozen blueberries
- ¾ cup sugar
- ½ cup water
- 1 tsp. almond extract

DUMPLINGS
- 2 cups all-purpose flour
- 4 tsp. baking powder
- 1 tsp. sugar
- ½ tsp. salt
- 1 Tbsp. cold butter
- 1 Tbsp. shortening
- ¾ cup 2% milk
  Vanilla ice cream, optional

1. Place blueberries, sugar, water and extract in a 3-qt. slow cooker; stir to combine. Cook, covered, on high 2-3 hours or until bubbly.
2. For dumplings, in a small bowl, whisk flour, baking powder, sugar and salt. Cut in cold butter and shortening until crumbly. Add milk; stir just until a soft dough forms.
3. Drop dough by tablespoonfuls on top of hot blueberry mixture. Cook, covered, until a toothpick inserted in center of dumplings comes out clean, about 30 minutes longer. Serve warm, with vanilla ice cream if desired.
1 CUP: 360 cal., 5g fat (2g sat. fat), 7mg chol., 494mg sod., 73g carb. (37g sugars, 3g fiber), 6g pro.

GINGERBREAD PUDDING CAKE

GINGERBREAD PUDDING CAKE

Sweet spices and molasses give my dessert a delightful old-fashioned flavor.
—Barbara Cook, Yuma, AZ

PREP: 20 min.
COOK: 2 hours + standing
MAKES: 8 servings

- ½ cup molasses
- 1 cup water
- ¼ cup butter, softened
- ¼ cup sugar
- 1 large egg white, room temperature
- 1 tsp. vanilla extract
- 1¼ cups all-purpose flour
- ¾ tsp. baking soda
- ⅛ tsp. salt
- ½ tsp. ground cinnamon
- ½ tsp. ground ginger
- ¼ tsp. ground allspice
- ⅛ tsp. ground nutmeg
- ½ cup chopped pecans
- 6 Tbsp. brown sugar
- ¾ cup hot water
- ⅔ cup butter, melted
  Sweetened whipped cream, optional

1. Mix molasses and 1 cup water. Cream softened butter and sugar until light and fluffy, 5-7 minutes; beat in egg white and vanilla. In another bowl, whisk together flour, baking soda, salt and spices; add to creamed mixture alternately with molasses mixture, beating well after each addition. Fold in pecans.
2. Pour into a greased 3-qt. slow cooker. Sprinkle with brown sugar. Mix hot water and melted butter; pour over batter (do not stir).
3. Cook, covered, on high until a toothpick inserted in center comes out clean, 2-2-½ hours. Turn off slow cooker; let stand 15 minutes. If desired, serve with whipped cream.
1 SERVING: 431 cal., 26g fat (14g sat. fat), 56mg chol., 377mg sod., 48g carb. (32g sugars, 1g fiber), 3g pro.

MIXED FRUIT & PISTACHIO CAKE

This cake is easy to make on a lazy day and a guaranteed-delicious dessert for several days—if you can make it last that long!
—*Nancy Heishman, Las Vegas, NV*

PREP: 20 min.
COOK: 2½ hours + cooling
MAKES: 8 servings

  1½ cups all-purpose flour
  1½ tsp. ground cinnamon
  ½   tsp. baking soda
  ½   tsp. baking powder
  ½   tsp. ground allspice
  ¼   tsp. salt
  1   can (8 oz.) jellied cranberry sauce
  ⅓   cup packed brown sugar
  ⅓   cup buttermilk
  ¼   cup butter, melted
  2   tsp. grated orange zest
  ½   tsp. orange extract
  1   large egg, room temperature
  1   cup mixed dried fruit bits
  1   cup pistachios
      Sweetened whipped cream, optional

1. In a large bowl, whisk together flour, cinnamon, baking soda, baking powder, allspice and salt. In another bowl, combine the cranberry sauce, brown sugar, buttermilk, butter. orange zest, extract and egg. Add cranberry mixture to flour mixture; stir until smooth. Add dried fruit bits and pistachios.
2. Pour batter into a greased 1½-qt. baking dish; place in a 6-qt. slow cooker. Lay a 14x12-in. piece of parchment over top of slow cooker under the lid. Cook, covered, on high until a toothpick inserted in center comes out clean, about 2½ hours.
3. Remove dish from slow cooker to a wire rack. Cool 30 minutes before inverting onto a serving platter.
4. Cut into wedges with a serrated knife; if desired, serve with sweetened whipped cream.
1 PIECE: 375 cal., 14g fat (5g sat. fat), 39mg chol., 349mg sod., 57g carb. (30g sugars, 4g fiber), 7g pro.

PUMPKIN PIE PUDDING

My husband loves anything pumpkin, and this creamy, comforting dessert is one of his favorites.
—*Andrea Schaak, Bloomington, MN*

PREP: 10 min. • **COOK:** 6 hours
MAKES: 6 servings

  1   can (15 oz.) pumpkin
  1   can (12 oz.) evaporated milk
  ¾   cup sugar
  ½   cup biscuit/baking mix
  2   large eggs, beaten
  2   Tbsp. butter, melted
  2½   tsp. pumpkin pie spice
  2   tsp. vanilla extract
       Optional: Sweetened whipped cream or vanilla ice cream

1. Combine the first 8 ingredients. Transfer mixture to a greased 3-qt. slow cooker.
2. Cook, covered, on low until a thermometer reads 160°, 6-7 hours. If desired, serve with whipped cream or ice cream.
1 SERVING: 229 cal., 9g fat (5g sat. fat), 76mg chol., 187mg sod., 33g carb. (25g sugars, 2g fiber), 6g pro.

SLOW-COOKED BREAD PUDDING

SLOW-COOKED BREAD PUDDING

This warm and hearty dessert is perfect on any cold, blustery winter evening. And the slow cooker fills your kitchen with an amazing aroma. My stomach is growling just thinking about it!
—*Maiah Miller, Montclair, VA*

PREP: 15 min. • **COOK:** 3 hours
MAKES: 8 servings

- 4 whole wheat bagels, split and cut into ¾-in. pieces
- 1 large tart apple, peeled and chopped
- ½ cup dried cranberries
- ¼ cup golden raisins
- 4 large eggs
- 2 cups fat-free milk
- ½ cup sugar
- 2 Tbsp. butter, melted
- 1 tsp. ground cinnamon
- 1 tsp. vanilla extract
  Confectioners' sugar, optional

1. In a 3-qt. slow cooker coated with cooking spray, combine the bagel pieces, apple, cranberries and raisins. In a large bowl, whisk the eggs, milk, sugar, butter, cinnamon and vanilla. Pour over bagel mixture and stir to combine; gently press bagels down into milk mixture.

2. Cook, covered, on low until a knife inserted in the center comes out clean, 3-4 hours. If desired, dust servings with confectioners' sugar.

1 SERVING: 293 cal., 6g fat (3g sat. fat), 102mg chol., 295mg sod., 51g carb. (31g sugars, 4g fiber), 10g pro.

FLAN IN A JAR

FLAN IN A JAR

Spoil yourself or the people you love with these delightful portable custards. They're a cute and fun take on the Mexican dessert classic. Tuck a jar into your lunchbox for a sweet treat.
—*Megumi Garcia, Milwaukee, WI*

PREP: 25 min.
COOK: 2 hours + chilling
MAKES: 6 servings

- ½ cup sugar
- 1 Tbsp. plus 3 cups hot water (110°-115°), divided
- 1 cup coconut or whole milk
- ⅓ cup whole milk
- ⅓ cup sweetened condensed milk
- 2 large eggs plus 1 large egg yolk, room temperature, lightly beaten
  Pinch salt
- 1 tsp. vanilla extract
- 1 tsp. dark rum, optional

1. In a small heavy saucepan, spread sugar; cook, without stirring, over medium-low heat until it begins to melt. Gently drag melted sugar to center of pan so sugar melts evenly. Cook, stirring constantly, until melted sugar turns a deep amber color, about 2 minutes. Immediately remove from heat and carefully stir in 1 Tbsp. hot water. Quickly ladle hot mixture into 6 hot 4-oz. jars.
2. In a small saucepan, heat coconut milk and whole milk until bubbles form around sides of pan; remove from heat.
3. In a large bowl, whisk condensed milk, eggs, egg yolk and salt until blended but not foamy. Slowly stir in hot milk; stir in vanilla and, if desired, rum. Strain through a fine sieve. Pour egg mixture into prepared jars. Center lids on jars; screw on bands until fingertip tight.
4. Add remaining hot water to a 6-qt. slow cooker; place jars in slow cooker. Cook, covered, on high until centers are set, about 2 hours.
5. Cool jars 10 minutes on a wire rack, then move to a 13x9-in. baking pan filled halfway with ice water; cool 10 minutes longer. Refrigerate until cold, about 1 hour. Run a knife around sides of jars; invert flans onto dessert plates to serve.
⅓ CUP: 224 cal., 10g fat (8g sat. fat), 100mg chol., 87mg sod., 28g carb. (27g sugars, 0 fiber), 5g pro.

BLUEBERRY COBBLER

This simple slow-cooked dessert comes together in a jiffy. If you like, you can substitute apple or cherry pie filling for the blueberry.
—*Nelda Cronbaugh, Belle Plaine, IA*

PREP: 10 min. • **COOK:** 3 hours
MAKES: 6 servings

- 1 can (21 oz.) blueberry pie filling
- 1 pkg. (9 oz.) yellow cake mix
- ¼ cup chopped pecans
- ¼ cup butter, melted
  Vanilla ice cream, optional

Place pie filling in a greased 1½-qt. slow cooker. Sprinkle with cake mix and pecans. Drizzle with butter. Cover and cook on high for 3 hours or until topping is golden brown. Serve warm, with vanilla ice cream if desired.
⅔ CUP: 449 cal., 14g fat (7g sat. fat), 20mg chol., 343mg sod., 79g carb. (57g sugars, 3g fiber), 2g pro.

BLUEBERRY COBBLER

CARAMEL
& PEAR PUDDING

CARAMEL & PEAR PUDDING

This is a lovely winter dessert that uses pears, which are seasonally available. It's easy to fix and a comforting treat after any meal. I enjoy snacking on it in front of the fireplace.
—*Diane Halferty, Corpus Christi, TX*

PREP: 20 min. • **COOK:** 3 hours
MAKES: 10 servings

- 1 cup all-purpose flour
- ½ cup sugar
- 1½ tsp. baking powder
- ½ tsp. ground cinnamon
- ¼ tsp. salt
- ⅛ tsp. ground cloves
- ½ cup 2% milk
- 4 medium pears, peeled and cubed
- ½ cup chopped pecans
- ¾ cup packed brown sugar
- ¼ cup butter, softened
- ½ cup boiling water
  Vanilla ice cream, optional

1. In a large bowl, combine flour, sugar, baking powder, cinnamon, salt and cloves. Stir in milk until smooth. Add pears and pecans. Spread evenly into a 3-qt. slow cooker coated with cooking spray.
2. In a small bowl, combine brown sugar and butter; stir in boiling water. Pour over batter (do not stir). Cook, covered, on low until pears are tender, 3-4 hours. Serve warm, with ice cream if desired.
½ CUP: 274 cal., 9g fat (3g sat. fat), 13mg chol., 164mg sod., 47g carb. (33g sugars, 3g fiber), 3g pro.

SPUMONI CAKE

SPUMONI CAKE

I created this cake for a holiday potluck one year. It has become one of my most-requested desserts. You can use all semisweet chips instead of a mix if you prefer.
—*Lisa Renshaw, Kansas City, MO*

PREP: 10 min.
COOK: 4 hours + standing
MAKES: 10 servings

- 3 cups cold 2% milk
- 1 pkg. (3.4 oz.) instant pistachio pudding mix
- 1 pkg. white cake mix (regular size)
- ¾ cup chopped maraschino cherries
- 1 cup white baking chips
- 1 cup semisweet chocolate chips
- 1 cup pistachios, chopped

1. In a large bowl, whisk milk and pudding mix for 2 minutes. Transfer to a greased 5-qt. slow cooker. Prepare cake mix batter according to package directions, folding the cherries into batter.
2. Pour batter into slow cooker. Cook, covered, on low until edges of cake are golden brown, about 4 hours.
3. Remove slow-cooker insert; sprinkle cake with baking chips and chocolate chips. Let cake stand, uncovered, 10 minutes. Sprinkle with pistachios before serving.
1 SERVING: 588 cal., 27g fat (9g sat. fat), 9mg chol., 594mg sod., 79g carb. (54g sugars, 3g fiber), 10g pro.

STRAWBERRY SODA CAKE

When you want a sweet cake without the heat of the oven, this slow-cooked strawberry-flavored spin on cola cake comes in handy. The topping smells divinely like chocolate-covered strawberries. (Remember this one for Valentine's Day!) It's delicious served with whipped cream or powdered sugar.
—*Laura Herbage, Covington, LA*

PREP: 30 min. • **COOK:** 2 hours
MAKES: 8 servings

- 1 cup 1% chocolate milk
- ½ cup butter, melted and slightly cooled
- 2 tsp. vanilla extract
- 2 cups all-purpose flour
- ½ cup sugar
- 2½ tsp. baking powder
- ½ tsp. salt
- ¼ cup semisweet chocolate chips

TOPPING

- 1 cup strawberry soda
- ¾ cup packed brown sugar
- ¼ cup sugar
- ¼ cup dark chocolate chips
- ¼ cup seedless strawberry jam
- ¼ cup molasses
  Whipped cream and sliced fresh strawberries

1. In a large bowl, mix chocolate milk, melted butter and vanilla until well blended. In another bowl, whisk flour, sugar, baking powder and salt; gradually mix into the chocolate milk mixture. Stir in chocolate chips. Spread into a greased 3- or 4-qt. slow cooker.
2. For topping, in a small saucepan, combine soda and sugars. Cook, stirring, over medium heat until sugar is dissolved; remove from heat. Stir in dark chocolate chips, jam and molasses; pour over batter.
3. Cook, covered, on high until a toothpick inserted in center comes out clean, 2-2½ hours. Serve with whipped cream and strawberries.
1 SERVING: 504 cal., 16g fat (10g sat. fat), 32mg chol., 423mg sod., 88g carb. (63g sugars, 2g fiber), 5g pro.

STRAWBERRY SODA CAKE

SLOW-COOKER BANANAS FOSTER

The flavors of caramel, rum and walnut naturally complement fresh bananas in this version of a dessert classic. It's my go-to choice for any family get-together.
—*Crystal Jo Bruns, Iliff, CO*

PREP: 10 min. • **COOK:** 2 hours
MAKES: 5 servings

- 5 medium firm bananas
- 1 cup packed brown sugar
- ¼ cup butter, melted
- ¼ cup rum
- 1 tsp. vanilla extract
- ½ tsp. ground cinnamon
- ⅓ cup chopped walnuts
- ⅓ cup sweetened shredded coconut
  Optional: Vanilla ice cream or sliced pound cake

1. Cut bananas in half lengthwise, then widthwise; layer in the bottom of a 1½-qt. slow cooker. Combine brown sugar, butter, rum, vanilla and cinnamon; pour over bananas. Cook, covered, on low until heated through, about 1½ hours.
2. Sprinkle with the walnuts and coconut; cook 30 minutes longer. Serve with ice cream or pound cake if desired.
1 SERVING: 462 cal., 17g fat (8g sat. fat), 24mg chol., 99mg sod., 74g carb. (59g sugars, 4g fiber), 3g pro.

FUDGY PEANUT BUTTER CAKE

FUDGY PEANUT BUTTER CAKE

I clipped this cake recipe from a newspaper years ago. The house smells heavenly while it's cooking. My husband and son enjoy this slow-cooked dessert with vanilla ice cream and nuts on top.
—*Bonnie Evans, Norcross, GA*

PREP: 10 min. • **COOK:** 1½ hours
MAKES: 4 servings

- ⅓ cup 2% milk
- ¼ cup peanut butter
- 1 Tbsp. canola oil
- ½ tsp. vanilla extract
- ¾ cup sugar, divided
- ½ cup all-purpose flour
- ¾ tsp. baking powder
- 2 Tbsp. baking cocoa
- 1 cup boiling water
  Chocolate or vanilla ice cream, optional

1. In a large bowl, beat the milk, peanut butter, oil and vanilla until well blended. In a small bowl, combine ¼ cup sugar, flour and baking powder; gradually beat into milk mixture until blended. Spread into a 1½-qt. slow cooker coated with cooking spray.
2. In a small bowl, combine cocoa and the remaining ½ cup sugar; stir in boiling water. Pour into slow cooker (do not stir).
3. Cook, covered, on high until a toothpick inserted in the center comes out clean, 1½-2 hours. Serve warm, with ice cream if desired.
1 SERVING: 348 cal., 13g fat (3g sat. fat), 3mg chol., 160mg sod., 55g carb. (39g sugars, 2g fiber), 7g pro.

OLD-FASHIONED TAPIOCA

My family loves old-fashioned tapioca, but I don't always have time to make it. So I came up with this simple recipe. It lets us enjoy one of our favorites without all the hands-on work.
—*Ruth Peters, Bel Air, MD*

PREP: 10 min. • **COOK:** 4½ hours
MAKES: 18 servings

- 8 cups 2% milk
- 1 cup pearl tapioca
- 1 cup plus 2 Tbsp. sugar
- ⅛ tsp. salt
- 4 large eggs, room temperature
- 1½ tsp. vanilla extract
  Optional: Sliced fresh strawberries and whipped cream

1. In a 4- to 5-qt. slow cooker, combine the milk, tapioca, sugar and salt. Cook, covered, on low for 4-5 hours.
2. In a large bowl, beat the eggs; stir in a small amount of the hot tapioca mixture. Return all to the slow cooker, stirring to combine. Cover and cook 30 minutes longer or until a thermometer reads 160°. Stir in the vanilla.
3. If desired, serve with sliced fresh strawberries and whipped cream.
½ CUP: 149 cal., 3g fat (2g sat. fat), 55mg chol., 86mg sod., 25g carb. (18g sugars, 0 fiber), 5g pro.

OLD-FASHIONED TAPIOCA

AMARETTO CHERRIES
WITH DUMPLINGS

AMARETTO CHERRIES WITH DUMPLINGS

Treat everyone to a dessert of comfort food—warm tart cherries drizzled with amaretto and topped with fluffy dumplings. A scoop of vanilla ice cream is the perfect finishing touch.
—Taste of Home *Test Kitchen*

PREP: 15 min. • **COOK:** 7¾ hours
MAKES: 6 servings

- 2 cans (14½ oz. each) pitted tart cherries
- ¾ cup sugar
- ¼ cup cornstarch
- ⅛ tsp. salt
- ¼ cup amaretto or
  ½ tsp. almond extract

DUMPLINGS
- 1 cup all-purpose flour
- ¼ cup sugar
- 1 tsp. baking powder
- ½ tsp. grated lemon zest
- ⅛ tsp. salt
- ⅓ cup 2% milk
- 3 Tbsp. butter, melted
  Vanilla ice cream, optional

1. Drain cherries, reserving ¼ cup of the juice. Place the cherries in a 3-qt. slow cooker.
2. In a small bowl, mix the sugar, cornstarch and salt; stir in reserved cherry juice until smooth. Stir into cherries. Cook, covered, on high for 7 hours. Drizzle amaretto over cherry mixture.
3. For dumplings, in a small bowl, whisk flour, sugar, baking powder, lemon zest and salt. In another bowl, whisk milk and melted butter. Add to flour mixture; stir just until moistened.
4. Drop by tablespoonfuls on top of hot cherry mixture. Cook, covered, 45 minutes or until a toothpick inserted in center of dumplings comes out clean. Serve warm, with ice cream if desired.

CHOCOLATE MALT PUDDING CAKE

¾ CUP: 369 cal., 6g fat (4g sat. fat), 16mg chol., 242mg sod., 71g carb. (48g sugars, 2g fiber), 4g pro.

CHOCOLATE MALT PUDDING CAKE

Whenever I make this comforting pudding cake, I "chop" the malted milk balls by putting them in a bag and pounding them with a rubber mallet. Doing this eliminates the mess.
—Sarah Skubinna, Cascade, MT

PREP: 25 min.
COOK: 2 hours + standing
MAKES: 8 servings

- ½ cup 2% milk
- 2 Tbsp. canola oil
- ½ tsp. almond extract
- 1 cup all-purpose flour
- ½ cup packed brown sugar
- 2 Tbsp. baking cocoa
- 1½ tsp. baking powder
- ½ cup coarsely chopped malted milk balls
- ½ cup semisweet chocolate chips
- ¾ cup sugar
- ¼ cup malted milk powder
- 1¼ cups boiling water
- 4 oz. cream cheese, softened and cubed
  Optional: Vanilla ice cream and sliced almonds

1. In a large bowl, combine milk, oil and extract. Combine flour, brown sugar, cocoa and baking powder; gradually beat into the milk mixture until blended. Stir in chopped milk balls and chocolate chips.
2. Spoon into a greased 3-qt. slow cooker. In a small bowl, combine sugar and milk powder; stir in water and cream cheese. Pour over batter (do not stir).
3. Cover and cook on high until a toothpick inserted in center of cake comes out clean, 2-3 hours. Turn off heat. Let stand 15 minutes. Serve warm. If desired, serve with ice cream and sprinkle with almonds.
1 SERVING: 430 cal., 17g fat (8g sat. fat), 19mg chol., 167mg sod., 67g carb. (50g sugars, 2g fiber), 6g pro.

PEACH CRUMBLE

I look forward to going on our family beach vacation every year, but I don't always relish the time spent cooking for everybody. This easy slow-cooker dessert (or breakfast!) gives me more time to lie in the sun and enjoy the waves.
—*Colleen Delawder, Herndon, VA*

PREP: 20 min. • **COOK:** 3 hours
MAKES: 8 servings

- 1 Tbsp. butter, softened
- 6 large ripe peaches, peeled and sliced (about 6 cups)
- 2 Tbsp. light brown sugar
- 1 Tbsp. lemon juice
- 1 Tbsp. vanilla extract
- 2 Tbsp. coconut rum, optional

TOPPING
- 1 cup all-purpose flour
- ¾ cup packed light brown sugar
- 1½ tsp. baking powder
- 1 tsp. ground cinnamon
- ½ tsp. baking soda
- ⅛ tsp. salt
- 1 cup old-fashioned oats
- 6 Tbsp. cold butter, cubed
  Whipped cream, optional

1. Grease a 6-qt. oval slow cooker with softened butter. Toss peaches with brown sugar, lemon juice, vanilla and, if desired, rum; spread evenly in slow cooker.

2. Whisk together first 6 topping ingredients; stir in oats. Cut in cold butter until crumbly; sprinkle over peaches. Cook, covered, on low until peaches are tender, 3-4 hours. If desired, serve with whipped cream.

¾ CUP: 339 cal., 11g fat (7g sat. fat), 27mg chol., 293mg sod., 57g carb. (36g sugars, 4g fiber), 4g pro.

PEACH CRUMBLE

BUTTERSCOTCH PEARS

This grand finale simmers during dinner and impresses as soon as you bring it to the table. Serve as is, or with vanilla ice cream and a slice of pound cake.
—*Theresa Kreyche, Tustin, CA*

PREP: 20 min. • **COOK:** 2 hours
MAKES: 8 servings

- 4 large firm pears
- 1 Tbsp. lemon juice
- ¼ cup packed brown sugar
- 3 Tbsp. butter, softened
- 2 Tbsp. all-purpose flour
- ½ tsp. ground cinnamon
- ¼ tsp. salt
- ½ cup chopped pecans
- ½ cup pear nectar
- 2 Tbsp. honey

1. Cut pears in half lengthwise; remove cores. Brush pears with lemon juice. In a small bowl, combine the brown sugar, butter, flour, cinnamon and salt; stir in pecans. Spoon mixture into pears; place in a 4-qt. slow cooker.
2. Combine pear nectar and honey; drizzle over pears. Cook, covered, on low for 2-3 hours or until pears are tender. Serve warm.
1 STUFFED PEAR HALF: 209 cal., 10g fat (3g sat. fat), 11mg chol., 109mg sod., 33g carb. (24g sugars, 4g fiber), 1g pro.

TEST KITCHEN TIP

What to do with the leftover pear nectar? Try adding it to sparkling wine or just pouring it over ice—it's heavenly!

INDIAN RICE & CARROT PUDDING

This recipe is rich in flavor and very easy to prepare.
—*Daljeet Singh, Coral Springs, FL*

PREP: 15 min. • **COOK:** 2¾ hours
MAKES: 9 servings

- 3½ cups 1% milk
- 1 cup shredded carrots
- ½ cup uncooked basmati rice, washed and drained
- ¾ tsp. ground cardamom
- ½ tsp. ground cinnamon
- ¼ tsp. ground ginger
- ¼ cup unsalted pistachios, chopped, divided
- ½ cup agave nectar
- ⅓ cup raisins
- ¼ tsp. rose water, optional

1. Combine milk, carrots, rice, cardamom, cinnamon and ginger in a 4-qt. slow cooker. Stir in half the chopped pistachios. Cook, covered, on high heat for 2½ hours, stirring occasionally.
2. Add agave and raisins; reduce heat to low. Cover and cook until rice is tender, about 15 minutes longer. If desired, stir in rose water.
3. Serve warm, or refrigerate and serve chilled. Garnish each serving with remaining pistachios.
½ CUP: 176 cal., 3g fat (1g sat. fat), 5mg chol., 66mg sod., 35g carb. (23g sugars, 1g fiber), 5g pro.

CHOCOLATE POTS DE CREME

CHOCOLATE POTS DE CREME

Lunch on the go just got a whole lot sweeter. Tuck jars of rich chocolate custard into lunch bags for a midday treat. These portable desserts are fun for picnics too.
—*Nick Iverson, Denver, CO*

PREP: 20 min.
COOK: 4 hours + chilling
MAKES: 8 servings

- 2 cups heavy whipping cream
- 8 oz. bittersweet chocolate, finely chopped
- 1 Tbsp. instant espresso powder
- 4 large egg yolks, room temperature
- ¼ cup sugar
- ¼ tsp. salt
- 1 Tbsp. vanilla extract
- 3 cups hot water
  Optional: Whipped cream, grated chocolate and fresh raspberries

1. Place whipping cream, chocolate and espresso in a microwave-safe bowl; microwave on high 4 minutes or until the chocolate is melted and cream is hot. Whisk to combine.
2. In a large bowl, whisk egg yolks, sugar and salt until blended but not foamy. Slowly whisk in hot cream mixture; stir in vanilla.
3. Ladle egg mixture into eight 4-oz. jars. Center lids on jars and screw on bands until fingertip tight. Add hot water to a 7-qt. slow cooker; place jars in slow cooker. Cook, covered, on low for 4 hours or until set.
4. Remove jars from slow cooker; let cool on counter for 30 minutes. Refrigerate 2 hours or until cold. If desired, top with whipped cream, grated chocolate and raspberries.
1 SERVING: 424 cal., 34g fat (21g sat. fat), 160mg chol., 94mg sod., 13g carb. (11g sugars, 1g fiber), 5g pro.

PUMPKIN LATTE CUSTARD

Here's a traditional slow-cooker pumpkin custard with some espresso powder for a latte effect.
—*Shelly Bevington, Hermiston, OR*

PREP: 10 min. • **COOK:** 6 hours
MAKES: 8 servings

- 1 can (29 oz.) pumpkin
- 1½ cups sugar
- 1 can (12 oz.) evaporated milk
- 4 large eggs, lightly beaten
- 1 Tbsp. pumpkin pie spice
- 1 Tbsp. instant espresso powder
- 1 tsp. salt
  Gingersnap cookies, crushed
  Whipped cream, optional

1. Pour 1 in. water into a 6-qt. slow cooker. Layer two 24-in. pieces of foil; roll up lengthwise to make a 1-in.-thick roll. Shape into a ring; place ring in slow cooker to make a rack.
2. Whisk the first 7 ingredients. Transfer to a greased 2-qt. baking dish; set aside. Fold an 18x12-in. piece of foil lengthwise into thirds, making a sling. Use the sling to lower the baking dish onto the foil rack, not allowing sides to touch slow cooker. Cover slow cooker with a double layer of white paper towels; place lid securely over the paper towels.
3. Cook, covered, on low 6-7 hours or until a thermometer reads 160°. Use the sling to remove baking dish from slow cooker. Top servings with crushed gingersnap cookies and, if desired, whipped cream.
1 SERVING: 280 cal., 6g fat (3g sat. fat), 108mg chol., 381mg sod., 52g carb. (46g sugars, 3g fiber), 7g pro.

PUMPKIN LATTE
CUSTARD

INDEX